Women in the United States Congress, 1917-1972

Women in the United States Congress, 1917-1972

Their Accomplishments; with Bibliographies

Rudolf Engelbarts

1974

Libraries Unlimited Inc., Littleton, Colo.

LIBRARIES UNLIMITED, INC.
P.O. Box 263
Littleton, Colorado 80120

PREFACE

This book has two main objectives. The first goal attempted is a picture of the Congressional accomplishments of each of the 81 subjects. In some cases this task is difficult since some of the women accomplished very little or nothing at all, either because their term of office was too brief to achieve any goal, or because they set themselves no goal to achieve, being willing to follow unquestioningly in their husband's footsteps. But there were a sufficient number of dynamic women who aimed at independence, who had ideologies and ideas, and who struggled to success. To give these women their due is, of course, even more important than to relate that some of their colleagues did not amount to much, because the hurdles that they had to surmount were even higher and more onerous than those the average, progressive Congressman has to clear. As a result of this disparity in achievements, some of the entries will be short and lacking in substance, while longer ones will reflect the careers of many-sided and successful achievers.

The second aim of the book is to provide a bibliography of books and articles for the help of those who may wish to pursue the study of a particular Congresswoman. It will be noted that some of the accounts will have only very brief bibliographies, while others have copious references to literature about the person; this again reflects the importance of the Congresswoman's accomplishments, although it also indicates how interesting or glamorous a personality she had, how good her public relations department was, and how much of an impact she made.

Serving as a basis for the evaluation of a Congresswoman's legislative accomplishments were *Congressional Quarterly Almanac*, the *Weekly Report* of the Congressional Quarterly Service, and the daily *Congressional Record* for 1972. The bibliographies were compiled from *Reader's Guide*, *International Index*, and *PAIS* (for articles) and the catalogs of the Library of Congress for books. References from newspapers have not been given, with the exception that in a few cases the *New York Times Index* has been referred to.

A secondary aim—that of supplying biographic detail—has not been emphasized. Anyone wanting to pursue the study of an individual Congresswoman has numerous tools at his disposal, beginning with the newspapers of her district. The need for biographic detail can be answered by a variety of who's who-type publications, which are listed and annotated in the bibliography. They include *Who's Who in America for 1972/73*; *Who's Who of American Women*; *Who's Who in Government*; *Who's Who in American Politics*. Other useful works are *Current Biography*, the *Official Congressional Directory*, *Biographical Directory of the American Congress, 1774-1971*, the *National Journal Intelligence Reports on Federal Policy Making*. Finally, mention should be made of *Notable American Women, 1607-1950*, *Women Studies Abstracts*, and *A Minority of Members: Women in the U.S. Congress*, by Hope Chamberlin.

Books and articles listed under each Congresswoman or Senator, as well as books and articles found in the general bibliography of this work, will also yield biographic detail. To all the preceding should be added the new periodical *Ms.*, which is not listed or analyzed anywhere in these pages. Other sources of biographical information include the *National Faculty Directory*; the *Index to Women of the World from Ancient to Modern Times*; Helen Astin's *Women: A Bibliography on Their Education and Careers*; the Library of Congress' *List of References Relating to Notable American Women*, compiled by Florence S. Hellman; *American Women*, the official who's who among the women of the nation, which started in 1935 as a biennial; *Foremost Women in Communications*; Krichmar's *The Women's Rights Movement in the United States, 1848-1970*; the *International Directory of Women's Organizations*, by the National Council of Women of the United States; and the Swiss book *Lexikon der Frau*, in two volumes. All of these could presumably be found useful in digging out biographic detail and other information on women in Congress.

For Henny again

TABLE OF CONTENTS

INTRODUCTION

WOMEN IN THE PAST

A man speaks jokingly of his better half, meaning his wife, but he will not willingly admit that women might be the better half, or more, of humankind. Some militant women will say that men have consistently and invariably treated women as being of little importance—and perhaps as slaves. That is perhaps exaggerated, since the great majority of men *and* women have been scarcely more than slaves for the very thin upper crust of mankind. But there is more than a little truth in what militant women assert: the female of the species has almost always played second fiddle to the male, in spite of matriarchal, matrilineal and matrilocal cultures, although Millett's charge of persistent patriarchal civilizations in which the male was unalterably the vehicle of all power may be of dubious authenticity. It has been asserted that only nomadic tribes accepted their female folk as being of the same worth and importance as the male. From the pastoral stage of civilization in the dim past, hundreds of thousands of years ago, to the most modern, post-industrial level, man has been the planner and ruler, the active one; woman has been the follower, the passive one.

What Nebuchadnezzar thought of women, I do not know; probably not much, because the Assyrian and Babylonian civilizations were warlike, with emphasis on cold-bloodedness and cruelty, which are male virtues. Other semitic civilizations also gave little prominence to women. In the Bible Eve is secondary to Adam, having been fashioned out of one of his ribs, and she was the seductress who was responsible for Adam's loss of his idyllic life in the garden of Eden. Throughout the times of the Old Testament women were the means whereby their lords filled the earth, although once in a while they were further distinguished by their courage and shrewdness in killing a wicked tyrant. Even today the Jewish prayer book has the men say, "Blessed art thou, o Lord, our God, king of the universe, who hast not made me a woman"; but the women say, "Blessed art thou, o Lord, our God, king of the universe, who hast made me according to thy will."

Christ made no such distinction between men and women and had kind words for the lowliest and those sunk most deeply in vice. Egypt's spirit was more gentle than Assyria's, and abundant with humor and a love for life. Women are frequently pictured in art and sculpture as doing their daily chores, and Egyptian gods and godesses are equally important and great. Kings sometimes married their sisters incestuously, and Nefertiti was outstanding in beauty and refinement; much later Cleopatra was a queen of great power. Greece distinguished three types of women. First was the virtuous one, the housewife and mother whose duty it was to oversee the domestic economy and to be the bearer of sons but who was allowed no participation in the artistic, intellectual and political life; Penelope was representative of this group of women. The other two segments of Greek womanhood were for the pleasure of men: the prostitutes, of whom there were several kinds; and, on a much higher scale, the hetairae, who were physically beautiful and intellectually challenging and who participated with the leading men in their symposia and in their intellectual and artistic life. In republican Rome women had distinguished and honored positions, but in the times of the Empire they sank in esteem as many of the women of the higher and highest classes participated in the dissoluteness and criminality of the men.

Early Christianity gave equal honor to men and women as they were steeled in the fires of persecution and cruelty, but throughout the Middle Ages with its incessant warfare women were no more than bearers of sons and beasts of burden, though they won adulation in the life of the courts and in the poetry of the troubadours and the minnesingers. The frugality and increasing prosperity of the developing bourgeoisie raised women to a higher place of importance and respect.

Great women rulers of old, such as Cleopatra, Boadicea, and Isabella of Spain, consort of Ferdinand, protectress of Columbus, were followed later by distinguished ruling women such as Elizabeth I, Catherine the Great, Maria Theresa, Queen Victoria, and in recent times the queens of England, the Netherlands, and Denmark. There had also been women in ruling positions at the courts of Italy and in France, and many ambitious and highly intelligent and gifted women gathered men of literature and philosophy about them in their salons. All these were women of the highest class; those of the middle classes achieved no such prominence and influence, and the toiling and sweating subject millions sometimes eked out a precarious livelihood, but more often lived in undescribable poverty and squalor; the women suffered even more than the men, died early, and were held in low esteem.

"Amerika, du hast es besser," said Goethe, and women especially were much better off in America than their European counterparts, from the earliest colonial times throughout the history of the United States. The reasons for their rise in esteem and treatment may have been their relative scarceness and their great value in the pioneering and westward movements of the nineteenth century; also a factor, however, was the religious feeling of the Puritans, which granted to women great respect and the privilege to participate with men in almost any endeavor. But they were not accorded many legal rights, nor did the fathers of the country ever think of granting them the vote. Abigal Adams desired her husband to think of women more highly than his ancestors did, and John Adams tried to humor this excellent woman, his wife; but he did nothing to advance the status of the female half of the country's population.

The women of the rich, thin upper crust were not interested in the lot of their fellow women; they were anglomaniacs and made their annual transatlantic travels to waste their husband's wealth in conspicuous display. The millions of men in the growing urban centers, joined from year to year by hordes of immigrants, lived hard lives; they had no thoughts to spare for the hardships of their wives and daughters, who struggled against even greater odds than the men. The men sought forgetfulness in drink and physical abuse of their female helpmates. It was up to women of the middle class to begin the long, arduous struggle toward real equality between the sexes, the struggle that has even now not been totally won, one and one-half centuries after it began.

Nearly fifty years after the founding of the new republic increasing industrialization and urbanization brought about tensions and problems that the simple agricultural order of the first four decades had not known. It was accompanied by rising prosperity and materialistic well-being, but also by heightened mobility and heterogeneity of the population, and by poverty and criminality among the urban masses. Agitation began concerning moral questions like slavery, the status of women, temperance, and prostitution. At first women were not greatly involved in the ferment that began to grip the country, but gradually events conspired to enlist their participation. Concern about slavery came first, followed by interest in temperance, and in the state of women's health. The Grimké sisters, Sarah and Angelina, daughters of a judge and slaveholder in South Carolina, became early appalled at the cruelty meted out to Negroes. They began to speak and write about the slavery question but since they were sometimes physically endangered, they moved to the North, to Pennsylvania and Massachusetts. Sarah was gloomy and guiltridden; Angelina, thirteen years younger, was a fighter, full of temperament and activity. She later married Theodore Weld, also a devoted antislavery fighter. Both sisters were very eloquent, and wrote and spoke beautifully and movingly; Angelina spoke before the Massachusetts legislature in favor of freeing of the slaves. Angelina may also be considered a forerunner of the women's franchise movement. Their days of glory were in the third and fourth decades of the nineteenth century. Amelia Bloomer is best known for her efforts to improve and simplify women's clothing, as well as for her interest in the temperance movement. The fight for women's rights, especially for their right to vote, began somewhat later, the outstanding figures being Susan Anthony, Elizabeth Stanton, Victoria Woodhull, and later Carrie Chapman Catt.

Mary Wollstonecraft, an English woman, was an early predecessor of the woman's movement in the United States. Born in 1759, she died at the age of 38, after having lived a stormy life. She was the granddaughter of a well-to-do manufacturer. Her father spent a fortune, tried farming, took to drinking, bullied his wife, and moved about much, gradually sinking lower. Mary and her sister Eliza, though they had little education, had much talent; Mary wrote many books and pamphlets, one of her first being "Thoughts on the Education of Daughters." She tried being a governess for a year, then moved to London where she became a reader and translator for a publisher. While traveling in France she met Godwin (who later became her husband) and Tom Payne. Back in London she lived with another man, and in 1794 gave birth to Fanny, who later became Shelley's wife. In 1797 she married Godwin, but after a few happy months she died in childbirth. An impulsive, enthusiastic woman of great charm, a believer in Rousseau, and unselfish but careless in her love affairs, she published many books. The most important of these was *A Vindication of the Rights of Woman*, first published in 1797 and since republished many times. Her influence on the thought of American women who became involved in the battle for women's rights was not great.

The involvement of some of the American suffragists came about rather fortuitously. While in London, Mrs. Mott and Mrs. Stanton were excluded, because of their sex, from the proceedings of the World Antislavery Convention; their disgust at this treatment caused them to take up the banner of women's liberation. The movement started in the 1840s and did not come to its conclusion until 1920. It involved several generations of militant fighters for women's rights—Susan Brownell Anthony, Elizabeth Cady Stanton and Victoria Woodhull, as perhaps the most important among a great many like-thinking women, were the earlier generation, and Carrie Chapman Catt and Charlotte Gilman were the outstanding personalities of the later generation who brought the movement to fruition.

Susan Anthony, born 1820, died 1906, was the second of eight children. Born in Massachusetts, she moved with her father to New York State, not far from Albany, where he managed a cotton mill. He met financial reverses in the 1837 panic, and Susan left home to teach in order to help her father. She was outraged when she learned that women earned less than men in teaching and in every other occupation. Later, men of distinction like Douglass, Wendell Philipps, and Garrison were frequent guests in the family's home and Miss Anthony learned all about the reform movements of the era: temperance, antislavery and women's rights. Through Amelia Bloomer she met Mrs. Stanton; in 1852 she attended the first women's rights convention at Syracuse. Women did not have the right to vote, to run for office, to hold property, or to inherit; they could not divorce, they were refused seats at meetings, they did not even have the right to retain their own children in case of the husband's death—and all this in a country that prided itself on its democratic freedom and that was praised by visitors from abroad for giving its women exceptional rights, liberties, and independence. Anthony, called the Napoleon of women's rights by William H. Channing, was ridiculed by men as a lean, cadaverous, bitter, frustrated woman though she was attractive, with a broad, generous nature. Throughout most of her long life she and Mrs. Stanton collaborated in furthering the rights of women, founding the National Woman Suffrage Association, which was more radical than the Boston-based American Woman Suffrage Association; the two of them eventually merged into the National American Woman Suffrage Association. Traveling widely to further women's rights and the rights of the oppressed, she finally saw vilification turn into respect for herself, but she never saw the successful end of her life-long battle.

This is true also of Elizabeth Cady Stanton, whose life was even longer than Miss Anthony's (1815-1902), and who shared her courage, intelligence, and amazing vitality. Born in New York State, where her father was a lawyer in a small town (he later served in the state legislature and as State Supreme Court judge), she was given as much freedom and as good an education as a boy. She developed a passionate interest in the fate of women when she overheard pitiful stories of women who came for help to her father when the law deprived them of their property and their children. She had an excellent education and became interested not only in women's rights, but in the temperance and antislavery movements; in 1840 she married H. B. Stanton, journalist and reformer, who shared her sympathies. She was chiefly responsible for the convention held in 1848 in Seneca Falls, New York, for which she drafted a Declaration of Sentiments modelled on the Declaration of Independence, explaining her aims in letters published in Horace Greeley's *New York Tribune*; she also wrote for Mrs. Bloomer's *Lily*. She was more radical than some of her co-fighters, demanding easier divorce, denouncing laws that treated wives as the personal property of men, and demanding immediate abolition of slavery. In 1866 she ran as an Independent for Congress; in 1869 she began a 21-year tenure as president of the National Woman Suffrage Association. She published, in collaboration with Miss Anthony and Matilda Joslyn Cage, a six-volume *History of Woman Suffrage*, lectured throughout the country, and even aided English and French women who became engaged in the same fight for women's rights.

Miss Anthony and Mrs. Stanton were women of immaculate moral integrity, hardworking, persevering, with excellent backgrounds and good education, progeny of the upper middle class. Victoria Woodhull, born Claflin, had none of these characteristics, but she shared with the two other women strength of spirit, courage, and intelligence—in addition, she could boast of great physical beauty. She also had the same amazing vitality and longevity which spanned almost a century, from 1838 to 1927. Born in obscurity, she and her sister Tennessee traveled the country with her parents, appearing at county fairs engaging in table rapping and other forms of spiritualism, and dispensing patent medicines; they even came under the cloud of causing the death of a patient, of fraud and prostitution. Victoria at 15 married Canning Woodhull, a physician, who later took to drink and drifted away. She met James Harvey Blood, a Civil War colonel, who introduced her to reform causes. In 1868 the spirit of Demosthenes told her to go to New York; there she met Cornelius Vanderbilt, financier and bold entrepreneur who helped her and Tennie set up in the brokerage business; they were known as the bewitching brokers, and did very well. Then she began to dabble in politics, inspired by Stephen Pearl Andrews, an aberrant philosopher and follower of Swedenborgianism. Victoria proclaimed herself a candidate for the presidency in 1870, and published a paper, *Woodhull and Claflin's Weekly*, which advocated short skirts, free love, legalized prostitution, tax reform, public housing, dietary reforms and world government. In 1871 the weekly published Marx and Engels' Communist Manifesto in English. In 1871 Victoria delivered an impassioned memorial to the House of Representatives urging Congress to legalize suffrage under the 14th amendment; her success impressed the leaders of the National Woman Suffrage Association sufficiently to invite her to address their convention. After an uproariously bold campaign for the presidency in 1872, Mrs. Woodhull received no votes; but she was arrested and jailed when Comstock got after her for passing obscene materials through the mails. This was a result of her quarrel with Henry Ward Beecher, whose extramarital intrigue (with the wife of his friend Theodore Tilton) she uncovered and publicized. Beecher was acquitted in the ensuing court case, and Victoria transferred her endeavors to England, where she married a banker and where her sister became Lady Cook. Mrs. Woodhull, now Mrs. John Biddulph Martin, still dabbled in humanitarian causes and published articles on eugenics, but both she and her sister became two eminently respectable ladies; she died at the age of 88. Strong-willed, of great beauty, impressionable, articulate, she was a force in women's fight for freedom, but the hard, persistent labor was performed by others. Carrie Chapman Catt (1856-1947), a native of Wisconsin, consolidated the gains made under Anthony and Stanton. A magnetic person and an able speaker, with rare organizational ability, she took over the presidency of the National American Woman Suffrage Association in 1900. With her tact and statesmanship she was responsible for a string of suffrage victories after 1910.

The House passed the 19th amendment in 1918, the Senate passed it on June 4, 1919. The final approval was won in Tennessee in June 1920, when one of the state senators cast the deciding vote because his mother had told the 24-year-old legislator to "be good and help Mrs. Catt," thus apparently ending the fight that had begun in 1848.

The nineteenth amendment reads as follows:

> Article XIX.
>
> Section 1.
>
> The right of citizens of the United States to vote shall not be denied or abridged by the United States or by any state on account of sex.
>
> Section 2.
>
> Congress shall have power to enforce this article by appropriate legislation.

WOMEN TODAY

But the battle is far from over. Betty Friedan and Kate Millett have written books to prove that women are still the second sex; in recent years women's liberation has become a catchphrase, and NOW can boast of a considerable membership, great publicity, and some influence. But what has been the reason for the comparative powerlessness of women in politics, as well as in other walks of life? In early times saloon keepers and liquor interests were the groups blamed; now big business and some politicians are held responsible—but the fact is that many women themselves think their place is in the home.

In the national election of 1920, only one-fourth of all eligible women voted; in 1949 the percentage had gone to 45 percent, in 1952 to 55 percent. In 1964, however, as many women as men voted, and in recent years more women than men are said to have voted. The lowest level of women voting is reached in the South and in rural districts; more college-educated women vote than college-educated men, and more Republican women vote than Democratic women.[1] Each of the two large political parties has had women's divisions, a fact which kept the women's influence weak; after 1952 both parties abolished separate women's divisions. Attendance of women at national party conventions has grown every four years, the Democrats giving more seats to women than the Republicans. Quite a few wives of Presidents in the twentieth century have greatly supported their husbands, and the same is true of the wives of Senators and Representatives. It is also true that more women have found political office in local government units and in state governments, and that Presidents have appointed increasing numbers of women to high posts, especially F. D. Roosevelt, John Kennedy and Lyndon B. Johnson. A small number of women have also held judgeships, and 4 percent out of a total of more than 7,500 state legislative seats have been held by women since 1920. On the local level women hold comparatively more seats on school boards and library boards, but do poorly in mayoral elections. Some women's organizations, like the various chapters of the League of Women Voters, make it their responsibility to educate women politically and to stimulate them to run for office, but most women's organizations are of a purely social nature and even the professional ones do not make it a point to interest women politically. Foreign countries do not do much better politically by their women than does the United States. The number of women in the British Parliament or in the Canadian House of Commons has been almost infinitesimal. The Weimar Reichstag had 41 women, and in the 1963 Bundestag there were 44 women in a total of 499; in Scandinavia, women accounted for about 10 percent of law givers, while France, Italy, Ireland, and Latin America had few. India's lower house had 35 of 509, the upper house had 27 of 236; the number of women in legislatures in Communist countries was not numerous. It seems that politically this is still a man's world, and the statement "in politics, American women have been virtually invisible"[2] is demonstrably accurate.

There seems to have been no breakthrough in the political role of women, nor has there been one in employment. Such a breakthrough will probably not even be achieved by passage and ratification of the Equal Rights Amendment passed by Congress in 1972 (largely through the efforts of Congresswoman Martha Griffiths). The Amendment has now been ratified by 23 states; the California legislature ratified in the summer of 1972 as the 22nd state, Wyoming in January 1973 as the 23rd state, which means 15 more to go to achieve the required 38 ratifications. But there has been much more aggressiveness by women in demanding better pay and better chances for promotion and really significant jobs; government, industry, and big business are still dragging their feet, however, while mouthing hypocritical protestations about their fair-mindedness. In life insurance for example, in 1950, 66 percent of employees on the lower rungs were women, but of the officers, the power-wielding executives, 98 percent were men. The same is true of labor unions; it seems ridiculous that in the Amalgamated Clothing Workers Union, which has a 75 percent female membership, the leadership is all male. Women themselves may be at fault; in a survey of 520 women workers who had worked for both male and female supervisors, 99 percent stated that they preferred a male boss. *Fortune* said that out of 250,000 real executives in the U.S. only 5,000 were women; a handful are on boards of directors of large banks, and it has been repeatedly stated that the number of women in positions of responsibility is declining.[3] Female professor-ships in universities and colleges are, at least percentage-wise, fewer now than 40 to 50 years ago. The federal government has taken American Telephone and Telegraph Company to task for alleged job discrimination; AT&T has not totally denied the charge but has laid it to the lack of ability of women job applicants,[4] and the firm promises that the proportion of women in Bell craft jobs will increase. An amendment to the Equal Pay Act, which took effect on July 1, 1972, has brought additional millions of female workers pay equal to that of men for equal work; among those benefitting are professors and teachers, personnel directors, attorneys, editors, and many, many more.[5] Millions are still excluded from protection, however, and that includes men and women. Arizona recently passed a harsh law that practically crushes farm workers' unions; big California growers sought to impose the same or similar draconian restrictions on field workers, but an initiative on the November 1972 ballot that was to accomplish this purpose was turned back by a large majority of voters; it has been intimated that a subservient legislature may yet try to nullify the intent of the initiative.

There are at present about 30 million women in the labor force. In the 1890s less than one American woman in 20 held a job outside the home; this had increased to one in four by 1950, and in 1960 it was one in three. Most of them are young unmarried women and women past the childbearing age, and most of them have little enthusiasm and motivation for improving their condition. But the lack of provision for child care service for working women and the unwillingness of employers to grant part-time employment are further roadblocks. It seems ironic that bowling alleys and supermarkets have nursing facilities, while schools, laboratories, and government offices have none.[6] Congress passed comprehensive child care facilities legislation in 1972, but Nixon, in his superior wisdom, vetoed it.

If one is to believe his extravagant claims, Nixon is also well on the way to giving women full equality in holding high executive posts in the federal government. There are a few: Mrs. Helen Bentley is Chairman of the Federal Maritime Commission; the U.S. Air Force has Brigadier-General Jeanne Holm; Mrs. Joyce Baker Spain is Vice-Chairman of the Civil Service Commission; Miss Barbara M. Watson is Administrator of the Bureau of Security and Consular Affairs; Mrs. Catherine Bedell is Chairman of the U.S. Tariff Commission; Mrs. Virginia Knauer is Special Assistant to the President for Consumer Affairs;[7] Marina Whitman, mathematician with a Ph.D. from Columbia University, is one of three members of the Council of Economic Advisers. There are now 79 women in the federal government who earn $28,000 to $42,000 per year, but Roosevelt, Kennedy and Johnson did more for outstanding women: in 1966 1.6 percent of the federal jobs paying $28,000 and more belonged to women (ridiculously few), but in 1970 the percentage had receded to 1.5 percent.[8]

Now that Congress has passed the Equal Rights Amendment, which states that "equality of rights under the law shall not be denied or abridged by the United States or by any state on account of sex," women may become more demanding. Chances for equality in employment look brighter, assuming that the necessary 38 states will ratify the amendment, but the real impact on the situation must be made by women themselves. That will be hard work, because the women's ranks are split as many ways as men's, and consensus is practically impossible. Yet militant women can overcome great odds, with persistence, and if there were more women in Congress like Abzug, Chisholm, Griffiths, and Mink, their job would be easier. The 93rd Congress has added several Congresswomen who may be expected to be militant on behalf of women's rights. But the women of the rank and file first must be awakened to the need for more women in Congress. Mrs. Medgar Evers, who herself ran unsuccessfully for political office (in a hopelessly uncongenial district), offers a ten-point test for women to get into politics. The characteristics needed are conviction, self-confidence, family support, financial support, flexibility, physical and mental stamina, ability to take defeat and try again, compatibility, a sense of politics (do you really enjoy politics?), and a sense of humor.[9] Margaret Mead said "more women must go into politics and many more women must actively support those who do." They must do what immigrants, religious and ethnic minorities, and labor unions have done—viz., break into politics.[10]

How difficult that is for women has been demonstrated. To cite only one example, a contender for the mayoralty of the city of Syracuse, New York, reported that: the press comment was constantly adverse; a local union, which had been requested to allow the aspirant to address the union members at one of its public functions, replied that women were not allowed at their clambakes; some women interrogated said "we belong in the kitchen"; and, to top it all, the final indignity was to be told to pose in the nude.[11] Lenore Romney is another contender who looks back with resignation on her unsuccessful try for a seat in the U.S. Senate.[12] Mrs. Griffiths says politics is a tough game;[13] another woman who ran and won says that politics is secretive, manipulative, and often enough dirty, and that anyone who can't take it shouldn't try to play the game.[14]

CONGRESS AND WOMEN

Woefully few women have gained access to the highest level of legislative activity in the United States: the Congress. Since 1916, when the first woman was sworn in as a member of the House of Representatives, through the 92nd Congress, which officially ended on the 3rd of January, 1973—that is, in nearly 60 years—only eleven women have gone to the Senate, and seventy have been in the House of Representatives, a total of 81 women.* When Congresswoman Martha W. Griffiths, who has represented Detroit since 1955, asked the Legislative Reference Service of the Library of Congress how long it would take for women to gain parity with men in representing constituencies in Congress, the answer was 432 years.

---

*There were 80 individual women, but Margaret Chase Smith served in both House and Senate, consecutively, and must therefore be counted twice.

The number of women elected to the Congress is indeed small. The total number of men serving as Senators or Representatives is calculated in the tens of thousands in the nearly two centuries since Congress started; the number of women serving does not even reach 100, abysmally low even when one recognizes that women have been in Congress scarcely more than one-fourth the time of men. Since 1917, when the first woman took her seat, through 1972 women have accounted for 12 Senators and 69 Representatives in our national legislature; the time span from 1917 through 1972 is the period under investigation in this survey. Some states have never sent any woman to Congress: they are Alaska, Delaware, Iowa, Mississippi, Nevada, New Hampshire, North Dakota, Rhode Island, South Dakota, Vermont, Virginia, Wisconsin and Wyoming. Wyoming, though, was the first to give the vote to women (as early as 1868); and having done so, Wyoming refused to be intimidated by the federal government's threats of expulsion from the Union. Alabama, Arizona, Idaho, Kansas, Kentucky, Maine, Maryland, Minnesota, Missouri, Montana, New Mexico, North Carolina, Ohio, Oklahoma, Utah and West Virginia each sent one woman to Congress. Connecticut, Hawaii, Indiana, Louisiana, Massachusetts, Michigan, Nebraska, New Jersey, Oregon, and Washington each elected two, while Arkansas, California, Georgia, South Carolina and Tennessee sent three, and Illinois and New York sent seven each. It seems, therefore, that representation is fairly evenly spread across the country, and that North and South, East and West have participated as equally as can be expected. During the first two decades more Republicans than Democrats made it, but later Democrats had an edge over the Republicans. During the last Congress surveyed in this book, of the total of 14 women Senators and Representatives, 11 were Democrats and 3 were Republicans. The length of service was very unequal: eleven served less than one year, three served between one and two years, ten had one two-year term, sixteen had two terms, seven had three terms, six served three terms, six four terms, four each had either five or six terms, two had seven terms; one each was in the Congress for eight, nine, and ten terms, and one each continued for thirteen, fourteen and eighteen terms. Most of the women were either married or widowed; only six were unmarried. About half of them succeeded their husbands after the latter's death while still serving as Congressman; and a number of these then sought successful re-election in their own right. The others sought and obtained election for themselves without having to walk over the dead bodies of their husbands, which has been increasingly the case in the last two decades. Twenty-four women had no previous political experience, while twenty-three had had political experience on the local, state, or national party level; a goodly number had previously served as elected government officials in their cities or states, such as judges, secretary of state, etc. Seventeen were housewives or socialites before going to Congress, thirteen had come from education, eleven from social work, eight from business, and nine from law. Three had been in the entertainment profession (actors), and reporters could not resist the temptation to call them glamour girls; this was the unfair stamp placed upon such able legislators as Clare Boothe Luce and Helen Gahagan Douglas. The overwhelming majority were superior in wealth, position, or education—in fact, most of them had better educational backgrounds than their male colleagues; only a few had received no education beyond college or university. Besides those who succeeded their congressman husbands, several others had men in their families who had served in legislative offices (fathers, uncles, etc.). Ruth Hanna McCormick frankly stated that she did not run as a woman, but as the daughter of Marc Hanna, and the wife of Medill McCormick, both United States Senators. Two widows who had no children dedicated their entire lives to public service—viz., Margaret Chase Smith and Mrs. Leonor Sullivan. Only one woman succeeded in being elected Senator after serving first as Congresswoman: Mrs. Smith, who served in the House from 1940 to 1948, and then was Senator from Maine for four full terms, 1949 to 1973. Mrs. Edith Nourse Rogers, a tremendous vote-getter, continued in the House for 18 full terms, 36 years, while Mrs. Smith had the second longest run, 32 years. One Senator served only one day.

Many Congresswomen were perfectly satisfied to remain obscure; their accomplishments were few or none. A substantial number rolled up good records, and some were real achievers, the most prominent being Mrs. Frances Bolton, Mrs. Helen Douglas, Mrs. Clare Luce, Mrs. Maurine Neuberger, Mrs. Mary Norton, and Mrs. Edith Rogers; Mrs. Bolton, Mrs. Norton, and Mrs. Rogers all had very long incumbencies. In the Congress just past Bella Abzug, Shirley Chisholm, Florence Dwyer, Edith Green, Martha Griffiths, Julia B. Hansen, Margaret Heckler, Patsy Mink, Senator Smith, and Mrs. Leonor Sullivan all made significant contributions. In all, women in Congress have done no better and no worse than men, although none of them could be called equal to men like Norris, La Follette, Sam Rayburn, Lyndon Johnson, or, to go back to the nineteenth century, Henry Clay. But then there have been so few of them and they have not had the opportunities that these men had. In ideology and accomplishment they have not differed from their male fellow legislators: they have been liberals, conservatives, or reactionaries; they have voted on issues much as Congressmen do; they have not been flighty, emotional or irresponsible; many have worked hard and earnestly; and not one has been involved in any reprehensible deals. Lobbyists with much money and influence to throw around have not ventured to approach them with selfish motives. Most of them have started as members of committees with low prestige. A larger proportion have been on the Education and Labor Committee than on any other committee, except perhaps the Veterans Committee, and only a handful have achieved membership on prestigious committees such as Appropriations, Armed Services, or Ways and Means; some have become chairmen of subcommittees that wield influence and power.

Congress, consisting of 100 Senators and 435 Representatives, convenes in January of each odd-numbered year in a first session to meet generally throughout the calendar year, with brief or long recesses. It reconvenes in January of the following, even-numbered, year for the second session. Representatives then must stand for re-election. Mrs. Griffiths has said that the important, substantial business coming before the Congress is taken up by the House; however, a quorum is often lacking on the floor, for various reasons—sometimes just because some Congressmen are lazy. The proceedings of Congress are published daily in the *Congressional Record*, separately for each

House. An enormous amount of verbiage is spouted. The *Daily Digest* for Wednesday, November 8, 1972, lists 21,926 pages of proceedings for the first session of the Senate (January 21 through December 17, 1971) and 18,665 pages for the second session (January 18 through October 18, 1972); the corresponding figures for the House are 12,759 and 10,503 pages, respectively, proving the House less verbose than the Senate. The latter was in session 186 days, or 1,157 hours and 14 minutes, and 162 days, or 1,137 hours and 23 minutes in the first and second session. Almost each daily issue also prints "Extensions of Remarks," speeches not made on the floor, but reported verbatim from printed or written matter provided by the members. Some of it is interesting and important, but most of it is drivel; this section of the daily record accumulated for each session was 13,942 and 9,264 pages for the 92nd Congress. One Congressman inserts daily the same little invariable sermon about man's cruelty to man, chiding the North Vietnamese for mistreating our POW's. Jack Anderson in his syndicated column says that he found, casually leafing through the pages of the Record, an essay on peanuts, a plea for needy beekeepers, an editorial (35 years old) criticizing FDR's policies, and similar matter.[15]

Some of the women in Congress also fill the pages of the Record with material of little interest, chiefly for pleasing their constituents by remembering some long-deceased baseball hero, or by celebrating the paper collection campaign of the students at an elementary school. Exceptions to this practice are Bella Abzug's columns in "Extension of Remarks"—always cogent, intelligent, to the point, and clearly and pungently expressed, they are on matters of primary interest to the welfare of the nation. She says that the report of the daily *Congressional Record* is light reading which she peruses after her 18-hour day.

CONGRESSIONAL COMMITTEES AND WOMEN

The real business of the Congress does not take place on the floor of each House. Much of it is done informally at meetings, lunches, in smoking rooms, or on the tennis and golf courses, where the wheeling and dealing for legislative projects takes place. But the substantial work is done in committees. Committees were established by Congress almost at the very beginning of our national history and in time they proliferated so wildly that there were hundreds of them. In the 1940s there was a sharp reduction to several dozen, but the zeal for multiplicity soon found a way around restrictions by giving birth to subcommittees. In 1970 there were a total of 305 in both houses, counting standing (i.e., permanent) committees and subcommittees.[16] The Senate has 17 standing committees, the House 21; some have no subcommittees (such as the Committee on Ways and Means, which does all its business in full committee). Membership is made up of Democrats and Republicans, roughly on the basis of the total membership of each party, the chairman being a representative of the majority party—that is, the person with the greatest seniority in length of service in the Congress. This gives great power to men from the South, who get re-elected year after year and decade after decade by their faithful constituents.

All of the chairmen are men, but some women have chaired sub-committees. Senator Smith was second-ranking minority member on the Aeronautical and Space Sciences Committee, third-ranking on Appropriations, and ranking (first) on the Armed Services Committee. Senators are usually on more than one committee, while Congressmen are confined generally to membership on one committee, although they retain places on one or more subcommittees. Mrs. Julia Butler Hansen was 17th on the majority side on the important House Appropriations Committee, which handles requests for expenditures of federal revenues; with its membership of 33 Democrats and 22 Republicans, it is the committee with the most members. Mrs. Leonor K. Sullivan was third on House Banking and Currency; Mrs. Dwyer and Mrs. Heckler, Republicans, were second and ninth, respectively, on the minority side. House Education and Labor had Mrs. Edith Green, second, and also Mrs. Mink, Mrs. Chisholm, Mrs. Grasso, and Mrs. Hicks; Government Operations had Mrs. Abzug and Mrs. Dwyer among its 39 members; Patsy Mink was the only woman on Interior and Insular Affairs; Leonor K. Sullivan was second on Merchant Marine and Fisheries; Bella Abzug, Democrat, with the lowest priority, on Public Works. Four women were on Veterans Affairs: Shirley Chisholm, Louise Day Hicks, Ella T. Grasso, and Margaret M. Heckler. Martha W. Griffiths was the only woman (and fifth in line of accession to the chairmanship) on the immensely important and powerful Ways and Means Committee, concerned with taxation, Medicare, tariffs, reciprocal trade, and Social Security.[17] Most women in recent Congresses have been on the less powerful committees (primarily education and veterans' affairs). These are not necessarily the committees on which they wanted to serve, for the committee assignments are made for the Democrats by the Democratic members of the Ways and Means Committee, for the Republicans by their Committee on Committees. Mrs. Chisholm was put on Agriculture but, in response to her objection that the only thing they knew in Washington was that a tree grew in Brooklyn, she was placed on a more appropriate committee. However, Bella Abzug, who wanted to be on Armed Services, was not similarly accommodated. Only two women are on the most crucial committees—Appropriations and Ways and Means—although several are on Education and Labor, an important committee torn by much internal dissention.

CONGRESSIONAL ACTION AND WOMEN

How a bill becomes a law is a rather simple procedure, diagrammatically, but in reality it is a most complex one. In the first session of the 92nd Congress, 18,146 measures were introduced (3,493 in the Senate, 14,653 in the House); in the second session 7,208 were introduced (1,403 in the Senate, 5,805 in the House). But only 224 and 383 public bills, respectively, were enacted into public law, three being vetoed by Nixon in the first session, and 17 in the second, with two overrides in the second session. Thus, slightly more than 1 percent of the introduced measures went onto the statute books. No wonder Congressmen get apathetic in the face of the immense odds against successful passage of what they consider very important issues.

Congress was the most vigorous branch of the federal government in the early decades of the present century. It has now abdicated its powers to the presidency, to the disadvantage of the electorate. Additionally, its most influential members are conservatives and reactionaries; many Congressmen and Senators are millionaires whose hearts go out to the rich. It is easy to get votes for the wealthy and their demands and for giant corporations that, through mismanagement, have fallen on evil times. Members of Congress are always ready to vote big salaries and pensions for themselves. Each of them now costs $42,500 a year; they intended to raise their pensions to $40,000 yearly, after a few years of incumbency, and to give themselves a paid-up $50,000 insurance. But they are reluctant to vote $1,600 a year for a poor family of four. The 92nd Congress has spent about $200 million for payroll and housekeeping, which amounts to $367,000 for each Senator and Congressman. Many of them are poorly informed about the needs of the country, and not too many care about the needs of the most unfortunate in the country. Members of Congress, however, also guaranteed themselves a profit on inflation. On March 1, 1969, they got themselves a 41 percent pay raise (from $30,000 to $42,500), which Nixon approved without complaining about its inflationary impact—as he does when federal employees' salaries or Social Security payments are to be raised 5 percent or 10 percent. Now they will get periodic pay boosts without voting for them. A special commission will set rules, and every four years new raises will go into effect. Their pensions entitle them to retirement at age 62 after 5 years of service; they may then take a job in private industry and not lose a penny. When the cost of living rises 3 percent a Congressman's or Senator's pension will automatically go up 4 percent.[18]

The same daily paper that reported this information presented noted about a year and a quarter later that politics, like crime, pays handsomely if it is of the right kind. Their "$42,500 annual salary is only the top of an iceberg of emoluments that come with the office."[19] Members of state legislatures, county supervisory boards, and municipal councilmen indulge in the same lucrative game. This is disgusting, but it will not stop until a new breed of people's tribunes replaces the old. The indications are that this may happen before too long.

Several good bills were introduced in both houses in the last session of the 92nd Congress. The Brademas-Dellenback Bill provided for a "comprehensive child development program" under HEW administration, and would have included quality education and day-care programs through school age. It gave priority to the lowest income groups at a cost of $700 million the first year (80 percent federally funded, 20 percent to be paid by states and counties). Javits was to introduce a "comprehensive program of community-based and co-ordinated child development," which paralleled the House bill, with direct funding to the local units, and which provided child care councils composed of parents and of public and private agencies within the community. Birch Bayh and Walter Mondale introduced programs similar to these.[20] There were good, positive programs for better health care (Kennedy bill), for better schools, education, transportation, and nutrition. But these bills had no chance of being passed by the last Congress. The day is coming when the electorate, no longer befuddled by prejudices, no longer ready to succumb to slogans, will elect a Congress that will do something for all—especially the poor—and not confine itself to benefiting the rich. There are many fine Congressmen and Senators, real tribunes of the people, but it is very hard for them to prevail against the coalition of conservative Republicans and Southern Democrats.

There has been only one multimillionaire Congresswoman; she gave good advice as to how the deprived classes could be taught responsibility; she also enjoyed many lengthy junkets to foreign countries as a member of committees to make investigations abroad, at taxpayers' expense. Almost all Congresswomen and Senators have come from the middle class—materially comfortable, but not individually wealthy or with enormous incomes. Only in recent years have the underprivileged sent some Representatives to Congress. Their income from congressional salaries and perquisites has not made them rich; in fact, some of them are penalized in relation to others. Mrs. Mink, for example, in order to keep in touch with her constituency, has to make many trips back to Hawaii, partially paying for them with her own money; Congresswomen from the East and Middle West do not face this same problem.

Congresswomen have made their impact in a limited sphere of problems, not in foreign affairs, defense needs, the judiciary, or science and astronautics, and only in a limited way as concerns appropriations or tax policies. Their contributions have been more in the social sphere—consumerism, education, veterans' needs and problems—and to some extent in economics as it applies to the daily life of the average citizen. Will this lopsided condition continue? It is likely to do so, but Congresswomen are rightly insisting on more influence in fields not traditionally considered to be theirs. Issues abound: unemployment (much larger than Nixon's figures reveal), poverty, insufficient health care for all, civil rights, the cities' decay, law and order, surveillance and oppression of free speech, ecologic damage, mass transit, taxes, the shaky dollar, unfavorable balance of payments and trade deficits, inflation, the accelerating cost of living, the frightening dependence on distant and unfriendly countries for fossil fuels, educational needs, child care, equality of opportunity for the underprivileged (including women)—the list is endless.[21] Members of Congress need to assert their independence from a President who demands hefty increases for bombers, missiles, submarines and space ventures, while cutting to the bone expenditures for social purposes. The 14 women in the 93rd Congress are too few to tip the scales, but at any rate it is hoped that they will align themselves on the side of the angels.

FOOTNOTES

1. Martin, Gruberg, *Women in American Politics* (Academia Press, 1968), p. 11.
2. Gruberg, p. v.
3. Gruberg, pp. 43-44.
4. *U.S. News & World Report*, Aug. 14, 1972, pp. 66ff.
5. *U.S. News & World Report*, Aug. 14, 1972, p. 69.
6. Betty Friedan, *The Feminine Mystique* (New York, 1963), p. 374.
7. *U.S. News*, Jan. 17, 1972, pp. 62-69.
8. *Time*, March 20, 1972, pp. 25-103 ("The New Woman," a *Time* special issue).
9. "Mrs. Medgar Evers: Petunia in an Onion Patch," *Ladies Home Journal*, Apr. 1972, p. 113ff.
10. Margaret Mead, "Women and Politics," *Redbook*, Nov. 1970, p. 50ff.
11. Karen de Crow, "Women and Politics," *Mademoiselle*, Feb. 1970, p. 34ff.
12. "Lenore Romney looks back on her unsuccessful campaign for Senator," *Look*, Apr. 6, 1971, p. 11.
13. "How women are doing in politics," *U.S. News*, Sept. 7, 1970, pp. 24-27.
14. Mary Anne Guitar, "An insider's guide for the politically innocent," *Mademoiselle*, June 1972, p. 132ff.
15. "Washington Merry-Go-Round," Monday, Nov. 27, 1972.
16. Marc J. Green, *Who Runs Congress?* (Grossman Publishers, 1972; Ralph Nader Congress Project), p. 54.
17. David Mayhew, *The 92nd Congress and Its Committees* (Washington, The Center of Information on America, 1971; Grass Roots Guide).
18. Vincent Burke in *Los Angeles Times*, Oct. 26, 1969, Sect. G, p. 3.
19. *Los Angeles Times*, Jan. 31, 1971, Sect. A.
20. *Saturday Review*, Feb. 20, 1971.
21. *Nation*, March 13, 1972, pp. 323-24.

HOUSE OF REPRESENTATIVES

(Congresswomen are listed chronologically
by year of arrival in the Congress)

JEANNETTE RANKIN
Republican, Montana
1917-19, 1942-43

The nineteenth amendment, which gave American women the right to vote, reads as follows:

Article XIX

Section 1

The right of citizens of the United States to vote shall not be denied or abridged by the United States or by any state on account of sex.

Section 2

Congress shall have power to enforce this article by appropriate legislation.

The nineteenth amendment was first submitted to Congress on January 10, 1878, and resubmitted for a vote in every subsequent Congress until it was passed by the 66th Congress in 1919; the House approved it on May 21, and the Senate on June 4. Secretary of State Bainbridge Colby proclaimed it part of the Constitution on August 26, 1920, when 36 of the then 48 states had ratified it. Illinois, Wisconsin, and Michigan were the first states to approve it, and Tennessee was the 36th state to pass it, on August 18, 1920.

Miss Jeanette Rankin, however, had beat the slow-moving machinery of voting and ratification; she was elected to the 65th Congress, in 1916, as Congresswoman-at-large, the only Republican representative from Montana. She held her seat from March 4, 1917, to March 4, 1919.

A graduate of the University of Montana, she became a social worker, but at the same time was very busy on behalf of woman suffrage, for which she campaigned in California, Washington, and Montana; the latter state had given women the right to vote as early as 1914. In 1917 Miss Rankin voted against America's entry into World War I; she was not reelected. She subsequently ran twice for Senator from Montana, both times unsuccessfully, then tried again for Representative, and in 1940 she was again elected as a pacifist. Once more she voted against United States participation in a World War, and once more was rewarded by defeat in the 1942 election. During her lifetime she remained active in her fight against wars, even when she was in her nineties. She was recently quoted as saying that she would do again what she did before, only she would be "more nasty." This grand old lady of courage and principle deserves our gratitude for her pioneer work.

Pacifism was her distinctive mark; but she was also struggling to aid other members of her sex. As mentioned above much earlier she had worked for woman suffrage; later, together with Jane Addams, she sought legislation to improve working conditions for women. Miss Rankin died in May 1973, at the age of 94.

Bibliography

"First Woman Elected to Congress," *Outlook* 114:623-24 (Nov. 22, 1916).
"First Woman Elected to Congress," B. Fligelman, *Sunset* 37:33 (Nov. 1916).
"Lady from Missoula," D. Wilhelm, *Independent* 90:25 (Apr. 2, 1917).
"Lady from Montana," Tattler, *Nation* 104:667 (May 31, 1917).
"Member from Montana," *Literary Digest* 53:1417 (Nov. 25, 1916).
"Our Busy Congress," *Literary Digest* 55:41+ (Aug. 11, 1917).
"Political Power in the Hands of a Woman," *Survey* 38:357 (July 21, 1917).
"What We Women Should Do," *Ladies Home Journal* 34:17 (Aug. 1917).
"Woman Against War," *Scribners Commentator* 11:27-30 (Nov. 1941).
Gruberg, Martin. *Women in American Politics: An Assessment and Sourcebook* (Oshkosh, Wisc., Academia Press, 1968), pp. 151-52.
Paxton, Annabelle. *Women in Congress* (Richmond, Va., Dietz Press, 1945), pp. 1-2.

ALICE M. ROBERTSON
Republican, Oklahoma
1921-23

The 66th Congress, which met from 1919-21, was an all-male Congress, but the 67th (1921-23) had four women representatives, three of them Republicans, and one Independent Democrat. While Miss Rankin was defeated because her antiwar stance was far ahead of its time, Miss Alice M. Robertson, Republican from the Second Congressional District of Oklahoma, incumbent from March 3, 1921, to the same date in 1923, was defeated in the 1922 general election because she had voted against the soldiers' bonus legislation.

She had studied at Elmira College, New York, and worked in the Indian Office from 1873 to 1879, thereafter had taught at Tallahassee Indian School as well as at Oklahoma Indian Territory Girls' School, later to become the University of Tulsa. Miss Robertson also later served as postmaster. While in the House of Representatives she was placed on the House Indian Affairs Committee, an assignment at which more politically ambitious women have balked; her parents had been missionaries to the Cherokees and Creeks. Amazingly, she expressed herself as being anti-suffragist. Since she was 66 years old at the time of her election to Congress, she willingly retired from politics after her defeat, saying that politics was too rough and immoral for women.

Bibliography

"Woman Who Got Into Congress Through the Want Ad Column," *Literary Digest* 67:56-58 (Dec. 4, 1920).
"A la Cherokee," *Delineator* 98:68 (Apr. 1921).
"Congresswoman Elected with Want Ads," *Current Opinion* 70:41-44 (Jan. 1921).
"Lady From Oklahoma," G. Forman. *Independent* 105:311 (Mar. 26, 1921).
"Miss Alice of Muskogee," *Ladies Home Journal* 38:21 (Mar. 1921).
"Women's Place in Politics," M. M. Marshall. *Woman's Home Companion* 48:15 (Oct. 1921).

Gruberg, p. 152.
Paxton, pp. 2-3.

MAE ELLA NOLAN (Mrs. John I. Nolan)
Republican, California
1921-25

Besides Senator Rebecca Felton and Representatives Huck and Robertson, the 67th Congress also seated Mae Ella Nolan, a Republican from California's Fifth Congressional District. Mrs. Nolan was reelected to the succeeding 68th Congress, its only woman member. A graduate of St. Vincent's Convent, San Francisco, she succeeded her late husband, John I. Nolan. After a pro-labor and anti-Prohibition campaign, she was reelected in November 1922 to serve until March 4, 1925. She did not seek renomination or reelection in November 1924.

Bibliography

Literary Digest 81:12 (Apr. 12, 1924).
Colliers 74:18 (Sept. 27, 1924).
Independent 115:727 (Dec. 26, 1925).
Gruberg, p. 152.
Paxton, p. 123.

WINIFRED SPRAGUE MASON HUCK (Mrs. Robert Huck)
Republican, Illinois
1922-23

Mrs. Huck was elected as Representative-at-large. Her term of office ran only from November 7, 1922 until March 4, 1923. A journalist and lecturer, she was elected to her late father's seat, which she never actually assumed, since Congress was not in session between the time of her election and the opening of the next Congress (the 68th); nor did she succeed in securing nomination and election for the 68th Congress. She campaigned once more in 1923 for the seat of another deceased Congressman, again without success.

Bibliography

"What Happened to Me in Congress," *Woman's Home Companion* 50:4 (July 1923).
Gruberg, pp. 121, 152.
Paxton, p. 123.

FLORENCE P. KAHN (Mrs. Julius Kahn)
Republican, California
1925-37

Another San Francisco woman who succeeded her late husband in Congress was Florence Prag Kahn; she represented California's Fourth Congressional District from 1925 to 1937. Like her mother she had been a teacher, but she kept herself closely involved with her husband's political interests and found little difficulty in representing her constituents' needs ably and articulately. She was first given a place on the Indian Affairs Committee, but because of her objections to serving on a committee that she considered of minor importance, the Congressional leaders (at that time Republicans) made her a member of the Education Committee. But she did not rest until she had convinced the party that she should be on the Military Affairs Committee; her husband Julius had been its chairman. Her remarks on the floor of the House were concise and logical; and she proved to be such a good parliamentarian that she was frequently chosen to preside over debate. She helped obtain authorization for a sum of $75 million for the building of the San Francisco Bay Bridge. Her term of 12 years in office was terminated by her defeat in the 1936 Roosevelt landslide over Alf Landon.

Bibliography

"New Congresswoman," E. N. Maddux. *Woman Citizen n.s.* 9:10 (Mar. 7, 1925).
"Gentlewomen of the House," D. Gilfond. *American Mercury* 18:158-59 (Oct. 1929).
"Lady from California," F. P. Keyes. *Delineator* 118:14+ (Feb. 1931).
"What Are the Women Up To?", A. R. Longworth. *Ladies Home Journal* 51:9+ (Mar. 1934).
"Women of the Year," M. R. Rinehart. *Pictorial Review* 36:7 (Jan. 1935).
"It Couldn't Happen in Congress Now," *Nations Business* 25:18-20+ (Feb. 1937).
Gruberg, pp. 152-53.
Paxton, pp. 3-4.

MARY TERESA HOPKINS NORTON (Mrs. Robert Francis Norton)
Democrat, New Jersey
1925-51

From Miss Rankin to Mrs. Rogers all Congresswomen had been Republicans; Mrs. Norton was the first Democrat elected to the House of Representatives. From 1925 to 1951, when she retired, she represented the Twelfth New Jersey Congressional District with great distinction.

She was born in 1875. Her father was a well-to-do roadbuilder, for whom she worked as stenographer and secretary until her marriage in 1909 to businessman Robert Francis Norton; when her only child died, she turned to welfare work and dabbled in politics; in 1920 she became a county representative of the New Jersey State Democratic Committee at the urging of Mayor Frank Hague of Jersey City. She advanced to state vice-chairman and in 1932 became chairman. Perceiving her political talent, Hague asked her to run for Congress, and with his powerful machine behind her she won a seat and began her incumbency in 1925, joining the 69th Congress.

As a freshman Congresswoman she was placed on the Veterans Committee; later, she advanced to the more important Labor Committee, which was subject to a great deal of internal strife; eventually she became its chairman. Called the dean of women representatives and a breaker of precedents, she adopted a responsible and progressive attitude as a friend of labor and a foe of prohibition. She introduced the first bill for repeal of the 18th Amendment (the Volstead prohibition amendment). Whatever she undertook she embraced with energy and resolution. As chairman of the House Committee on the District of Columbia, she was called the mayor of Washington and under her vigorous leadership many ameliorative bills passed through: for slum clearance, legalization of boxing, and selling of liquor.

In the 75th Congress (1937 and 1938), she resigned from this committee to become chairman of the Labor and Education Committee. "Aunt Mary" steered Franklin D. Roosevelt's pending Wage and Hours Bill through the House against the stubborn opposition of conservatives. She considered this one of the most important bills passed by Congress, and tried to shame her detractors by arguing that members of Congress who took home $833 a month, dare not face workers whose wages were $12.60 a week. Some of her male colleagues resented her being committee chairman and they were willing to sabotage legislation originating in her committee; she complained that much important legislation had been "stolen" from the Labor Committee because it was headed by a woman.*
While the Wage and Hours Bill was adopted, she was unable to get a permanent Fair Employment Practices Commission established, though she pushed strongly for it. Her bill remained bottled up in the Rules Committee. She had no kind words for Carl Vinson, whose Committee on Naval Affairs she said was infringing on labor legislation.

Other legislation that she originated asked for an annual authorization of $5 million to set up state agencies for the administration of labor laws; this would have established a three-man Industrial Safety Commission. Another bill, HR3864, would have required the creation of four new positions in the Labor Department; both bills were stricken from the Consent Calendar. In the 79th Congress, meeting in 1946, she introduced maternal and child welfare bills; none of this legislation was passed by a hostile Congress. The same fate befell a bill that would have raised the minimum wage from 40 to 65 cents an hour; this rejection was also given to what was called a "labor extension bill," whose purpose was to provide labor with a service similar to the one provided for agriculture by the Agricultural Extension Service.

The years after World War II and those of the beginning of the Cold War were heartbreaking years of frustration and failure for Mrs. Norton and other progressives trying to stem the flood of legislation unloosed by Republican and Democrat reactionaries. Labor- and communist-baiters had a field day, but Mrs.

*Gruberg, p. 154.

Norton was able to turn back the Mundt-Nixon bill, which would have required registration of all Communist front organizations and of all Communist Party members—legislation endorsed by many patriotic societies, such as the American Legion; it failed to get through the second session of the 80th Congress, in 1948. In the first session of the 81st Congress, meeting in 1949, the House Administration Committee reported HR3199, which called for outright repeal of the poll tax; this bill was ably put forward by the Committee's chairman Mary T. Norton. Southerners moved for adjournment, claiming that such a law was unconstitutional. In a counterspeech Mrs. Norton took up this contention, saying that Senate lawyers had accepted previous bills as constitutional; nine law professors also signed a document attesting to the constitutional power of Congress to outlaw the poll tax; furthermore, the Attorney General expressed his opinion that the bill was constitutional. Mrs. Norton was successful: the final vote in the House was 273 to 116 for her bill. In the Senate SJRes34 called for a constitutional amendment to outlaw the poll tax, but its discussion was postponed indefinitely, thus negating Mrs. Norton's efforts on behalf of civil rights. President Truman pledged that there would be no retreat from his civil rights stand, but it took a dozen more years and several more presidents to accomplish the grant of full civil rights.

Mrs. Norton was always easily reelected. Her district was urban, without farm population, and organized labor was and is strong there. Of Hague, who is generally evaluated a scoundrel, she said that he was a great and noble leader. It is true that he never once tried to dictate her vote, and she may have uttered this praise only for practical reasons, because politicians cannot always be held to their words. She was pessimistic about women's support for women in elections; "women won't vote for women." But although she said she believed that woman's place was in the home, she was vigorous in organizing women.

Genial and unassuming, cool, witty, competent, and hardworking she was one of the best of woman representatives in Congress, and she worked so hard and devotedly that she cared for no social life outside her home; she had this singleminded devotion in common with several other women lawmakers, such as Congresswoman Leonor Sullivan and Senator Margaret Chase Smith.

Bibliography

"Politics is a Business," *Colliers* 89:22 (May 21, 1932).

"Should Legal Barriers Against Birth Control be Removed?", *Congressional Digest* 10:106-107 (Apr. 1931).

"Gentlewomen of the House," D. Gilfond. *American Mercury* 18 :159-60 (Oct. 1929).

"Five Democratic Women," M. Davis. *Ladies Home Journal* 50:117 (May 1933).

"Her Honor, the Mayor of Washington," D. T. Lynch. *Literary Digest* 119:24 (Mar. 30, 1935).

"Truly Democratic," F. P. Keyes. *Delineator* 122:12+ (Mar. 1933).

"What Are the Women Up To?", A. R. Longworth. *Ladies Home Journal* 51:9+ (Mar. 1934).

"Headliners in American Affairs," *Scholastic* 30:10 (May 15, 1937).

"Wage and Hours Legislation; Object of the Law," *Vital Speeches* 4:485-86 (June 1, 1938).

"Aunt Mary's Applecart," *Time* 31:14-15 (May 16, 1938).
"Congresswoman Who Learned How From a Master," *Newsweek* 9:17-18 (June 26, 1937).
"Women in Two Big Labor Posts," R. A. Black. *Independent Woman* 16:200+ (July 1937).
"Woman's Next Step," interview, S. B. Anthony, 2d. *New York Times Magazine,* p. 11+ (Jan. 12, 1941).
"Democracy's Stepchild," *Woman's Home Companion* 71:19 (Aug. 1944).
"Ladies of Congress," A. Porter. *Colliers* 112:22-23 (Aug. 28, 1943).
"Biography of Mary T. Norton" in *Current Biography* (Nov. 1944).
"Arguments in Favor of Fair Employment Practices Bill," *Congressional Digest* 24:172+ (June 1945).
"Remarks on Anti-Poll Tax Measure," *Congressional Digest* 29:60+ (Feb. 1950).
"Battling Mary Retires," *Independent Woman* 29:198-200 (July 1950).
"Women in Congress," *National Education Association Journal* 38:283 (Apr. 1949).
Gruberg, pp. 67, 104, 111, 153-54, 241, 279, 291.
Paxton, pp. 29-37.

EDITH FRANCES NOURSE ROGERS (Mrs. John Jacob Rogers)
Republican, Massachusetts
1925-60

Mrs. Rogers, who represented the Massachusetts Fifth Congressional District, had the longest incumbency of all women in Congress; she entered into service on June 3, 1925, and died in office on September 10, 1960, piling up fully 35 years, an even longer stretch than Mrs. Bolton's and Senator Margaret Smith's, who served 29 and 32 years, respectively. And at the beginning of her career, when she succeeded her husband, it was prophesied that her career would be brief.

On her mother's side she descended from a woman who came on the Mayflower, on her father's side from Rebecca Nourse, the last "witch" to be hanged at Salem, Massachusetts. During World War I, from 1917 on, she worked for the American Red Cross and for the YMCA. She did so well that three presidents sought her help and named her personal representative in charge of assistance to disabled veterans, for their care, hospitalization and compensation. In this capacity she served Harding, Coolidge and Hoover, and it was a concern that was to stay with her throughout her long legislative career. She became one of the sponsors of the GI Bill of Rights and she supported veteran's interests from her first year in Congress. She said it was a "national scandal" that veteran's hospitals had not enough beds for disabled veterans. She also introduced bills for pensions for widows of veterans, and as the only woman member of the House Foreign Affairs Committee she sponsored legislation creating the WAAC's (Womens Army Auxiliary Corps) which passed in 1942 and attained a strength of 150,000 members.

She always voted the strict Republican line, was a strong proponent of neutrality, and was much opposed to the State Department's reciprocal trade treaties; she tried to curb import of Japanese goods and she opposed changing cotton tariffs. Her district was predominently industrial and residential, consisting of cities and small towns bordering the Boston area, with a highly diverse population. Industry consisted of textile and shoe manufacturing and food processing, and Mrs. Rogers worked for both sides—owners and mill hands—pushing for protective tariff laws for the mill owners and for benefits for millhands and their families. For this she won her constituency's appreciation, receiving 120,435 votes to her opponent's 37,593 in the 1940 election. She was also interested in the status of women. In the first session of the 80th Congress in 1947 she introduced a bill to secure an amendment for equal rights for women; the bill, however, remained unreported by the Judiciary Committee, a fate shared by other bills introduced for the same purpose.

There was one exception to her strict adherence to the demands of the Republican leadership: in the first session of the 86th Congress in 1959, Congress voted for public works projects, legislation that was vetoed by President Eisenhower. Rogers then voted with members who wanted to override the President's veto. Thereafter, Congress passed a revised version which was again vetoed, but the veto was overriden by both Houses; this version carried appropriations of $1,176,579,834 for army and civil functions and the Department of the Interior.

To summarize her accomplishments: although she was first of all a friend of veterans and their dependents, she also untiringly stood up for business interests, and she promoted aviation, the Women's Army Corps, and foreign service. She was conservative in her ideology and hard-working in office. She lived to be almost 80 years old.

Bibliography

"Widow in Politics," *Literary Digest* 86:13 (July 18, 1925).
Address. *American Society for International Law. Proceedings.* 1928:148-54.
"Does Naval Preparedness Prevent War?", *Congressional Digest* 8:18-19 (Jan. 1929).
"How the Kellogg Peace Pact Can be Made Effective," *Annals American Academy* 144:51-54 (July 1929).
"Gentlewomen of the House," D. Gilfond. *American Mercury* 18:157-58 (Oct. 1929).
"What Are the Women Up To?", A. R. Longworth. *Ladies Home Journal* 51:9+ (Mar. 1934).
"Tragedy of the Highways," *Vital Speeches* 2:439-40 (Apr. 6, 1936).
"Women's Army?", *Independent Woman* 21:38 (Feb. 1942).
Current Biography, 1942, pp. 898-99.
"Time Is Now," *Woman's Home Companion* 70:25 (Aug. 1943).
"Ladies of Congress," A. Porter. *Colliers* 112:22-23 (Aug. 28, 1943).
"Veterans Voice in Congress," *U.S. News* 22:70 (Feb. 28, 1947).
"New Notes in Scandals," *Newsweek* 33:24 (Apr. 4, 1949).
"Women in Congress," *National Education Association Journal* 38:283 (Apr. 1949).
Address on executive military power, March 15, 1951; excerpts: *Congressional Digest* 30:317+ (Dec. 1951).

"Women in the 83rd Congress," M. L. Temple. *Independent Woman* 32:59 (Feb. 1953).

"Women in the 84th Congress," *Independent Woman* 34:23+ (Jan. 1955).

"People of the Week," *U.S. News* 45:20 (July 11, 1958).

Gruberg, pp. 122, 153.

Paxton, pp. 39-51.

U.S. 86th Congress, 2nd sess., 1960.
> Memorial services held in the House of Representatives and Senate of the United States, together with remarks presented in eulogy of Edith Nourse Rogers, late a Representative from Massachusetts. Washington, U.S. Govt. Print. Off., 1961. 92p. port.

KATHERINE LANGLEY (Mrs. John Wesley Langley)
Republican, Kentucky
1926-31

Katherine Langley, a Republican, represented Kentucky's Tenth Congressional District in the 70th and 71st Congresses, 1926 to 1931. Her term ran from December 5, 1926, to March 4, 1931. She had attended the Woman's College, Richmond, Virginia, and the Emerson College of Oratory in Boston; thereafter she taught at the Virginia Institute in Bristol, Tennessee. Her knowledge of political life was intimate: her father had been a Congressman from North Carolina, and her husband served 19 years in Congress; she was his secretary for most of this time. In 1927 Mr. Langley was convicted of violation of the prohibition law; thereupon his wife was elected to fill his seat. She ran for reelection in the general election in 1930, but was defeated. During her incumbency her daughter served as her secretary; she thus continued the family tradition of a small intimate group keeping a tight grip on the political fortunes of tens of thousands of voters.

Bibliography

"Will It Be Congresswoman Langley?", *Literary Digest* 88:9 (Jan. 30, 1926).

"Kentucky's First Congresswoman," *Literary Digest* 90:14-15 (Aug. 21, 1926).

"Gentlewomen of the House," D. Gilfond. *American Mercury* 18:159-60 (Oct. 1929).

Gruberg, p. 154.

Paxton, pp. 123, etc.

FANNY PEARL PEDEN OLDFIELD (Mrs. William Allan Oldfield)
Democrat, Arkansas
1929-31

Mrs. Oldfield succeeded her husband as representative of Arkansas' Second Congressional District. She did not aspire to a second term, saying that a woman's place is at home.

Bibliography

Current History 30:426 (June 1929).
Gruberg, p. 154.
Paxton, p. 123.

RUTH HANNA McCORMICK   (Mrs. Medill McCormick)
Republican, Illinois
1929-31

Mrs. McCormick represented Illinois as a Representative-at-large in the 71st Congress. She knew politics from the ground up. She was the daughter of Senator Marc Hanna, for whose election she is said to have rung the doorbells of voters, and she married another politician, Medill McCormick. She took a prominent part in the Bull Moose movement, and before her entry into politics she had been chairman of the Congressional Committee of the National American Woman Suffrage Association. After her husband's death she engaged in two quite dissimilar enterprises: farming and newspaper publishing. In her campaign for Congress she traveled about in great style in a gleaming automobile. She seems to have been an isolationist and attacked the World Court while she was in Congress. But her political career came to a quick end in the 1930 general elections when she ran for the Senate. She achieved victory in the primary, but she lost out to her opponent in the November election. Political life seems to have been a necessary ingredient in her life style, however; in 1932 she married Congressman Albert G. Simms.

Bibliography

"Backstage in Washington," *Outlook* 156-58 (Sept. 10, 1930).
"Buying the Right to Govern," *Christian Century* 47:710-12 (June 4, 1930).
"Court, Beer and Politics," *Nation* 130:480 (Apr. 23, 1930).
"Deneen vs. Mrs. McCormick," *Christian Century* 47:390-92 (Mar. 26, 1930).
"Expenditures for Republican Nomination for Senator," *New Republic* 63:29 (May 28, 1930).
"First Woman Senator; Does Mrs. McCormick's Candidacy Reflect Those Ideals Which Women Will be Proud to See Represented?", *Christian Century* 47: 425-26 (Apr. 2, 1930).
"Gentlewomen of the House," D. Gilfond. *American Mercury* 18:153-55 (Oct. 1929).
"Illinois Referendum," C. C. Morrison. *Christian Century* 47:119-23 (Sept. 17, 1930).
"Marc Another Hanna," *Colliers* 85:10-11+ (Mar. 15, 1930).
"Marc Hanna's Little Girl," E. P. Keyes. *Delineator* 117:14+ (Oct. 1930).
"Mrs. McCormick of Illinois," D. Gilfond. *New Republic* 62:95-97 (Mar. 12, 1930).
"Mrs. McCormick Wins," *Outlook* 154:652-53 (Apr. 23, 1930).
"Mrs. McCormick's Trick," *Christian Century* 47:1055-56 (Sept. 3, 1930).
"New Newberry Case," *Outlook* 155:54-55 (May 14, 1930).

"Ominous Political Figures," *Christian Century* 47:1078-80 (Sept. 10, 1930).
"Out for the Senate," *Outlook* 153:218 (Oct. 9, 1929).
"Ruth Hanna McCormick's Victory," *Literary Digest* 105:9 (Apr. 19, 1930).
"Ruth McCormick Smashes Through," F. Babcock. *Nation* 130:484 (Apr. 23, 1930).
"She Snoops to Conquer," *Literary Digest* 106:5-7 (Sept. 20, 1930).
"Three Ruths in Congress," A. Hard. *Ladies Home Journal* 46:13 (Mar. 1929).
"What Price Public Office?", *Literary Digest* 105:14 (May 17, 1930).
"Woman of the Month," *Woman's Journal n.s.* 15:4 (May 1930).
"Woman Senator?", A. Hard. *Review of Reviews* 81:62-67 (Mar. 1930).
"Woman's Inglorious Adventure in Politics," *Christian Century* 47:1406 (Nov. 19, 1930).
Gruberg, pp. 121, 154-55, 203.
Paxton, pp. 6-7.

RUTH BRYAN OWEN (Mrs. Reginald Owen; Mrs. Boerge Rohde)
Democrat, Florida
1929-33

Ruth Bryan Owen, the daughter of William Jennings Bryan, was born in Florida. Her father, Wilson's Secretary of State, was the silvertongued orator who thought free coinage of silver would be the remedy for the ills besetting the country. He was a tireless champion of populist causes, and many times the presidential standard bearer for the Democrats, was always frustrated in his attempts for the aid of the underdog.

Ruth Bryan Owen studied at the University of Nebraska and was a great help to her father in his political crusades; she turned, like her father, to the Chautauqua platform to appeal for reforms and to support causes in aid of the common man. She married a British army officer, Reginald Owen, an engineer, who died in 1927. She then turned resolutely to a political career and served from 1929 to 1933, in the 71st and 72nd Congresses, as Democratic representative for Florida's Fourth Congressional District. She had a place on the House Foreign Affairs Committee; her male colleagues are said to have been enchanted with her. Her father had been a free trader; she did not follow him in this respect, but supported protective tariffs.

It is not surprising that she did much in support of causes to better the condition of women; she spoke out for mothers' pensions, and for the creation of a federal Department of Home and Child. Her Congressional career came to an end in the 1932 election, when she supported prohibition and was defeated in the primary. Franklin D. Roosevelt appointed her United States Minister to Denmark, the first woman appointed to a high foreign service post. She resigned in 1936, when she married Boerge Rohde of the Danish army, and she wrote several books in her leisure time.

Bibliography

Works about Ruth Bryan Owen

"Department of Home and Child," *Woman's Journal n.s.* 16:8-9 (Feb. 1931).
"Everglades From the Air," *Review of Reviews* 85:46-47 (Mar. 1932).
"Uncle Sam and the Children," *Good Housekeeping* 92:24-25+ (Jan. 1931).
"Woman in the House," *Woman's Home Companion* 58:11-12+ (Nov. 1931).
"Ask Your Congressman," interview, M. M. Marshall. *Colliers* 88:29+ (July 18, 1931).
"Gentlewomen of the House," D. Gilfond. *American Mercury* 18:152-53 (Oct. 1929).
"Some Are Born Great," F. P. Keyes. *Delineator* 119:14+ (Nov. 1931).
"Three Ruths in Congress," *Ladies Home Journal* 46:13 (Mar. 1929).
"Woman of the Month," *Woman's Journal n.s.* 15:6 (Jan. 1930).
"Lady Lame Duck's Farewell Verse," *Literary Digest* 115:32 (Feb. 25, 1933).
"My Daughter and Politics," *Woman's Home Companion* 60:27+ (Oct. 1933).
"Peace the Goodwill Way," *Rotarian* 43:5 (Dec. 1933).
"Men of State," W. F. Palmer. New *Outlook* 163:37 (Mar. 1934).
"Mr. Roosevelt's New Deal for Women," *Literary Digest* 115:24 (Apr. 15, 1933).
"New Minister to Denmark," *Newsweek* 1:18-19 (Apr. 15, 1933).
"Our First Woman Diplomat," C. Lowe. *Pictorial Review* 35:4+ (Feb. 1934).
"Ruth Bryan Owen, Our First Woman Diplomat," *Christian Century* 50:549-50 (Apr. 26, 1933).
"Women of the Year," M. R. Rinehart. *Pictorial Review* 36:6 (Jan. 1935).
"Double Helpings of Fame; Children of Famous People," E. Ramsay. *Delineator* 130:11 (Jan. 1937).
"Inunguak, or America's Entertaining Envoy to Denmark," *Newsweek* 6:22-23 (Sept. 28, 1935).
"Madame Minister's No. 3," *Time* 28:21 (July 20, 1936).
"Stateswoman's Shin," *Time* 28:16 (Oct. 5, 1936).
Gruberg, pp. 144, 147, 155, 276.
Paxton, pp. 4-6.

Works by Ruth Bryan Owen

"Caribbean Caravel," New York, Dodd, Mead, 1949. viii, 222p. illus.
"Look Forward, Warrior," New York, Dodd, Mead, 1942. vii, 108p.

RUTH BAKER PRATT (Mrs. John T. Pratt)
Republican, New York
1929-33

Ruth Baker Pratt represented the 17th New York State Congressional District in the 71st and 72nd Congresses. She was a graduate of Wellesley College and as Congresswoman received honorary degrees from Mt. Holyoke and

New York University. Widow of a Standard Oil executive, she had been active in civic affairs and as a woman's suffrage leader; before her entry into Congress she had also been a member of the New York City Board of Aldermen, the first woman member to be thus distinguished. She took great interest in Republican Party affairs and served five times as a delegate to Republican national conventions. Even after her unsuccessful try for reelection in 1932, which was not a Republican year, she continued her role in party politics. She also took part in the administration and furtherance of the New York Philharmonic Orchestra. She was the mother of six children.

Bibliography

"Ask Your Congressman," interview, M. M. Marshall. *Colliers* 88:29+ (July 18, 1931).
"Gentlewomen of the House," D. Gilfond. *American Mercury* 18:155-57 (Oct. 1929).
"Lady of the House," *Outlook* 152:377 (July 3, 1929).
"Three Ruths in Congress," A. Hard. *Ladies Home Journal* 46:13 (Mar. 1929).
"Republican Case," *North American Review* 234:389-93 (Nov. 1932).
Gruberg, pp. 155, 206, 242.
Paxton, pp. 10-11.

EFFIEGENE LOCKE WINGO   (Mrs. Otis Theodore Wingo)
Democrat, Arkansas
1930-33

Effiegene Wingo represented the Fourth Arkansas Congressional District from November 4, 1930, to March 4, 1933. She had attended several women's colleges in the south and entered educational work after completing schooling. November 4, 1930, was a good day for her: she was elected to fill the unexpired term of her husband, and on the same date she was also elected on her own to a full two-year term in the 72nd Congress. She did not seek reelection in 1932.

Bibliography

New York Times Index, 1930.
New York Times Index, 1932: "Will Not Seek Reelection."
Woman's Journal n.s. 15:6 (Dec. 1930). Portrait.
Gruberg, p. 155.
Paxton, p. 131.

WILLA B. ESLICK   (Mrs. Edward Everett Eslick)
Democrat, Tennessee
1932-33

Mrs. Willa B. Eslick attended several colleges, including the Metropolitan College of Music. She was a member of the Tennessee Democratic State

Committee and after her husband's death acceded to his Congressional seat, in which he had represented the state's Seventh District. Her term was only from August 4, 1932, to March 4, 1933; she was not reelected.

Bibliography

Literary Digest 114:9 (July 2, 1932). Portrait.
Gruberg, p. 156.
Paxton, p. 128.

VIRGINIA ELLIS JENCKES (Mrs. Ray G. Jenckes)
Democrat, Indiana
1933-39

Mrs. Jenckes represented Indiana's Sixth Congressional District from March 4, 1933, to January 3, 1939, during the 73rd, 74th, and 75th Congresses. She was one of the few Congresswomen who lacked a college education, but she was busily engaged in the work of civic improvement associations. While in Congress she made flood control legislation her chief concern; her election had come about because of her anti-prohibition stand. She lost her bid for reelection in 1938.

Bibliography

"Five Democratic Women," M. Davis. *Ladies Home Journal* 50:117 (May 1933).
"What Are the Women Up To?", A. R. Longworth. *Ladies Home Journal* 51:9+ (Mar. 1934).
"Portraits" in *Literary Digest* 121:29 (Jan. 25, 1936).
National Republic 24:17 (Aug. 1936).
Gruberg, p. 156.
Paxton, p. 11.

KATHRYN O'LOUGHLIN McCARTHY (Mrs. Daniel McCarthy)
Democrat, Kansas
1933-35

Mrs. Kathryn McCarthy, Democrat, who represented the 6th Congressional District of Kansas, served one term, in the 73rd Congress, from 1933 to 1935. She was in Congress while still unmarried as Miss O'Loughlin; she had attended Kansas State Teachers College and then went on to graduate from the law school at the University of Chicago. Shortly after starting her term in Congress she married one of her former opponents, Kansas State Senator Daniel McCarthy. In the primary election she had beaten eight male adversaries, but she was unable to win reelection to the 74th Congress. Her interest in politics continued, however, and she served as delegate to state and national Democratic conventions until 1944.

Bibliography

"Five Democratic Women," M. Davis. *Ladies Home Journal* 50:117 (May 1933).

"What Are the Women Up To?", A. R. Longworth. *Ladies Home Journal* 51:9+
    (Mar. 1934).
Gruberg, p. 156.
Paxton, p. 124.

MARIAN WILLIAMS CLARKE   (Mrs. John D. Clarke)
Republican, New York
1933-35

Mrs. Clarke represented New York State's Thirty-fourth Congressional
District from December 18, 1933, to January 3, 1935, having won election to
her late husband's seat. She intended to run again for the next, the 74th Congress, but changed her mind before entering the primary. She had graduated from
Colorado College.

Bibliography

Gruberg, p. 157.
Paxton, p. 124.

ISABELLA SELMES GREENWAY   (Mrs. John Campbell Greenway)
Democrat, Arizona
1933-37

Mrs. Greenway, a Democrat, represented her state as a Representative-at-
large in the 73rd and 74th Congresses, from October 3, 1933, to January 3, 1937.
She filled the vacancy left by the resignation of a male Congressman and gained a
seat of her own in the 1934 general election. She was a successful businesswoman
and a large property owner. Her husband was a copper magnate, but Mrs. Greenway did much to help unemployed miners. She was powerful in the Democratic
state organization, but did not choose to run for reelection after completion of
her second term. She was a schoolmate of Eleanor Roosevelt and was her brides-
maid in 1905.

Bibliography

Gruberg, pp. 120, 156.
Paxton, p. 28.
"Portraits" in *Literary Digest* 121:29 (Jan. 25, 1936); *Newsweek* 6:18 (Aug. 31,
    1935); *Newsweek* 7:12 (Feb. 29, 1936).

CAROLINE GOODWIN O'DAY   (Mrs. Daniel O'Day)
Democrat, New York
1935-43

Caroline Goodwin O'Day, a Democrat, served her state of New York as a
Representative-at-large from 1935 to 1943, in the 74th, 75th, 76th and 77th

Congresses. She was the widow of a Standard Oil executive; Eleanor Roosevelt helped campaign for her.

Mrs. O'Day had studied art in Paris and Munich and in Holland, and had exhibited her paintings. Having been a pacifist during World War I, she learned politics the hard way, organizing women and working for her party. For 11 years she also functioned as a Commissioner of the New York State Board of Social Welfare, was president of a local school board in New York State, and was active in both the Consumers' League and the League of Women Voters. After serving her apprenticeship in practical politics, she held offices in the hierarchy of the New York State Democratic Party. She did not want renomination for a fifth term; she died one day after her fourth term expired on January 4, 1943. She was progressive and generous with her fortune on behalf of deserving unfortunates.

Bibliography

"Congresswoman," *Vital Speeches* 1:381-83 (Mar. 11, 1935).
"Should Congress Pass the Dies Bill to Deport Alien Fascists and Communists?", *Congressional Digest* 14:283 (Nov. 1935).
"Obituary," *Current Biography*, 1943; *Time* 41:56 (Jan. 11, 1943).
Gruberg, pp. 96, 108, 157.
Paxton, pp. 8-10.
"Portraits" in *Good Housekeeping* 102:38 (Jan. 1936 etc.).

NAN WOOD HONEYMAN   (Mrs. David T. Honeyman)
Democrat, Oregon
1937-39

Mrs. Honeyman, a Democrat, represented Oregon's Third Congressional District in the 75th Congress, from January 3, 1937, to January 3, 1939. She had worked her way up in state party politics, and before going to Congress had served a term in Oregon's House of Representatives. She ran again for Congress in the November elections of 1938 and 1940, but both times failed to win. However, she went once more to the state legislature, this time to fill a vacancy in the Senate. She was also at one time in the Pacific Coast Office of Price Administration and later became a customs collector.

Bibliography

Gruberg, p. 157.
Paxton, p. 129.

BESSIE HAWLEY GASQUE   (Mrs. Allard H. Gasque)
Democrat, South Carolina
1938-39

An author and lecturer, Mrs. Gasque was elected to fill the vacancy left by her husband's death. She was never sworn in to take up her seat, however, because Congress was not in session between September 13, 1938, the date of her election, and the final day of the 75th Congress, January 3, 1939. Her district was South Carolina's Sixth Congressional District.

Bibliography

New York Times Index, 1938, p. 1873.
Gruberg, pp. 157-58.
Paxton, p. 128.

JESSIE SUMNER
Republican, Illinois
1939-47

Miss Sumner, who represented the Eighteenth Congressional District for four full terms, from the 76th through the 79th Congress, had enjoyed a very thorough education, having studied at Smith College, and at the universities of Chicago, Columbia, and Oxford. She was a lawyer, later a judge and also a business executive.

She was a member of the Banking and Currency Committee, and both in Committee and on the floor of the House she was one of the best "rough and tumble" arguers; she has been characterized as a skilled parliamentarian wanting more production, less spending, no wage increases, and selective price controls. In her foreign policy stance she was an isolationist. She led the House opposition to the bill for enacting the conclusion of the Breton Woods monetary conference, which was called by Franklin D. Roosevelt, and which sat from July 1 to July 22, 1944. The proposals before the Breton Woods meeting called for the establishment of an International Monetary Fund and an International Bank for Reconstruction and Development; 44 nations participated in the conference. The plans, the culmination of several years of consideration, were aimed at removing some of the monetary disorders that had stifled world trade in the 1920s and 1930s. Miss Sumner, together with two other Republicans who led the opposition to the bill, aired arguments expressing the views of the American Bankers Association, saying that it was foreign to the thinking of the American people to pay tribute to foreign governments, and calling the agreement the worst swindle in world history. However, the bill became law by a majority of 348 to 18 (all the negative votes were those of Republican members, ten of whom ultimately changed their vote to yea). Miss Sumner also voted against price control, against veterans' temporary housing, against housing subsidies for veterans, against the British loan, and against Congressional pensions. She was not a candidate for reelection in 1946, but preferred to return to her business interests.

Bibliography

"Ladies of Congress," A. Porter. *Colliers* 112:22 (Aug. 28, 1943).
"Biography," *Current Biography* (Jan. 1945).
Gruberg, p. 158.
Paxton, pp. 55-62.
"Portraits," *Independent Woman* 17:371 (Dec. 1938); *Newsweek* 13:13 (Jan. 16, 1939); *New York Times Magazine*, p. 21 (Apr. 1, 1945).

CLARA G. McMILLAN   (Mrs. Thomas S. McMillan)
Democrat, South Carolina
1939-41

Mrs. McMillan succeeded her late husband to represent the First Congressional South Carolina District in the 76th Congress from November 7, 1939, to January 3, 1941. She had studied at colleges in North and South Carolina. Mrs. McMillan did not seek reelection in 1940.

Bibliography

New York Times Index, 1940.
Gruberg, p. 158.
Paxton, p. 123.

FLORENCE R. GIBBS   (Mrs. Willis B. Gibbs)
Democrat, Georgia
1940-41

Mrs. Gibbs was chosen to fill a vacancy left by the death of her husband. She held office only from October 1, 1940, to January 3, 1941, representing the Eighth Georgia Congressional District. She had attended Brenan College in Gainesville, Georgia.

Bibliography

Gruberg, p. 158.
Paxton, p. 129.

* * *

As one surveys the 55 years from 1917 to 1972, the period seems to divide itself into three unequal parts. The first 23 years might be seen as an era of preparation. Twenty-four Congresswomen appeared on the legislative stage, the majority of them serving for brief periods—for one or two Congresses, or for even shorter time spans. Many of them seemed to have no genuine liking for the political life and apparently bowed out without regret. The exceptions were Miss Rankin, an opponent of war; Mrs. Kahn, an able parliamentarian and shrewd politician; Mrs. Norton and Mrs. Rogers, both with long-service terms—the first a champion of labor, the latter known for work on behalf of veterans. There were also Ruth McCormick and Ruth Owen, both of whom received a lot of publicity, but without staying long or rolling up a good solid achievement record. Mrs. O'Day served well for eight years, as did Miss Sumner, but neither wanted reelection. Most of the others served for shorter periods and left little if any impression on the nation's legislative life.

The 1940s seem to bring a change. There were still quite a few who served only for short periods, and a number of short-term appointments of Congressmen's wives to fill vacancies. But there are more Congresswomen with longer terms and with substantial achievements, among them Frances Bolton, Margaret Chase Smith, Clare Boothe Luce, Helen Gahagan Douglas, Chase Going Woodhouse, Katherine St. George, Cecil M. Harden, Edna Kelly, and Marguerite Stitt Church, all of whom came in the 1940s or early 1950s.

From about 1955, almost all Congresswomen served long terms and several became nationally known; a number of them are still active in Congress, with strong personalities, ideas, commitments, and independence of action.

Party-wise, they were almost equally divided between Republicans and Democrats from 1917 to 1940, though a good number of the Democrats were from the South and were ideologically more akin to Republicans than to Northern Democrats. In the second period, 1940 to about 1955, there were almost twice as many Democrats as Republicans; while in the third period, from 1955 to 1972, there were considerably more Democrats than Republicans. The ideological difference between them, however, seems to be much smaller than before, some Democrats being at least as conservative as the Republicans if not more so. The second time period may be considered to begin with Frances Bolton.

FRANCES PAYNE BOLTON (Mrs. Chester C. Bolton)
Republican, Ohio
1940-69

Born in 1885, Mrs. Bolton started her long Congressional career in the 76th Congress as a representative for Ohio's Twenty-second Congressional District. Her husband, Chester Bolton, was serving his fifth term in Congress when he died; Mrs. Bolton served out his term, then proceeded to win many reelections to succeeding Congresses. Her husband, reputed to be the richest man serving in Congress, had made a fortune in steel.

Mrs. Bolton was one of the few women in Congress who had not attended college, but she amassed numerous honorary degrees from colleges and universities for her outstanding performance as a Congresswoman and participant in civic concerns, in public health, nursing education, philanthropic activities, and general education. Her forebears had been judges, city council members, and U.S. Senators. She was wealthy when she married her industrialist husband, being the daughter of a Cleveland banker and industrialist. As a young woman she radiated energy and enthusiasm. She learned to speak French and German fluently and volunteered to practice nursing work among poor tenement families without her father's knowledge. When her father, Charles Bingham, learned of his young daughter's activities he said that he would not have allowed her to do that kind of work, but then encouraged her to continue: "It's the only way you'll learn how most of the world has to live."* Her youthful experience may have given her a clearer outlook on life and may have tempered her conservative upbringing with an injection of progressivism. Although she mostly voted loyally with her Republican confreres, she took at times a remarkably independent course. Lamson credits her with poise, self-assurance, intelligence, energy, and an amazing memory. She was also generous with her wealth. In 1929 she provided a gift of $1,250,000 for a school of nursing at Western Reserve University; later she developed an interest in the preservation of our country's historical sites and invested generously in their acquisition and upkeep.

When she first came to Congress, her district was the most populous one in the United States; later it was split up and reduced by 300,000 voters, these being added to the Eleventh District, which was represented by one of her three sons, Oliver Bolton, who sometimes voted in opposition to his mother. She had started her committee assignments as a member of the Indian Affairs Committee; later she came to the prestigious House Foreign Affairs Committee. As a member she did much traveling abroad, at the federal government's expense. In 1947 she headed a Congressional mission to the Middle East, the Soviet Union, and Poland; she had already made one trip to Russia in 1945. In connection with her Near East trip she expressed her unhappiness about the partition of Palestine. In 1955 she made a three-month trip to Africa, and in 1957 she returned as a member of an official U.S. delegation to celebrate the independence of Ghana.

In her first 14 years she proposed scores of bills, many of them concerned with social, educational, and industrial matters and with public hygiene. The Bolton Act of 1943 established the United States Cadet Nurse Corps, which had a membership of 70,000 on its first anniversary (July 7, 1944). In 1941 she had opposed the selective service bill then before the House, but she voted for the soldier vote bill. She voted against Lend Lease, and against the Smith-Connally bill outlawing strikes, but for Taft-Hartley. On the other hand favorable votes were cast for the anti-poll tax bill and for the bill that became the 22nd amendment, which restricts a president to two terms. She also voted for maintaining 90 percent farm price supports, for Hawaii's statehood, and for extending the excess profits tax, and she advocated the inclusion of women in the draft. She voted to end federal rent controls, saying that "people must be responsible." In 1955, when economy-minded Congressmen wanted to cut appropriations for the Departments of State and Justice and for the judiciary and related agencies, she objected because this would include the State Department's student program and would eliminate a very important group that contributed significantly to international good will. Economists also had refused appropriations for the State Department information program and for cultural relations in 1947. George Marshall, Secretary of State, and Bedell Smith, ambassador to Russia, had

---

*Peggy Lamson, *Few are Chosen: American Women in Political Life Today* (Boston, Houghton Mifflin, 1968), p. 38.

supported such programs (which included the periodical *Amerika*, much sought after by Russian readers); Karl Mundt, who was then a Representative, managed the bill on the floor of the House. Mrs. Bolton was one of his supporters; after prolonged debate and filibustering by the opposition and the tacking on of 32 amendments, the bill was finally passed on June 24, 1947, after several months of obstruction. Ninety Representatives had voted against it, the majority of them Republicans. Mrs. Bolton had also opposed a cut in funds for the Children's Bureau; Helen Gahagan Douglas was another Congresswomen who supported full funding. In 1946 two bills, one introduced by Senator Claude Pepper in the Senate, the other by Mrs. Bolton in the House, would have authorized the Federal Security Administration to continue work done during the war to help states and localities prevent the spread of venereal diseases by combatting prostitution. The Senate bill passed, but Bolton's bill failed in the House.

Even the Peace Corps, favorite punching bag of Republicans, endeared itself to Mrs. Bolton, who said that she was very dubious about it when it started but that she had followed its course closely and that a little to her surprise she had found herself enthusiastic; she also voted $2.06 billion for OEO in 1967. Strangely, she was rated zero on the ADA scoreboard.

Mrs. Bolton was not a strong supporter of equal treatment for women. Ironically, a bill of hers submitted in 1951 made her a champion of equal rights for men, because it provided for the appointment of male citizens as nurses in the Armed Forces. This bill later became law; the Army complied with its clauses, while the Navy allegedly continued to discriminate against male nurses. But she had warm feelings for her fellow Congresswomen; she was indignant about the treatment given Representative Helen Douglas by Nixon in the 1950 senatorial campaign, calling it "shocking, perfectly shocking." She expressed her pride in Mrs. Martha Griffiths' election to the powerful Ways and Means Committee.

Conservative, but open-minded and capable of independence, articulate, and dynamic, she was one of the better Congresswomen. She left her mark on federal legislation.

Bibliography

Works about Frances Payne Bolton

"Congressional Quarterly Almanac," 1941-69.
"Ohio Omens," *Life* 8:28 (Mar. 11, 1940).
"Rich Widow," *Time* 36:20 (Feb. 12, 1940).
"Ladies of Congress," A. Porter. *Colliers* 112:22-23 (Aug. 28, 1943).
"Women in Congress," *National Education Association Journal* 38:283 (Apr. 1949).
"Women in the 83rd Congress," M. L. Temple. *Independent Woman* 32:59 (Feb. 1953).
"Hard Work; She Likes It," V. R. Batdorff. *Independent Woman* 32:441-42 (Dec. 1953).
"He Followed Mom to Congress," H. F. Pringle and K. Pringle. *Saturday Evening Post* 226:25+ (Aug. 15, 1953).

"Lady Congressman from Ohio," M. Cartright. *Negro History Bulletin* 17:155-56 (Apr. 1954).

"Women in the 84th Congress," *Independent Woman* 34:21 (Jan. 1955).

"View of Africa," *Annals American Academy* 306:121-27 (July 1956).

"People of the Week," *U.S. News* 39:18 (Sept. 9, 1956).

"Nursing Answers," *American Journal of Nursing* 42:138-40 (Feb. 1942).

"Private Agency Today," *Public Health Nursing* 32:471-74 (Aug. 1940).

"New Day for Health and Welfare," *Journal of Social Hygiene* 35:104-109 (Mar. 1949).

"Presentation of the 1949 Award of the Snow Medal [to F. P. Bolton with her reply]," *Journal of Social Hygiene* 35:115-16 (Mar. 1949).

Gruberg, pp. 122, 147, 158.

Lamson, Peggy. *Few Are Chosen*, 1968. p. 38ff.

Loth, David. *A Long Way Forward: The Biography of Congresswoman F. P. Bolton.* Longmans, 1957. 302p. illus.

Paxton, pp. 65-73.

Works by Frances Payne Bolton

"World Impact of U.S. Policy: Fundamental Defenses" (with Karl Earl Mundt), *Vital Speeches* 14:503-505 (June 1, 1948).

"Women Should Be Drafted," *American Magazine* 147:47+ (June 1949).

"Assembly Votes to Recess," *U.S. Department of State Bulletin* 29:910 (Dec. 28, 1953).

"Educational Needs in Non-self-governing Territories," *U.S. Department of State Bulletin* 29:686-88 (Nov. 16, 1953).

"Ewe-Togoland Unification Question," *U.S. Department of State Bulletin* 29:876-77 (Dec. 21, 1953).

"Nature of U.S. Puerto Rican Relations," texts of Statements Made in Committee IV (Trusteeship), *U.S. Department of State Bulletin* 29:797-98, 802-805 (Dec. 7, 1953).

"Requests for Oral Hearings Concerning Trust Territories in Fourth Committee. U.S. Opposition to Request for Puerto Rican Independence Party," *U.S. Department of State Bulletin* 29:498-99 (Oct. 12, 1953).

"Treatment of Indians in South Africa," statement, Oct. 26, 1953. *U.S. Department of State Bulletin* 29:728-30 (Nov. 23, 1953).

"U.N.: A Family of Nations," address, Oct. 18, 1953. *U.S. Department of State Bulletin* 29:628-29 (Nov. 9, 1953).

"U.S. Position on Question of Southwest Africa," *U.S. Department of State Bulletin* 29:805-806 (Dec. 7, 1953).

U.S. Congress. House. Committee on Foreign Affairs. Subcommittee on the Near East and Africa.

Report of the special study mission to Africa, south and east of the Sahara, comprising Hon. F. P. Bolton, ranking minority member submitted pursuant to H.Res.29, A5, 1957. Washington, D.C., U.S. Govt. Print. Off., 1957. xxi, 151p. tables, maps. (85th Congress, 1st session, H. rept. no. 307) (Union Catalog No. 97)

U.S. Congress. House. Committee on Foreign Affairs. Subcommittee on the Near East and Africa.

Report of the special study mission to the Near East and Africa. Hon. F. P. Bolton, ranking minority member, pursuant to H.Res.29, 1958. Washington, D.C., U.S. Govt. Print. Off., 1958. v, 14p. (85th Congress, 2d session, H rept. no. 2214) (Union Calendar No. 909)

U.S. Congress. House. Committee on Foreign Affairs.

The strategy and tactics of world communism. Report of Subcommittee no. 5, national and international movements, Frances P. Bolton, Chairman, with supplement I, One Hundred Years of Communism, 1848-1948, and supplement II, Official Protests of the United States Government against Communistic Policies or Actions, and Related Correspondence. [July 1945-December 1947.] Washington, D.C., U.S. Govt. Print. Off., 1948. 1v. (various pagings). U.S. 80th Congress, 2d session, 1948. House document no. 619.

"Letters From Africa, 1955," Washington, D.C., 1956. 33p. illus. map.

KATHARINE EDGAR BYRON   (Mrs. William D. Byron)
Democrat, Maryland
1941-43

Like so many other women Mrs. Byron succeeded her late husband in the 77th Congress, representing Maryland's Sixth Congressional District. She served from May 27, 1941, to January 3, 1943, and did not ask to be reelected.

Bibliography

"Widow's Might," *Time* 37:16 (June 23, 1941).
Gruberg, p. 159.
Paxton, p. 128.

VERONICA GRACE BOLAND   (Mrs. Patrick J. Boland)
Democrat, Pennsylvania
1942-43

Mrs. Boland took her late husband's seat briefly in the 77th Congress, from the 19th of November, 1942, to January 3, 1943. She did not run for reelection.

Bibliography

Gruberg, p. 159.

CLARE BOOTHE LUCE   (Mrs. Henry Robinson Luce)
Republican, Connecticut
1943-47

Born in 1903, Mrs. Luce was the stepdaughter of a Congressman. She was editor of *Vanity Fair*, a playwright, an actress, and a war correspondent for *Life*, *Time* and *Fortune*, before marrying the owner of this famous chain of mass circulation journals. She came to Washington for four years to represent the Fourth Congressional District of Connecticut in the 78th and 79th Congresses. It is claimed that she consistently voted as a liberal, but there were contradictions in her words and actions. She engaged in the woman's movement and, being very articulate, made many speeches. As a member of the important House Military Affairs Committee, she is said to have studied the issues before it carefully and assiduously. But she has been branded as an isolationist who characterized all plans for collective security as "globaloney": she probably meant this epithet to apply to impractical ideas and was not cynically refuting all efforts at international harmony. For her it was "America first, but not only." Also accused of being an anglophobe, she pleaded consistently for Indian independence.

In the first session of the 79th Congress, in 1945, she favored naturalization of natives of India, which was supported by members of both parties; although the idea met strong opposition in Committee, a bill, HR3517, was passed by voice vote in the House, while the measure did not emerge from the Senate Committee on immigration for a vote on the floor of the Senate. She had voted against the Smith-Connally anti-labor, anti-strike legislation. In the second session of the 79th Congress, in 1946, Mrs. Luce voted with arch-conservative Senator Dirksen, Republican from Illinois, whose amendment to the UNRRA bill prohibited use of its supplies in countries that failed to give representation to the American press to observe and report UNRRA activities without censorship; this was aimed primarily at Russia. Although many of her fellow Congressmen were against loans for Britain, Mrs. Luce supported such loans, thereby refuting her reputation as anglophobe. She also never deserted the military. The atomic energy act, as drawn up by Representative May, would have given the military much more control over atomic energy; Mrs. Luce favored this.

On the other hand, in internal affairs she kept her heart open for the weak and needy, and for developments that were to benefit the country at large. In the second session of the 79th Congress she proposed HR5960 for a Department of Children's Welfare, which was to include health, educational, and welfare services. She also proposed HR5332 to create a Department of Science and Research. Neither of these bills was reported by its committee; thus both measures were killed. Other bills offered by Mrs. Luce were also killed in committee: HJRes365, offered June 11, 1945, for the purpose of providing for popular election of U.S. representatives to the U.N. Security Council; a woman's equal pay bill requiring equal pay for equal work regardless of sex or color; and a bill calling for liberalization of the loan guarantee provisions of the GI bill. This must have been very frustrating for an intelligent, progressive, and active Representative like Mrs. Luce; no wonder she did not care to continue the agony of having her legislation consistently buried. She did not consider running for another House term, but in later years tried for the U.S. Senate, first from Connecticut and later from New York. Her opinions seem to have become more conservative in the meantime; she did not succeed in capturing a Senate seat. Under the Eisenhower administration she served as ambassador to Italy.

Bibliography

Works about Clare Boothe Luce

"Beauty and the East," F. Davis. *Saturday Evening Post* 216:6 (July 17, 1943).
"Connecticut's Clare," Potomacus. *New Republic* 109:72-74 (July 19, 1943).
"Here the Gavel Fell," weekly column in the CBI Roundup. *Time* 42:62 (Aug. 2, 1943).
"Ladies of Congress," A. Porter. *Colliers* 112:22-23 (Aug. 28, 1943).
"Soldier's Letter to Mrs. Luce," W. J. Caldwell. *Nation* 159:35-36 (July 8, 1944).
"Soldier's Letter to Mrs. Luce," reply P. D. Robinson. *Nation* 159:139 (July 29, 1944).
"Starvation; Eyewitness," Interview. *Newsweek* 25:39 (Jan. 15, 1945).
"Through the Mill," *Time* 44:23 (Nov. 20, 1944).
"The Audience Was Polite," *Newsweek* 26:89 (Aug. 20, 1945).
"Candida; Congresswoman Luce's Performance in Famous Shaw Play," *Life* 19:65-66 (Aug. 20, 1945).
"Congresswoman U.S. Russia," *Time* 46:23 (July 30, 1945).
"Good Governor and Fighting Lady," *Time* 48:19-20 (Aug. 26, 1946).
Gruber, pp. 43-47 and passim.
Paxton, pp. 81-91.
Hatch, Alden. *Ambassador Extraordinary Clare Boothe Luce*. Illustrated with photos. New York, Holt [c1956], 245p.
"Excursion; Candida," W. Gibbs. *New Yorker* 21:36 (Aug. 18, 1945).

Works by Clare Boothe Luce (Political Writings)

"Arguments Against the 4th Term," *Congressional Digest* 23:152+ (May 1941).
"A Greater and Freer America," address to the Republican National Convention, June 27, 1944. *Vital Speeches* 10:586-88 (July 15, 1944).
"News Blackout of the Fifth Army," radio broadcast, February 9, 1945. *Vital Speeches* 11:305-307 (Mar. 1, 1945).
"Search for An American Foreign Policy," *Vital Speeches* 10:550-54 (July 1944).
"Speech in the House," excerpts. *Time* 42:18 (July 5, 1943).
"Victory is a Woman," *Woman's Home Companion* 70:34+ (Nov. 1943).
"Waging the Peace," *Vital Speeches* 11:43-44 (Nov. 1, 1944).
"Why a Get-out-the-vote Campaign," *Independent Woman* 23:298+ (Oct. 1944).
"America and the World Community," *Vital Speeches* 11:647-49 (Aug. 15, 1945).

"China's Government," *Vital Speeches* 12:94-96 (Nov. 15, 1945).
"Fifth Army, the Infantry, and Combat Rotation," excerpts. *Infantry Journal*
    56:54-56 (Mar. 1945).
"In Italy the 4 Horsemen Outride the 4 Freedoms," *Life* 18:40a (May 14,
    1945).
"Saintly Scientist," *Vital Speeches* 13:241-45 (Feb. 1, 1947).

Works by Clare Boothe Luce (Non-Political Writings)

The Valor of Ignorance. With specially prepared maps. By Homer Lea.
    Introduction by Clare Boothe. New York and London, Harper and
    Brothers [c1942], 343p.
The Day of the Saxon. By Homer Lea. New York and London, Harper and
    Brothers [c1942], 31p. "The Valor of Homer Lea," by Clare Boothe.
    First published 1912.
Europe in the Spring. New York, Knopf, 1941 [c1940]. xi, 324p.
Kiss the Boys Good-bye. (In the Best Plays of 1938-1939), 1939. pp. 357-97.
Margin for Error. (In the Best Plays of 1939-1940), 1940. pp. 317-49.
Margin for Error. Satirical melodrama in 2 acts. [New York] Dramatists
    Play Service, Inc. [c1940]. 96p.
*Schedule of Exhibitions 1970: March–Arizona State University, Tempe,
    Arizona*. Catalogue by Philip C. Curtis. Comments by John Russell and
    Clare Boothe Luce. Flagstaff, Ariz., printed by Northland Press [1970].
    72p. illus., ports.
Saints for Now. London, New York, Steed and Ward [1952]. 277p.
The Women; a play. New York, Random House [c1937]. xvi, 215p.

WINIFRED C. STANLEY
Republican, New York
1943-45

Miss Stanley served a full term in the 78th Congress, elected as a
Representative-at-large for the state of New York by nearly two million
votes. She was the youngest person, at that time, ever to serve as Representative in Congress. Graduated from the University of Buffalo summa cum laude,
she then attended its law school. As a practicing lawyer she argued for woman's
rights to serve on juries. Later, as assistant district attorney of Erie County at
the age of 29, she tried many cases in city and county courts and before the
State Supreme Court. While in Congress she served on the Civil Service Committee, among others. She crusaded for gainful employment for all, regardless
of race, religion, and sex, and she demanded equal remuneration for women,
being certain that women would play an increasingly important role in community, national, and world affairs. Miss Stanley also thought that everybody,
no matter how crowded his schedule, should devote some time to an interest
in good government. For her concern with women's rights, full employment,
and world peace, she was awarded by having her seat reapportioned out of
existence. However, her interest in civic matters continued.

Bibliography

"Ladies of Congress," A. Porter. *Colliers* 112:22-23 (Aug. 28, 1943).
Current Biography, 1943.
Portraits: *Independent Woman* 21:357 (Dec. 1942); *Ladies Home Journal* 61:
34 (Nov. 1944).
Gruberg, p. 159 and passim.
Paxton, pp. 93-101.

WILLA L. FULMER   (Mrs. Hampton P. Fulmer)
Democrat, South Carolina
1944-45

Mrs. Fulmer represented the Second Congressional District of South
Carolina in the 78th Congress. She completed her late husband's twenty-third
year but was an incumbent only from November 16, 1944, to January 3,
1945. A graduate of Greenville, South Carolina Female College, she was the
mother of three married daughters. She did not seek reelection.

Bibliography

Gruberg, p. 160.
Paxton, pp. 103-106.

EMILY TAFT DOUGLAS   (Mrs. Paul Howard Douglas)
Democrat, Illinois
1945-47

Mrs. Douglas was elected as Representative-at-large to represent Illinois
in the 79th Congress, from January 3, 1945, to January 3, 1947. Born in
Chicago, she was the daughter of sculptor Lorada Taft. She wanted to go on
the stage, but her parents insisted that she attend college, so she attended the
University of Chicago, graduating in three years. Her post-graduate work was
in economics and political science. She married Paul Douglas, an economist
who later became United States Senator from Illinois. As an actress she toured
the country in a number of plays, and was in the cast of Eugene O'Neill's
Emperor Jones. She was politically active for the Illinois League of Women
Voters. While in Congress she managed to become a member of the House
Foreign Affairs Committee. In the second session of the 79th Congress she
voted for the school lunch bill, HR3370, which was passed by both House
and Senate (with amendments) and was widely backed bi-partisanly by people
of all races, creeds, and sections of the country. She also favored Senator
Monroney's housing amendment, which called for an authorization of $600
million to be used in making premium payments to increase the supply of conventional and new types of building materials. A library demonstration bill
offered by Mrs. Douglas, similar to one submitted in the Senate by Lister Hill
of Alabama, remained unreported by the Education Committee; it would have

authorized $25,000 a year for the demonstration of public library services in areas without such service. She submitted a labor practices bill to outlaw oppressive labor practices (such as the use of labor spies, strikebreakers, etc.); similar to legislation introduced in the Senate by Senators Robert M. La Follette, Jr., and Elbert D. Thomas, it remained unreported in the Education and Labor Committee. Mrs. Douglas was not reelected in November 1946.

Bibliography

Works about Emily Taft Douglas

"America's Good Chance," *Annals American Academy* 240:7-10 (July 1945).
"Biography" in *Current Biography* (Apr. 1945).
Gruberg, pp. 20, 160.
Paxton, pp. 107-110.

Works by Emily Taft Douglas

Margaret Sanger; Pioneer of the Future. New York, Holt, Rinehart and Winston [c1970]. viii, 274p. illus. ports.

HELEN GAHAGAN DOUGLAS   (Mrs. Melvyn Douglas)
Democrat, California
1945-51

Mrs. Douglas was the first Democrat sent to Congress from California. She represented the Fourteenth Congressional District in the 79th, 80th, and 81st Congresses. Her husband is actor Melvyn Douglas; they have three children.

Mrs. Douglas attended Barnard College. She had held important offices in state and national Democratic committees, freely giving her time and money to the Democratic cause. Even before she entered Congress she had acquired the reputation of being liberal and progressive; she had an interest in migratory farm labor, and she talked with farmhands about their problems, visiting their camps and sponsoring and supporting farm legislation in California. Hollywood celebrities induced her to enter politics; her platform included respect for the rights of organized labor, but also full opportunity for private enterprise, if honestly conducted; taxation based on ability to pay; prevention of unemployment and depression; the return of excess and unjust profits to the government; and renegotiation of war contracts. She also stood for food subsidies for the poor, price control and price rollback where necessary, and she stressed protection of small business.

She kept faith with her promises during the six years she was in Congress. She was a member of the House Foreign Affairs Committee. In the 79th Congress she opposed cuts in funds for the Children's Bureau as well as cuts in NLRB funds. Another cut, or rather the deletion of $215,000 for a Shasta Dam survey, was vigorously assailed by her; she wanted to break the monopoly held by PG&E on electric power distribution. Other positive commitments: she favored the anti-poll tax bill and voted for the Monroney Housing

Amendment. On the Un-American Activities Committee her one-minute speech touched off an acrimonious two-hour debate. She said the Committee was coming to be known for acts thoroughly un-American; Rankin of Mississippi replied that her criticism reflected on the integrity of the members of the Committee. She also fought for increased federal contributions under the Social Security Act, taking on the powerful Ways and Means Committee which, after one bill had been abandoned, brought in another bill with the rule that permitted no amendments; over her protest, however, the rule was adopted. She also supported a cancer research bill which carried an appropriation of $100 million and was supported even by Everett M. Dirksen, who was then in the House; however, three doctors testified against it and the bill had no chance. With Clare Boothe Luce she was one of the proponents of an Atomic Energy Commission, recommending that complete control over the development and use of atomic energy be placed in the hands of five civilian members appointed by the President and confirmed by the Senate. After long debate the House finally accepted a conference report that incorporated these recommendations. Other legislation that she supported, but that was generally defeated because of conservative opposition, included the FEPC bill; the labor extension service bill; and the bill by Vito Marcantonio, ALP, New York, to abolish the poll tax. This last bill passed the House, but was not acted on by the Senate and thus had to wait for another Congress for passage.

In the first session of the 80th Congress, in 1947, there was introduced a so-called portal-to-portal pay bill, whose purpose was to ban portal-to-portal pay suits by labor unions against employers; Mrs. Douglas, like McCormick of Massachusetts and many other Democrats, felt that most such suits were unjustified, but that the bill jeopardized other essential rights of labor. She therefore voted against it. An amendment to the rent control bill, on which hearings were held before the House Banking and Currency Committee with a view to extending federal rent and construction controls, brought a formidable list of witnesses on both sides. HR3203, introduced by chairman Jesse Wolcott, Republican from Michigan, provided for continuation of rent controls to the last day of December 1947, with the proviso that the President could extend them for another three months if necessary, but that rents could be increased by 15 percent if both landlord and tenant agreed to this; Mrs. Douglas offered an amendment calling for a restoration of rent controls as provided in the Price Control Act of 1942; this amendment was defeated 195 to 52.

Mrs. Douglas approved of aid for foreign countries. She was opposed to the loyalty oath bill for federal government employees, reported by the Civil Service Commission. This bill encountered opposition on several grounds: (1) that it was unconstitutional; (2) that the Loyalty Board to be set up would be prosecutor, judge, and jury, all in one; (3) that it contained incrimatory phrases; (4) that there was no court review and appeal of the Loyalty Board decision. These and similar arguments were made by Mrs. Douglas and others who were opposed to this type of witchhunting. Other bills considered in the 80th Congress dealt with farm labor, FHA mortgages, kindergarten youngsters, cancer research, fair employment practices, and wage discrimination on the basis of sex. There came before Congress a veterans' housing bill, and an anti-lynching bill, brought in by Representative Emanuel Celler, which called for fines or imprisonment for state and local government officers failing to prevent or prosecute lynchings; it remained unreported in the Judiciary Committee. Mrs. Douglas had brought in a similar bill, which also remained in Committee.

The foregoing should evidence her energy, courage, and sympathy with the underdog. But with the outbreak of the Korean War in 1950 and the hardening of the Cold War, a spirit of reaction began to grip the country. When Sheridan Downey, California's Democratic Senator, resigned in late 1950 because of ill health, Douglas and Nixon, who was also a Congressman representing a nearby district, contended for his seat. Nixon, charging Douglas with a soft approach to Communism, won the seat, forcing her into retirement.

Bibliography

Works about Helen Gahagan Douglas

"Keep Atomic Energy Free!" *New Republic* 114:366 (Mar. 18, 1946).
"Weapons of Peace," *Nation* 161:705-706 (Dec. 22, 1945).
"Congress' Week," *Time* 49:22-23 (Mar. 24, 1947).
"Leaders Are Readers," M. L. Becker. *Scholastic* 48:20 (Feb. 4, 1946).
"If I Were Seventeen," *American Magazine* 144:214 (Sept. 1947).
"Impressions of the United Nations," *Annals American Academy* 252:45-52 (July 1947).
"The World I Want for Children," *Parents Magazine* 24:24-25+ (Mar. 1949).
"Helen Gahagan Douglas," *New Republic* 119:10 (Sept. 20, 1948).
"Helen Gahagan Douglas," reply with rejoinder. C. B. Baldwin. *New Republic* 119:30 (Oct. 18, 1948).
"Why I Voted for Arms for Europe," *New Republic* 121:9-10 (Aug. 29, 1949).
"California Foot Race," *Newsweek* 35:25-26 (June 5, 1950).
"Helen Douglas and Tobey," H. L. Ickes. *New Republic* 123:18 (Oct. 16, 1950).
"Nixon vs. Douglas," R. Moley. *Newsweek* 36:84 (Aug. 28, 1950).
"Red Smear in California," H. W. Flannery. *Commonweal* 53:223-25 (Dec. 8, 1950).
"Roaring Races," R. de Toledano. *Newsweek* 36:21 (Oct. 30, 1950).
"Warren Touch," *Time* 55:21 (June 19, 1950).
"Women in Congress," *National Education Association Journal* 38:283 (Apr. 1949).
"How I Conceive the Congresswoman's Role During the Next Two Years," *Free World* 8:425-27 (Nov. 1944).
Gruberg, pp. 120, 160.
Paxton, pp. 111-16.

Works by Helen Gahagan Douglas

The Eleanor Roosevelt We Remember. Pictures by Aaron J. Erickson. New York, Hill and Wang [1963]. 173p. illus.

CHASE GOING WOODHOUSE   (Mrs. Edward J. Woodhouse)
Democrat, Connecticut
1945-47, 1949-51

Mrs. Woodhouse twice represented the Second Connecticut Congressional District, first in the 79th Congress (from January 3, 1945, to January 3, 1947) and again, after having been defeated for election to the 80th Congress, from January 3, 1949, to January 3, 1951, as a member of the 81st Congress.

Her father had been a railroad engineer and she traveled with him up and down the Pacific Coast. She studied at McGill University, Montreal, became a professor at Connecticut College, New London, Connecticut, and also taught at Smith College in Massachusetts. She lectured in every state of the union, and authored several technical books, also contributing regularly to professional journals. Senior economist of the Federal Bureau of Home Economics, president of the Connecticut League of Women Voters, several times president of the Connecticut Federation of Democratic Women's Clubs, Executive Director of the Women's Division of the Democratic National Committee, Secretary of State for Connecticut from 1941 to 1942, she was a very busy teacher, civic leader and legislator. Her son said: "Dad talks about Thomas Jefferson, and Mother talks about better jobs for women." (Paxton, p. 120).

Her legislative and voting records were liberal. In the second session of the 79th Congress, Mrs. Woodhouse voted for housing subsidies and for the Monroney amendment, which authorized $600 million to be used in making premium payments to increase supplies of conventional and new types of building materials. She voted for the Connecticut River Bridge bill, which passed both Houses in March and April 1946; she favored the British loan, and supported bills for equal pay for women and for liberalized immigration. The women's equal pay bill submitted in the House was identical with a bill, S1178, submitted in the Senate by Senators Pepper and Morse, which stipulated equal pay for equal work by women. Consideration was blocked by objectors; the bill introduced by Woodhouse was reported by the Labor Committee, but was not acted upon by the House. President Truman wanted immigration rules liberalized to admit displaced persons. A proposal by Mrs. Woodhouse to use the unfilled quotas of England, Iceland, and other northern European nations for reassignment to Poland, Austria, and the Balkans was opposed; most bills on immigration proposed to tighten rather than ease laws—specifically, the DAR was against weakening of existing laws. A housing stabilization bill pushed by the Truman administration faced an opposition coalition of Southern Democrats and Republicans. They wanted to abolish OPA, and raise ceiling prices on building materials. Woodhouse agreed with Lyndon Johnson that subsidies would be the most economic method of stimulating production. Republican Woolcott's legislation required that ceiling prices should reflect the cost of production plus a reasonable profit for producers, processors, distributors, and retailers; Patman and Woodhouse agreed that such a move would double the cost of living, and that it would add an impossible administrative burden because of lack of effective cost accounting systems.

In the first session of the 81st Congress, in 1949, Woodhouse voted for the anti-poll tax bill, which made it unlawful to require the payment of a poll tax or any other charge of any kind on registering and voting. As to economic policy, Truman submitted 11 proposals, which Woodhouse supported; among them were an increase in the minimum wage and in unemployment compensation, an extension of its coverage, an increase in Social Security benefits, etc. In the second session of the 81st Congress, in 1950, the House Education and Labor Committee opened hearings on two bills asking for equal pay for equal work by women–one by Woodhouse, a similar one by Helen Gahagan Douglas–but the National Association of Manufacturers opposed equal pay for equal work. The Senate never acted on the proposal, and the House Education and Labor Committee never reported its bill to the House. The reaction of Congress was a sad environment for progressives like Woodhouse, and a similarly reactionary constituency refused to reelect her in 1950.

Bibliography

Works about Chase Going Woodhouse

"Biography" in *Current Biography* (Mar. 1945).
"Consumer and Congress," *Journal of Home Economics* 38:388-91 (Sept. 1946).
"Need for the W.E.T. [Wagner-Ellender-Taft] Bill as Supplement to Federal Housing Policy," *Congressional Digest* 25:272+ (Nov. 1946).
"Experiment in Educational Techniques," *Annals American Academy* 251: 153-56 (May 1947).
"Women of Berlin," *Survey Graphic* 37:495-98 (Dec. 1948).
"Women in Congress," *National Education Association Journal* 38:283 (Apr. 1949).
Gruberg, pp. 56, 160, 184, 194.
Paxton, pp. 117-21.

Works by Chase Going Woodhouse

Married College Women in Business and the Professions. Philadelphia, 1929. 14p.
Occupations for College Women: A Bibliography. By Chase Going Woodhouse and Ruth Frances Yeomans. Greensboro, N.C., The North Carolina College for Women, 1929. 290p. (Institute of Women's Professional Relations, Bulletin No. 1.)

HELEN DOUGLAS MANKIN   (Mrs. Guy Mankin)
Democrat, Georgia
1946-47

Mrs. Mankin served briefly in the 79th Congress, from February 12, 1946, to January 3, 1947, succeeding to a vacancy caused by the former member's resignation. She was a lawyer, her husband an engineer; her parents had also been lawyers. Before she went to Congress she had served ten years in the Georgia State Legislature, pressing for "better salaries for teachers, modern health legislation, segregation of youthful offenders, a state department of labor and a truly secret ballot," (Gruberg, pp. 160-61) and a progressive attitude awake to the needs of modern times. She won a popular majority in the 1946 primary, but the cards were stacked against her under the Georgia election system, which favored rural areas; so she lost. Two years later, in 1948, she tried again but again suffered defeat.

Bibliography

"Biography" in *Current Biography* (Apr. 1946).
"Congressman Helen J. Walz," *New York Times Magazine*, p. 24 (Apr. 28, 1946).
"Georgia's Black Ballots," *Newsweek* 27:28 (Feb. 25, 1946).
"Good News Down South," *New Republic* 114:304-305 (Mar. 4, 1946).
"Member Atlanta Club Elected to Congress," *Independent Woman* 25:44 (Mar. 1946).
"Precinct 3-B," *Time* 47:22 (Feb. 25, 1946).
CQA, 1946: Truman vetoes labor bill passed by Congress, with long message explaining his opposition; Mankin votes to sustain veto; labor had urged veto.
Gruberg, pp. 160-61.

ELIZA JANE PRATT
Democrat, North Carolina
1946-47

Miss Pratt served about eight months in the 79th Congress, in the state's Eighth Congressional District. She succeeded the late Representative Burgin, whose secretary she had been. She had served various Congressmen representing the Eighth District for more than 20 years, and had been a newspaper editor before being employed in this capacity. Miss Pratt did not run for reelection in the 1946 Congressional election campaign.

Bibliography

Gruberg, p. 161.

GEORGIA LEE WITT LUSK (Mrs. Dolph Lusk)
Democrat, New Mexico
1947-49

Mrs. Lusk represented her state as a Representative-at-large in the 80th Congress, from 1947 to 1949. After graduating from state teachers' college, she became a teacher and later attained the post of state superintendent of public instruction. In Congress she joined those representatives who approved relief aid for war-devastated countries; she also favored State Department information programs. And although she was from a state where copper mining was of some importance, she reluctantly acceeded to a two-year suspension of a 4-cent tax on imported copper. She failed in her bid for reelection to the 81st Congress. From 1949 to 1953 she was a member of the War Claims Commission.

Bibliography

"Biography" in *Current Biography* (Oct. 1947).
Gruberg, pp. 161, 198.

KATHARINE COLLIER ST. GEORGE   (Mrs. George Baker St. George)
Republican, New York
1947-65

Mrs. St. George, wife of a banker and businessman, participated intensely in local and national political affairs before her election to the 80th Congress. A Representative of the Twenty-seventh District of New York State, she served nine full terms, from 1947 to 1965.

In the realm of foreign politics she favored prohibiting the sale of certain strategic materials to Russia. Later she voted for setting up a joint watchdog committee in Congress to supervise the administration of the Defense Production Act of 1950; after the outbreak of the Korean War a group of three Republicans joined in a fight for imposition of an excess profits tax, threatening opposition to adjournment until the proposal was acted upon. Mrs. St. George was a member of this group.

As for economic and social policies in the country, one can say that some of her votes are quite acceptable while others seem unreasonable. In 1963 she opposed a pay increase for federal government employees, which would have benefitted 1.7 million persons. Mrs. St. George said that such action was "premature, unjustified, extravagant and inequitable"; in consequence of great opposition, Congress failed to complete action on the bill. The 88th Congress, however, enacted a bill to increase salaries for government employees which became PL88-426 in 1964; Mrs. St. George and other opponents charged that blatant and callous pressure had been used in ramming it through Congress. In 1963 she was the only Congresswoman to vote against a broadened 1951 ban on interstate transportation of gambling devices. In the same Congress, in 1964, a bill to exempt railroads and water carriers from ICC-regulated rates for hauling certain commodities was killed by the House Rules Committee's refusal to clear the bill; Mrs. St George had sided with representatives voting to clear the bill for passage. Although her political stance is obviously conservative, pro-business, and in favor of austerity for the wage earner, as if to counterbalance this favoritism toward the status quo she proved herself a strong supporter of equal rights for women. She urged passage of an equal pay bill as early as 1950. Wide-ranging pay differentials had been noted, and Congresswoman St. George had objected to the term "comparable" used in the wording of a bill to remedy inequities; her amendment substituting the word "equal" for "comparable" was accepted. In the 88th Congress an equal pay bill for women was finally enacted; Senate and House bills became PL88-38, signed on June 10, 1963, by President Kennedy. Supporters of the bill expressed little elation, saying it might be too weak, too late, and too little. Mrs. St. George expressed her lack of total acceptance by quipping that it was only one bite of the cherry, while Mrs. Bolton warned that the legislation by no means covered all women workers.

Representative St. George served on the Post Office and Civil Service Committee; later she was the first woman to serve on the powerful Rules Committee, which can exert great leverage either toward getting bills to the floor of Congress for final action or toward keeping them stalled in the originating Committee. As a loyal Republican she was also placed on the GOP Policy Committee as well as on the GOP Committee on Committees, which makes assignments of Republican Congressmen to various House committees.

Representative St. George was very active and outspoken during her years in Congress, presenting great numbers of bills to each Congress; but the constituency in her district denied her another term, giving her opponent, a liberal Democrat, a victory with a rather thin margin, 48.4 percent to 51.6 percent.

Bibliography

"Biography" in *Current Biography* (Dec. 1947).
"FDR's Republican Cousin in Congress," E. B. Lockett. *Colliers* 126:26-27+ (Aug. 19, 1950).
"Women in Congress," *National Education Association Journal* 38:283 (Apr. 1949).
"Women in the 83rd Congress," M. L. Temple. *Independent Woman* 32:59 (Feb. 1953).
"Women in the 84th Congress," *Independent Woman* 34:38 (Jan. 1955).
Gruberg, pp. 161-62 and passim.
Congressional Quarterly Almanac, 1947-64.

REVA BECK BOSONE   (Mrs. Joseph P. Bosone)
Democrat, Utah
1949-53

Mrs. Bosone, who studied at various colleges and universities, became a lawyer after teaching high school for seven years; her husband also was a lawyer. While she was a member of Utah's House of Representatives from 1933 to 1936, she authored and had passed into law several important pieces of social legislation: a minimum wage law, a maximum hour law for women and children, an unemployment insurance law, and a water control law. After her term in the state legislature she was elected municipal judge of Salt Lake City and gained appreciation for instituting measures to reduce the traffic death toll.

She served in Congress from 1949 to 1953, in the 81st and 82nd Congresses, and worked for admission of Hawaii and Alaska to statehood, emphasizing that both Nevada and Utah were states with small populations but that they had poured great wealth into the country. She also authored a bill to establish a commission to study a national health insurance program. Another of her efforts was to increase self-government for our Indian tribes; she wanted to cut off the apron strings which bound them tightly to the federal government. She worked hard for her constituents and her state, supporting river development and reclamation projects, and the eradication and control of weeds, and working to increase knowledge about the history and important personalities of her state. In the 82nd Congress she turned her attention more to social questions—such as increased provision for maternity and hospital benefits for servicemen's dependents—but she also continued to stress the need for reclamation projects, as she had done in preceding Congressional sessions. In May 1952 the Justice Department ordered an investigation into accusations against Representative Bosone that she had violated the federal Corrupt Practices Act by accepting a $630 campaign contribution from two paid government employees in her office; while acknowledging receipt of these funds, however, she insisted that she had done nothing culpable. Justice then decided not to press the case for further inquiry. Mrs. Bosone was defeated in the general election of 1952.

Bibliography

"Biography" in *Current Biography* (Jan. 1949).
Gruberg, pp. 122, 162, 179.
"New Faces in Congress," *New Republic* 120:8 (Jan. 24, 1949).
"Women in Congress," *National Education Association Journal* 38:283
    (Apr. 1949).

CECIL M. HARDEN   (Mrs. Frost Revere Harden)
Republican, Indiana
1949-59

Mrs. Harden was a member of Congress for ten years, from 1949 to 1959, representing the Sixth Congressional District of Indiana in the 81st, 82nd, 83rd, 84th and 85th Congresses. She was 56 when she came to Congress. After attending Indiana University, she became a school teacher, while at the same time taking an active interest in Republican Party matters; she was a national committeewoman from 1944 to 1959.

Her assignments in Congress were to the committees for Government Operations and for Post Office and Civil Services. She was friendly to business interests; as chairman of the Subcommittee on Intergovernment Relations she said that government enterprise is a "real threat to private enterprise" and reported that the National Coffee Association had recommended closing government coffee-roasting facilities and that such a move, if adopted, would save millions of dollars. Her investigation had shown that the federal government had dozens of commercial and industrial activities (such as 31 manufacturing enterprises, engaged in making sleeping bags and dentures and producing aluminum and atomic energy, besides coffee roasting) as well as facilities for transportation, commissaries, power plants, insurance, fish hatcheries, and many more. She had no labor backing. Her service was rather undistinguished and she did not introduce many bills. She was unsuccessful in her attempt to gain a sixth term, but she was rewarded for her staunch Republicanism by being appointed Special Assistant to the Postmaster General in 1959 by the Eisenhower administration; her husband had been a postmaster in the 1930s.

Bibliography

"Women in Congress," *National Education Association Journal* 38:283 (Apr. 1949).
"Women in the 83rd Congress," M. L. Temple. *Independent Woman* 32:59 (Feb. 1953).
"Women in the 84th Congress," *Independent Woman* 34:23 (Jan. 1955).
Congressional Quarterly Almanac, 1950-58.
Gruberg, pp. 25, 162.

EDNA FLANNERY KELLY   (Mrs. Edward Leo Kelly)
Democrat, New York
1949-69

Mrs. Kelly's incumbency was one of the longest of all Congresswomen; she represented New York City's Tenth District for twenty years, from the 81st through the 90th Congress. Her husband was a New York City court judge, his father had been a postmaster in Brooklyn. Mrs. Kelly became a widow when she was only 35 years old, but from then on she took a very active interest in borough and state Democratic politics.

In 1949, because of the death of the incumbent, Mrs. Kelly emerged as the victor in a special election, and entered upon her long Congressional career on November 8, 1949. A recurrent feature of her actions in Congress is her lack of sympathy with nations in the Communist bloc; this can be understood if it is remembered that at the height of the Cold War, when Communists and Communist sympathizers were being found under everyone's bed, any other course would have been political suicide for a Democratic Representative in a district that had formerly been consistently Republican. In 1951, when President Truman requested aid for India, his request was greeted with fast approval and bi-partisan sponsorship; Mrs. Kelly acted and voted affirmatively on this legislation, which became PL48. In the second session of the 82nd Congress, in 1952, however, Mrs. Kelly rejected all aid for Yugoslavia, and in the following Congress she favored cutting off all carry-over aid for that country. Somewhat later, in 1954, when there were large farm surpluses on hand for disposal to needy nations, legislation (to become PL480) excluded Russia and its satellites from the definition of "friendly nations"; Mrs. Kelly was one of the sponsors of the amendment that accomplished this exclusion. In the 84th Congress, her bias against Tito came to the fore in both Sessions. The Mutual Security Act, introduced in 1955, was enacted into law on July 8 of that year; Mrs. Kelly offered an amendment to this barring any aid to Yugoslavia, but this time it was rejected.

In 1954, in the second session of the 83rd Congress, at the age of 48, she had attained a seniority of 46; although this was still pretty far down the line of importance, she was already a member of the important House Foreign Affairs Committee. As a member she made several trips to other countries—one to Montreal and Ottawa for joint meetings with a Canada-U.S. Interparliamentary Group—of course, at government expense. No enemy of the United Nations, she was a member of a delegation to the 18th session of the United Nations Assembly. Later she favored passing legislation that would have reimbursed New York City for the sum of $3,063,500 for police protection of Khrushchev, Castro, and heads of ten other nations; the bill passed the House, and was amended by a Senate Committee, but no further action was taken on it.

In the first session of the 88th Congress, in 1963, the foreign aid program began to suffer setbacks. One of Mrs. Kelly's amendments, which just failed of acceptance, required that developmental loans should be given only if the recipient country agreed to allow inspection and auditing to insure that loans were properly administered. Another of her amendments—to prohibit aid to countries that did not permit reviews by the United States teams—was accepted. In 1966 she again traveled abroad, this time to hold hearings on the future of NATO. De Gaulle had threatened to withdraw France from the alliance, and there was great fear that NATO might collapse. General Eisenhower sent letters to Senator Jackson and to Mrs. Kelly, as chairmen of their respective committees of the Senate and House on foreign affairs, saying that in spite of the seriousness of developments in NATO and in spite of the expenses involved, it would be a grave mistake for the other member countries to abandon the alliance.

In the area of internal politics, Mrs. Kelly's actions and votes were liberal. In 1952 when tax revision was emphasized, more than 500 witnesses testified on 40 major tax subjects; tax relief for working mothers was one of the subjects, and Mrs. Kelly testified in support of it. Around 1956 civil rights legislation began to make headlines. In legislation passed by the House a six-man committee was established and directed to report within two weeks on what the Justice Department plans were in enforcing civil rights. Adam Clayton Powell and Mrs. Kelly were among the committee's members.

In 1967 Mrs. Kelly introduced 50 bills on such subjects as truth in lending, drug abuse, conservation, crime, prisons, and public health. In addition to her position on the Foreign Affairs Committee, she was also elected to the House Ethics Committee, set up as a first step toward a guide for official conduct; its membership consisted of six Democrats and six Republicans. Some of the cases that led to the formation of this committee were the following: Adam C. Powell was excluded from the House, having been found guilty of misusing funds; Senator Dodd had incurred Senate censure because of irregularities in using moneys obtained as campaign contributions; Senator Long of Missouri was accused of aiding Jimmy Hoffa; and Bobby Baker, Secretary of the Senate Majority Party, was convicted and sent to prison, guilty of income tax evasion, theft, and conspiracy.

Mrs. Kelly also became secretary of the House Democratic Caucus. In the last Congressional session that Representative Kelly attended (the second session of the 90th Congress, in 1968), the conservative coalition of Republicans and

Southern Democrats shaped all the major bills dealing with budget cutting, civil rights, gun control, crime bills, student disorders, and the Abe Fortas nomination to the Supreme Court; Mrs. Kelly, like most Northern Democrats, was opposed to the goals of this coalition.

Mrs. Kelly never had difficulties in being reelected; in fact, she piled up ever-larger winning majorities, once receiving 81.7 percent of the total votes cast in her district for the office of Congressman.

Bibliography

"Biography" in *Current Biography* (Mar. 1960).
"People of the Week," *U.S. News* 27:39 (Nov. 18, 1949).
"Women in the 83rd Congress," M. L. Temple. *Independent Woman* 32:36+ (Feb. 1953).
"Women in the 84th Congress," *Independent Woman* 34:23 (Jan. 1955).
"Principles of International Law Concerning Friendly Relations and Cooperation Among States: Peaceful Settlement of Disputes," address, Nov. 19, 1963. *Department of State Bulletin* 50:57-66 (Jan. 13, 1964).
"Principles of International Law Concerning Friendly Relations Among States: Sovereign Equality of States," statement, Dec. 3, 1963. *Department of State Bulletin* 50:264-67 (Feb. 11, 1964).
Congressional Quarterly Almanac, 1950-68.
Gruberg, p. 162.

VERA D. BUCHANAN   (Mrs. Frank Buchanan)
Democrat, Pennsylvania
1951-55

Mrs. Buchanan's husband, Frank Buchanan, a Democratic Representative, died on April 27, 1951; in a special election held on July 27, 1951, his wife was elected his successor and sworn in on August 1 of the same year, representing Pennsylvania's Thirtieth District in the 82nd and 83rd Congresses (which met from January 3, 1951, to January 3, 1955). She was then reelected to the next Congress. Mrs. Buchanan was given membership on the Banking and Currency Committee, whose concern is with banking and currency generally, and with financial matters other than taxes and appropriations, as well as with public and private housing plans; this committee is supposed to take anti-inflation measures. Representative Buchanan introduced bills dealing with these subjects–namely, bills to combat inflation, to increase railroad retirement benefits, to provide housing for elderly persons of low income, and to deal with problems affecting consumer interests. Congresswoman Buchanan died on November 26, 1955, while in office.

Bibliography

"Women in Congress Now Number Eleven," *Independent Woman* 30:311 (Oct. 1950).
"Women in the 83rd Congress," M. L. Temple. *Independent Woman* 32:36 (Feb. 1953).

"Women in the 84th Congress," *Independent Woman* 34:22 (Jan. 1955).
Congressional Quarterly Almanac, 1951-55.
Gruberg, p. 162.
U.S. 84th Congress, 2nd Session, 1956

Memorial services held in the House of Representatives and Senate of the United States together with remarks presented in eulogy of Vera Daerr Buchanan, late a Representative from Pennsylvania. Washington, U.S. Govt. Print. Off., 1956. 48p. port.

MAUDE ELIZABETH FRAZIER KEE   (Mrs. John Kee)
Democrat, West Virginia
1951-65

Elizabeth Kee, whose husband John represented the Fifth Congressional West Virginia District, and who died on May 8, 1951, was elected to fill his vacancy on July 17, 1951. She was sworn in on July 26, and was reelected six times to serve in the 82nd through 88th Congresses. She had been her husband's secretary while he was in office, and during her own Congressional career she appointed her son as her administrative assistant; her age was 57 when she began her service.

She was first a member of the Committee on Veterans' Affairs; she then added the Committee on Government Operations, which she held through the major part of her incumbency, but which she exchanged for membership on the Internal and Insular Affairs Committee during the session of the 88th Congress. Although she introduced many bills, few of them were enacted into law, and many were meant to be for the benefit of her constituency—e.g., an authorization for appropriations to erect a courthouse and post office in Bluefield, West Virginia. In 1952, when a number of bills were introduced in the Congress to provide for national presidential primaries, Mrs. Kee submitted one with identical purpose. She also sponsored libraries for handicapped children.

Bibliography

"Women in the Congress Now Number Eleven," *Independent Woman* 30:311 (Oct. 1951).
"Women in the 83rd Congress," M. L. Temple. *Independent Woman* 32:36+ (Feb. 1953).
"Women in the 84th Congress," *Independent Woman* 34:23 (Jan. 1955).
Congressional Quarterly Almanac, 1952-64.
Gruberg, p. 163.

MARGUERITE STITT CHURCH   (Mrs. Ralph Edwin Church)
Republican, Illinois
1951-63

Mrs. Church succeeded her husband in the representation of the Thirteenth Illinois Congressional District, Cook County, from 1951 (the 82nd Congress) to

1963 (the 87th Congress) for a total term of 12 years. She had graduated from Wellesley and Columbia University, taught psychology at Wellesley and was a practicing psychologist during World War I.

She became a member of the House Foreign Affairs Committee in 1955, at a time when a record number of women (17) were in the Congress; 31 had run for election. One of the first bills she introduced called for provision of annuities for widows of certain former federal employees who had rendered 30 years of service or more. Another had for its purpose the creation of a commission to study the administration of the federal government's overseas activities. She authored a bill to prohibit transportation of fireworks into any state or political subdivision thereof in which the sale of such fireworks was prohibited, as well as several bills authorizing the Postmaster General to acquire post office buildings by making lease-purchase agreements with private contractors; one of these was passed by both Houses, but died by pocket veto. Another bill provided for state and local taxation of real property owned by the federal government and leased to private persons.

A Church amendment to the Mutual Security Act of 1953 (which had appropriated $5,157,232,500 for foreign aid in fiscal 1954), requiring deletion of a provision of a $100 million authorization for French arms and ammunition manufacturers, was rejected. On the other hand, an amendment of hers to HR 5246 to increase funds for Howard University was accepted. In 1954 she again sponsored a bill that forbade transportation of fireworks into states where they were prohibited; 36 states limited or prohibited their use, because they caused deaths and thousands of injuries annually. This time the bill was accepted and became public law. A provision in the Mutual Security Act of 1955, which increased funds earmarked for Spain, drew the ire of Mrs. Church and other members of a minority group; she insisted that Congress should not provide a blank check for the Mutual Security program. In 1957 the Middle East was a very dangerous international troublespot and political leaders of the country were in favor of giving Eisenhower authority to undertake a program of economic and military cooperation in the Middle East; Mrs. Church was one of two members of the Foreign Affairs Committee to dissent.

In her reelection to the 85th Congress she had received 71.6 percent of all votes cast in her district. Being a hardworking and conscientious Congresswoman she scored 100 percent voting participation in the second session of that Congress. In 1959, during the 86th Congress, she traveled to Mexico as a House delegate to participate in the inauguration of the new Mexican president. In reference to the 1959 Congressional authorization of $3,556,200,000 for mutual security, she again expressed her displeasure; in her minority report she lambasted the Congress for its continued abdication of responsibility and control over the foreign aid program. She also expressed opposition to the 1960 Mutual Security Act and chided Congress for wrangling more than a month over members' franking privileges which she said was a luxury that members of Congress might well sacrifice. From October 18 to December 4, 1960, she made a long overseas trip, with other members of the House Foreign Affairs Committee, to Japan, Korea, Okinawa, Formosa, Hong Kong, Saigon, the Philippines, Australia, New Zealand, Indonesia, Thailand, India, Pakistan, Cyprus, Israel, Turkey, Greece, Spain, and Morocco; this trip was made at government expense, with military transportation.

Swastika daubings on synagogues, which had started in West Germany and spread to other countries, caused Mrs. Church to ask Congress to make religious desecration in the United States a federal offense. In 1961 she expressed once more her displeasure with certain phases of the foreign aid program. She said she supported foreign aid but opposed financing developmental loans through Treasury borrowing, which, she said, was not needed since Congress had appropriated 92 percent of the $43.6 billion authorized for that purpose in the past ten years. She called this a back-door spending device to avoid annual scrutiny and control of the program by Congress. And in her last year in Congress she repeated her expression of disagreement with the administration of foreign aid, claiming that the program had failed to accomplish the expected results, that it had become an indiscriminate instrument of United States foreign policy, characterized by poor planning and faulty administration, and that the bill failed to provide clear guidelines and vigorous checks on poor administration.

One gets the impression of an honest, hard-working, clear-minded Congresswoman; if there had been more like Mrs. Church in the past, many of our sad experiences overseas might have been avoided or mitigated.

Bibliography

"Biography" in *Current Biography* (Feb. 1951).
"Women in the 83rd Congress," M. L. Temple. *Independent Woman* 32:59 (Feb. 1953).
"Women in the 84th Congress," *Independent Woman* 34:22 (Jan. 1955).
Congressional Quarterly Almanac, 1951-62.
Gruberg, pp. 122, 163.

RUTH THOMPSON
Republican, Michigan
1951-57

Ruth Thompson served three full terms in Congress, representing the Ninth Michigan Congressional District in the 82nd, 83rd and 84th Congresses. A graduate of Muskegon, Michigan, Business College who also studied law, she served three terms as probate judge (from 1925 to 1937) and thereafter was a member of the Michigan State Legislature for four years; this was followed by several positions in the federal government—in the Labor Department, on the Social Security Board, and with the Army of Occupation in Europe.

She was 63 years old when she entered Congress, where she was given assignments on the Committee on the Judiciary and on Immigration and Nationalities Policies. She was not greatly interested in improving immigration legislation. On HR6481, which became PL203 and which called for the admission of 214,000 refugees over a three-year period, Miss Thompson said that it would take considerable persuasion to get the bill through Congress; she may have agreed with Representative Frances Walters of Pennsylvania, who feared that Iron Curtain refugees might be planted as spies in the United States. Miss Thompson's real interests lay in flood control and drainage projects. She was defeated for reelection in November 1956.

Bibliography

"Biography" in *Current Biography* (Nov. 1951).
"Women in the 84th Congress," *Independent Woman* 34:38 (Jan. 1955).
"Michigan's Wandering Airbase," P. Southwick. *Reporter* 14:20-24 (June 14, 1956).
Congressional Quarterly Almanac, 1951-56.
Gruberg, p. 163.

LEONOR KRETZER SULLIVAN   (Mrs. John Berchmans Sullivan)
Democrat, Missouri
1953-

Mrs. Sullivan has represented the Third Missouri Congressional District continuously since 1953, from the 83rd through the 92nd Congresses; she was reelected to the 93rd Congress, which convened in 1973, and she has the longest record of service among the 14 Congresswomen presently in the 93rd Congress. She is one of the few women Representatives who did not have the means and the time to attend college in her youth; she was one of nine children, and her parents had a small income. So Mrs. Sullivan had to postpone her higher education until she was employed in business; she then attended Washington University in St. Louis.

While her husband, a liberal Democrat, represented the Third District from 1942 to 1950, she served as his assistant. After his death she hoped to fall heir to his seat, but the St. Louis Democrats put up a man who lost to a Republican. In 1952 Mrs. Sullivan tried again, without party support, and was elected with a large majority; she has been reelected with large majorities ever since, because she has represented her constituents well and has acquired national prominence for her liberal social record and her strong championship of the consumer.

Her district covers South St. Louis and some suburbs. It is 88 percent central city, and her constituency is 40 percent white collar and 60 percent blue collar, with 10 percent blacks and a total foreign-born stock of 15 percent. The population has decreased from 1960 to 1970 and the area has been repeatedly redistricted without hurting Mrs. Sullivan's ability to be reelected. There are large-scale federal military-industrial commitments, including McDonnell-Douglas Aircraft and IBM, as well as food and beverage manufacturing, printing and publishing, banking and insurance; St. Louis University is also located there. She has received consistently high ratings from ADA, COPE, and the National Farmers Union, an organized group of small farmers. (COPE is the Committee on Political Action of the AFL-CIO, and ADA is Americans for Democratic Action, a liberal group believing in international cooperation and in freedom and economic security for the average citizen.)

Mrs. Sullivan is a member of the Banking and Currency Committee, second in line after chairman Wright Patman, and she is chairman of the Committee's subcommittee on consumer affairs; in addition, she is on the subcommittees for Housing and Small Business. The whole committee's concern is with banking and currency legislation, public and private housing laws, and other financial matters.

In 1972 she was second from the top on the Committee for Merchant Marine and
Fisheries, with membership on three subcommittees: Coast Guard and Geodetic
Survey and Navigation; Merchant Marine; and Panama Canal. Mrs. Sullivan, one
of the Congressional leaders of the consumer movement, fought for the truth-in-
lending law. She is a thorough, orderly, and courageous person who does not
shrink from a stiff fight in committee or on the floor; she is forthright and lucid
in her arguments.

Mrs. Sullivan is also a member of the Joint Committee on Defense Production; a member of the National Commission of Consumer Finance, which was
created by the Consumer Credit Protection Act of 1968; and a member of the
United States Territorial Expansion Commission, which oversees the Jefferson
National Expansion Memorial, and the Gateway Arch in St. Louis. She is on the
Democratic Steering Committee, serving as its secretary; she is the only woman
on it. She might be called Dean of Women, because she is the oldest and the one
with the longest Congressional record among Congresswomen; also, she has what
must be one of the largest workloads of any woman in Congress.

Mrs. Sullivan's outstanding record as a proponent of consumerism goes
back almost to the first year she served in Congress. She initiated the Poultry
Products Inspection Act of 1957, establishing for the first time compulsory
federal inspection of poultry sold in interstate commerce. Next was the Food
Additives Act of 1958, which requires pretesting for safety of all chemical
additives used in or on foodstuffs, while 1960 saw her engaged in a battle to pass
the anticancer provisions of the Color Additives Act, dealing with artificial color-
ing used in foods, drugs, and cosmetics. In 1961 came the Hazardous Substances
Labelling Act. The far-reaching Drug Control Act of 1962 included the major
provisions relating to prescription drugs that she first proposed 18 months earlier
as part of an omnibus bill to rewrite the Food, Drug and Cosmetics Act of 1938
and bring it up to date. The Wholesome Meat Act of 1967 and the Wholesome
Poultry Act of 1968 authorize compulsory federal inspection of such products
sold in intrastate commerce. She introduced and guided to passage the Consumer Credit Protection Act of 1968 (known as truth-in-lending). In 1970 she
introduced in the House and helped to pass a "Fair Credit Reporting Act,"
which would enable consumers to protect themselves against arbitrary,
erroneous, and malicious information given out and sold by credit reporting
companies to users of their service for credit, employment, or insurance purposes. To do these things took courage and required everlasting watchfulness
and ingenuity. Proxmire had succeeded in having the Senate pass a truth-in-lending
bill, but it had been so watered down in the legislative process that it was virtually
useless. Mrs. Sullivan had to fight fierce battles against giant retail chains like
Montgomery Ward, Sears, and Penney's. The Fair Credit Reporting Act is opposed
by credit card companies and other monied interests with well-financed lobbies,
and Mrs. Sullivan will have to wage a battle royal to get a good bill passed.

In 1955 she offered an amendment to a bill intended to close a serious gap
in statistical information involving America's biggest import item: coffee. She
said hundreds of millions of dollars had been taken out of the pockets of consumers in tribute to a shortage that never existed because we didn't know that
statistics formerly kept had been discontinued. In 1959 Congresswoman Sullivan

was the author of the first Food Stamp Law, enacted in the same year. Six years earlier she had introduced HR7876 to set up a food stamp plan through which up to $1 billion in surpluses would be distributed to needy persons. Others had said surpluses should be used abroad and the Assistant Secretary of Agriculture had opined that Congress should go slow on food stamp disposal of surplus food. "Too costly, too complicated" were the facile objections, but Mrs. Sullivan doggedly pursued her aim and since 1959 distribution of surplus commodities to needy Americans through regular grocery stores would have been commonplace if the Eisenhower administration had not decided not to implement the law. A modified food stamp plan was instituted by Kennedy, which led to Representative Sullivan's introduction in the 88th Congress of an administration food stamp bill that was enacted into law on August 31, 1964.

Congresswoman Sullivan has also played a leading role in the preparation of housing bills passed by the House since 1955. She has opposed high-rise public housing for families with children, stressing the desirability of garden-type homes for such families. But she is not weak-kneed toward the poorer classes, and stresses that they have responsibilities too; she has advocated regulations that would require tenants in public housing to be more responsible for the maintenance and ordinary care of their housing units. In the 91st Congress the Congresswoman was chairman of an ad-hoc subcommittee of the House Banking and Currency Committee to investigate alleged irregularities of federally insured activities in inner-city residential properties. Among other concerns of the House Banking Committee she initiated legislation in 1969 that gave the President and the Federal Reserve Board authority to regulate rates and forms of any type of credit; in 1970 she co-sponsored the standby Price and Wage Control Act which Nixon implemented in Summer 1971. And she successfully offered proposals to raise maximum limits on federal insurance of deposits in banks and savings and loans, first from $10,000 to $15,000 and then from $15,000 to $20,000.

She has also been active in promoting educational policies and activities. In another line, as chairman of the Panama Canal subcommittee of the Merchant Marine and Fisheries Committee, she has taken strong stands in favor of retaining U.S. supremacy in the Canal Zone. In the woman's sphere she co-sponsored and worked for the Equal Pay Act of 1963; worked to eliminate job discrimination against women under the Civil Rights Act of 1964; and introduced bills to provide full Social Security benefits for women retiring at age 62. But she was the only woman in the House to reject the Equal Rights Amendment of 1972. She did so because of her fear that women might lose the protection that is now theirs under the law. May she be proved wrong on this score.

Besides being the only, and the first woman to serve on the Democratic Steering Committee of the House of Representatives, she was also the elected member and secretary of the House Democratic Caucus in the 84th, 86th, 88th, 90th and 91st Congresses and, finally, was the senior House member of the National Commission on Food Marketing, which conducted a two-year investigation from 1964 to 1966 into all aspects of food marketing from farmer to consumer. During the 92nd Congress she introduced, co-sponsored, or worked for a list of 17 major projects in health, employment, taxation, environment protection, Social Security, women's rights and food and drug protection, including sponsorship of the bill introduced in the House by Martha Griffiths to create a national system of complete health security (HR23).

In 1973 Mrs. Sullivan will be the third woman ever to serve in the House as chairman of a full committee: the Committee on Merchant Marine and Fisheries; Mary Norton, Democrat from New Jersey, was chairman of the Committee on Education in the 1940s, and Edith Nourse Rogers, Republican from Massachusetts, was chairman of the Veterans Affairs Committee for one term in the 1950s.

Mrs. Sullivan is deeply disturbed about Congress' loss of standing and the ever-increasing monolithic power of the executive branch. But she is very patriotic and has never refused to vote for the defense establishment. She voted against SST, but for giving plane manufacturers a rebate of $58 million for their alleged investments in the supersonic plane. She also voted against the welfare legislation of the 92nd Congress and its Family Assistance Plan perhaps because it left the "mess" much as it was before. She is a law-and-order Congresswoman; she was for no-knock, but also for giving the vote to 18-year-olds, for clean water appropriations, and for compensation for migratory agricultural workers. This is a mixture of progressivism and conservatism, but her record leans more to the liberal side. Wherever the average citizen is concerned, Congresswoman Sullivan has a solid record of beneficial accomplishments.

Bibliography

"Women in the 83rd Congress," M. L. Temple. *Independent Woman* 32:35 (Feb. 1953).

"Increase in Coffee Prices," *U.S. Department of State Bulletin* 30:257 (Feb. 15, 1954).

"Women in the 84th Congress," *Independent Woman* 34:38 (Jan. 1955).

"Lack of Leadership in Washington," address, April 25, 1957. *Vital Speeches* 23: 489-92 (June 1, 1957).

Excerpt from debate, April 7, 1964. *Congressional Digest* 43:180+ (June 1964).

"Citizens Role in Furthering Consumer Interests," address, April 21, 1966. *Vital Speeches* 32:498-501 (June 1, 1966).

Excerpt from debate, January 30, 1968. *Congressional Digest* 47:82+ (Mar. 1968).

Congressional Quarterly Almanac, 1954-70.

Congressional Quarterly Weekly Report, 1970-71.

Almanac, pp. 432-34.

Congressional Record, especially Monday, February 7, 1972, no. 15, E896 on cosmetics; Tuesday, March 7, 1972, no. 34, E2119 National Housing Conference; Monday, June 19, 1972, no. 99, H5773; Wednesday, August 2, 1972, no. 122, E7273; Friday, August 11, 1972, no. 129, E7436-37; Thursday, September 28, 1972, no. 153, E8225, etc.

Gruberg, p. 164.

Sussman, Robert. *Leonor K. Sullivan, Democratic Representative From Missouri*. [Washington, D.C., Grossman Publishers, c1972] [1p.] (Ralph Nader Congress Project. Citizens Look at Congress.) Biographical and legislative material received from Representative Sullivan.

GRACIE PFOST (Mrs. John W. Pfost)
Democrat, Idaho
1953-63

Gracie Pfost, representing the First Idaho Congressional District, was 48 when she was elected to the 83rd Congress meeting in January 1953. She was greatly interested in irrigation and power projects. During her first session in Congress she offered amendments to legislation concerning the Bonneville Dam, to increase appropriations for its construction, but she was unsuccessful in her attempts. A five-member commission to which she was appointed by Speaker Joseph Martin was to undertake a foundations probe to investigate the tax exempt status of educational, philanthropic, and other foundations. The probe seems to have born some fruit only much, much later. This 83rd Congress also wrangled about the Hells Canyon Project in Idaho. The Truman administration wanted to build a multiple-purpose dam and power projects in Hells Canyon at a cost of $356.8 million. But the Idaho Power Company filed application to build several smaller dams instead of a high one; Eisenhower, who had just started his administration, favored private construction. Wayne Morse, Gracie Pfost, and several others favored the federal project; they also intended to investigate the Federal Power Commission for its handling of the Idaho Power Company. No action was taken on any of the bills concerning the projects in the 83rd Congress' first session. In the second session of the 83rd Congress, in 1954, Mrs. Pfost again strongly favored public bodies over private ones in another area; she urged approval of amendments to give preference to public bodies and cooperatives in the development of atomic power plants and in the sale and distribution of power, asking, "Does it not seem fair and logical that those of us who have paid for these vast projects should receive the benefits for them?" In the continuing foundations probe alluded to before, one witness claimed that Paul Douglas while at Columbia University some forty years before had been a Socialist, which Douglas denied; Gracie Pfost was among the representatives who walked out in disgust at this type of questioning and testimony. Another subject that drew lively argument concerned a ban on liquor advertising; two bills would have banned interstate advertising of alcohol in the press, on the radio, and on TV. Mrs. Pfost spoke in support of these measures.

In the following Congress her assignments continued as before: with the Internal and Insular Affairs Committee and with the Committee on the Post Office and Civil Service. In this Congress the Hells Canyon Project received further airing; Mrs. Pfost again supported a federal project which aimed at a storage capacity of 3.9 million acre feet, while private construction would have supplied only 1 million; the federal project would have generated 900,000 kilowatts and additional capacity on eight downstream dams, with water available for irrigation, but private construction could supply no more than 610,000 killowatts. Mrs. Pfost was joined in urging federal construction by other forward-looking Democrats: Metcalf, Magnusson, and Edith Green. Again Mrs. Pfost met with defeat, and she fared no better in the 85th Congress: the ten-year history of delays and defeats that surrounded Hells Canyon legislation continued when bills were put off until 1958, but Congresswoman Pfost was undeterred and said that she would introduce new legislation. In the meantime she raised her voice against Eisenhower's wish to increase postal rates; she said that first class and air mail rates should not be raised for the benefit of so-called junk mail.

In 1958 she joined a 15-member commission to make a survey of national outdoor recreational resources; it was the first such inventory signed into law in PL470. Seven of the members were civilians, while the other eight were public officials appointed by the President, the Senate, and the Speaker of the House. Her committee assignment on the Internal and Insular Affairs Committee took her, with other members, on a trip to Puerto Rico and the Virgin Islands in 1960; on the Public Works Committee, which she had exchanged for membership on the Post Office and Civil Service Committee, she went with other congressmen to Italy, France, and England to attend the International Road Conference, with commercial transportation at government expense. Once more in the second session of the 87th Congress, in 1962, she took up the cudgels for a public works project, called the Burns Creek Project on the Upper Snake River Valley in Idaho, saying that the dam planned was not a partisan issue in Idaho, and should not be a partisan issue on the floor of the Congress. But the item was deleted on the House floor and not reinstated in conference.

Mrs. Pfost had an excellent record as a legislator and her voting participation was sometimes 100 percent. Her election campaigns were spirited and colorful, and her reelection margins, sometimes with the aid of labor, were substantial. When she was 56 years old, she ran for the Senate and was narrowly defeated by Len B. Jordan, the interim Republican Senator.

Before going to Congress, Mrs. Pfost had been a chemist, and she later held posts as county clerk, auditor and recorder; in 1950 in her first try for Congress she was defeated, but in 1952 she defeated the man who had beaten her two years before. Idaho voters could have done better than defeating her in favor of mediocrities.

Bibliography

"Women in the 84th Congress," *Independent Woman* 34:23 (Jan. 1955).
House wilderness hearings May 7-11, 1962, with text of substitute Wilderness
  Bill. *Living Wilderness* 80:14-35 (Spring 1962).
Wilderness hearings May 7-9, 1962. *Living Wilderness* 79:28-30 (Winter 1961).
Congressional Quarterly Almanac, 1953-62.
Gruberg, pp. 163-64.

ELIZABETH FARRINGTON   (Mrs. Joseph R. Farrington)
Republican, Hawaii
1954-57

Mrs. Farrington, a Hawaii territorial delegate to Congress, succeeded her husband, Joseph Rider Farrington, as of July 31, 1954, and won a full two-year term in the November 1954 election, serving until January 3, 1957, in the 83rd and 84th Congresses. She was defeated for reelection in November 1956. She had attended the University of Wisconsin and was thereafter active in local and national Republican Party organizations. She had three committee assignments in the House—Agriculture, Armed Services, and Internal and Insular Affairs—an unusually heavy load. In the 84th Congress she pressed for statehood for Hawaii, as well as for Alaska. She was anxious to support an increase in the sugar marketing quotas for domestic producers, saying "Hawaii needs and expects to share pro rata with its sister areas in the increase in sugar marketing"; a bill to that purpose was passed, as amended by the House on July 30, 1955, by a vote of 194 to 44. Mrs. Farrington introduced numerous bills. Some of them dealing with statehood for Hawaii; another embodied a proposed amendment granting equal rights to men and women; and others were on military and veterans affairs, and on taxes and economic policy.

Bibliography

"Call on the President," *U.S. News* 37:8 (Aug. 20, 1954).
"Women in the 84th Congress," *Independent Woman* 34:22 (Jan. 1955).
Congressional Quarterly Almanac, 1955-56.
Gruberg, p. 164.

IRIS FAIRCLOTH BLITCH (Mrs. Erwin Blitch)
Democrat, Georgia
1955-63

Mrs. Blitch, who had studied at the University of Georgia, became a businesswoman together with her husband, who had diversified business interests. At the same time she engaged in politics and served several terms in the Georgia State Senate. She was the chief proponent of a bill to permit women to serve on Georgia juries; she was also a member of the Democratic National Committee for eight years, until 1956. During her four terms in the U.S. House of Representatives (to which she was first elected in the general election of November 1954) in the sessions of the 84th, 85th, 86th, and 87th Congresses, she represented Georgia's Eighth Congressional District. Her committee assignment was Public Works, which ranges in scope from public buildings and roads to flood control and improvement of rivers and harbors, and from water power to stream pollution; she was also on its subcommittees for Rivers and Harbors and for Public Buildings and Grounds.

Congresswoman Blitch introduced bills concerning highway programs, and expressed the views of a minority of committee members who objected to a provision that would have authorized payment for relocation of utility lines at the cost of "almost $1 billion during the next thirteen years, at the expense of funds sorely needed for highway construction." In the area of agriculture she introduced a bill to amend the Agricultural Adjustment Act of 1938 in order to exempt certain wheat producers from liability under the act when the entire wheat crop was fed or used for seed on the producing farm. Concerning tax and economic policy, she introduced legislation to amend the Watershed Protection and Flood Prevention Act so as to provide that the federal government should pay a portion of the costs of certain improvements constructed for purposes of water conservation. In the same general area she introduced legislation in the circle of interests taken care of by the Ways and Means Committee, with the purpose of reducing the rate of import duty on jute yarn when it was to be used wholly in the manufacture of backing for tufted rugs and carpets.

In the first session of the 85th Congress she was one of the co-signers of a segregation manifesto issued by Southern Representatives in answer to HR627. HR627 proposed to establish a Committee on Civil Rights, to provide for additional Assistant Attorney Generals to further strengthen civil rights, and to protect the right to vote for every citizen. One hundred and one Representatives from Alabama, Arkansas, Florida, Georgia, Louisiana, Mississippi, North and South Carolina, Tennessee, Texas, and Virginia called this legislation "an iniquitous and flagrant violation of states rights." They (19 Senators and 82 Representatives) also presented a Declaration of Constitutional Principles to Congress criticizing the Supreme Court for the 1954 decision that called for desegregation of schools: they characterized the decision as an "abuse of judicial powers" and commended states that "have declared their intention to resist forced integration by any lawful means."

Beyond affixing her signature to this instrument she again introduced bills on taxes and economic policy. In the area of education and welfare, she suggested legislation providing for supplementary benefits for needy recipients of public assistance through the issuance of certificates to be used for acquiring surplus agricultural foods and fiber products. Other legislation offered by her was concerned with repayment of money lost because of damage to crops from fire and drought, and she was sufficiently interested in environmental matters to bring in a bill for further protection of the Okefenokee National Wildlife Refuge in Georgia. In the 86th and 87th Congresses Representative Blitch remained on the Public Works Committee and continued to introduce bills in the areas of her main concern.

She had had little difficulty being reelected, although in general she neither received nor spent any election funds. There is nothing of interest concerning her activities in the last session of the 86th and the two sessions of the 87th Congresses, meeting in 1960, 1961, and 1962. A controversy on nepotism in Congress that flared up in 1959 apparently did not damage her reputation in the eyes of her constituents. It was revealed that there were dozens of Representatives who had namesakes on their payroll. Mrs. Blitch had Brooks E. Blitch on her payroll at a salary of $5,177 per year, but assistants of many other Congressmen received payments in excess of $10,000.

Mrs. Blitch was a rather colorless lawmaker, conservative and never attempting to strike out on her own. No particular friend of civil rights, and not outstanding in social legislation, she brought in the usual crop of bills chiefly beneficial to agricultural producers—which is, of course, perfectly legitimate. Very little has been written about her or her activities.

Bibliography

Congressional Quarterly Almanac, 1955-62.
Gruberg, pp. 165-66.

EDITH STARRETT GREEN
Democrat, Oregon
1955-

Edith Green has represented Oregon's Third Congressional District for more than 18 years. She was first elected to the 84th Congress in 1955 and has been regularly reelected every two years.

Representative Green attended the University of Oregon and Stanford University; after graduation she was for 14 years a teacher and a leader in the Oregon Education Association. In the Congress she holds an appointment to the Committee on the District of Columbia, where she has taken a stand against unconditional home rule. Her main appointment—and the one she treasures most and in which she has done outstanding work— is as a member of the Committee on Education and Labor, where she is second in rank on the Democratic side; she is also on the general subcommittee on education, and on the select subcommittees on labor, and is chairman of the special subcommittee on education. Because of her dedication and her expertise in matters educational, she has been called Mrs. Education. In the 92nd Congress there were four other women on the Education and Labor Committee: Patsy Mink, Shirley Chisholm, Ella Grasso, and Louise Hicks, in the order of their seniority.

Mrs. Green's district comprises most of the city of Portland and some of its suburbs; it is 100 percent metropolitan and 66 percent central city, having a 1970 population of 522,000. Unemployment is high; the employment figures show that the white collar component is 48 percent, the blue collar 52 percent. Foreign-born stock is 24 percent of the population, but blacks make up only 5 percent. Representative Green's district consists chiefly of lower and middle income neighborhoods. It includes industry engaged in manufacturing transportation equipment and in ship and boat building; the processing of food and dairy products, and the manufacturing of metal products; it has also institutions for higher education (Portland State University). Mrs. Green has two sons and is divorced.

In the area of economic concerns Mrs. Green voted for a boost in the minimum wage to $2.00 per hour. Together with two Republicans on her committee, she voted against OEO extension, while 32 other members voted for it. Neither did the Welfare Reform Bill, HR1, passed by the House, get her assent; she objected to the provision for $4,320 for a family of four. Mrs. Green demanded more consideration for middle-income people, saying that it was high time the House and the Senate gave more attention to these groups of wage and salary earners; she insisted that she was not opposed to helping the poor, but was rather in favor of raising everyone up—but not at the expense of those who were trying desperately to make ends meet and who perhaps actually had less to support themselves after paying taxes than families getting the benefit of public assistance. She expressed more concern for the 750,000 to 800,000 Vietnam War veterans coming into the tight labor market looking for jobs, stating: "We are faced with a major social problem, potential social dynamite." She pointed out that HR3613, which Nixon sponsored, did not provide enough jobs; but she was afraid that if more money were appropriated for creating employment, Nixon would veto the bill on the grounds that it cost too much.

Congresswoman Green has worked diligently for improving education, but has in recent years opposed busing as a desegregation aid. Again, her concern has been primarily for the middle-class citizens who generally make up the population of her district. But she is not at all satisfied with what Nixon sets aside for education. If Nixon has decided that it is necessary to use federal funds to rescue Penn Central from financial disaster and seems willing to use federal funds to bail out Lockheed, she says, why does he not propose some federal aid to save America's failing colleges and universities from financial disaster?

On the busing question she spoke out on the floor of the House on November 4, 1971: "I have opposed busing for several years. . . I oppose busing because I don't think it is workable. We had prohibition when I was a small child and it did not work. We repealed the prohibition law. I think the evidence is overwhelming that busing is not the answer to a very complex school problem of today. The schools are deteriorating before our eyes. They are decaying. We cannot find enough money for our classrooms. We cannot find enough money for our teachers. We cannot find enough money to do the things we ought to be doing. Instead we go on this busing binge and spend hundreds of millions of dollars on buying buses and hiring bus drivers." To illustrate her point, she alluded to the situation in Los Angeles where integration was forced by court order. If the order is upheld after appeal, she calculated that to implement it would cost $42 million during the first year to buy buses and hire drivers, and each year thereafter it would cost an additional $20 million to $24 million. Her stand may please the majority, but it does not present positive suggestions for arriving at absolute equality of educational opportunity for all. The amendment Mrs. Green offered to the Education Act of 1971 says that neither HEW nor any other agency of the executive branch can impose upon any local school district or state any requirements for any programs that require the expenditure of state or local funds for those purposes for which federal funds cannot be spent. (*Congressional Record*, November 4, 1971.)

She enlarged upon her point of view in an interview with representatives of *U.S. News and World Report* (April 3, 1972). She maintained that desegregation must be brought about by some means other than busing, which she said had been the easy answer to a complex problem. What she seems to take for more fundamental reforms is "in terms of housing and other opportunities in the ghettos." While she agrees with Nixon in her anti-busing stand, she claims that his proposals for equalizing educational opportunities fall far short of the needs. "It will take more money than the President proposes." She thinks that the votes in the House "clearly demonstrate a feeling that busing has gone too far." Her amendment was co-sponsored by Ashbrook of Ohio and Broomfield of Michigan, both Republicans. In all this one detects a lack of positive statement, a scarcity of creativity.

Mrs. Green has been opposed to the Vietnam War since 1965. On May 11, 1965, she said in the *Congressional Record* that she and six of her colleagues dissented from the vote of the majority of the House which approved the government's policy of escalating the Indochina War. During the years 1966 to 1968 she continued to express her opposition to the war by speaking out on and voting against all proposals aimed at widening the war, and in 1970 she cast her vote against ABM. On April 26, 1972, she introduced her war powers legislation, HR14592, co-sponsored by her colleague from Oregon, Wendell Wyatt, which essentially aimed at the following: the President is allowed, without the prior consent of Congress, to commit troops to a combat area, volunteers without limit, draftees for the first 90 days only. Within 90 days Congress by resolution or declaration of all-out war must endorse the original presidential action to permit continuation of assignment of draftees to combat areas, or they must be promptly withdrawn. Within 180 days of the President's initial commitment of troops to a combat area, all are to be promptly withdrawn unless the Congress has formally declared a state of war to exist. That bill was introduced because she thought it had certain advantages over S2956, the so-called War Powers Bill recently passed by the Senate. (*Congressional Record*, April 26, 1972.)

When the OEO extension bill was before the House in 1971, Representative Green opposed it and offered legislation whose purpose was to strengthen state economic opportunity offices and to provide for a positive, affirmative vote for the states through the implementation of a state developmental and coordination program.

Mrs. Green was the author of equal pay for equal work legislation, the Library Services Act, the Higher Education Act of 1965 and 1968, and much other legislation; among other Social Security Act improvements, she co-sponsored legislation for hospital and nursing home care for the aged, nurses' training, liberalized immigration, aid to handicapped children, national school lunch program, etc. In the 91st Congress (1969-1970), she introduced the federal Coal Mine Health and Safety Act of 1969, a cost of living increase for Social Security recipients, the College Assistance Act of 1969, the omnibus Post-Secondary Education Act of 1970, equal pay for equal work amendments of 1970, and other bills.

Congresswoman Green is a former member of President Kennedy's Commission on the Status of Women, a former member of the U.S. Commission to UNESCO; she was a delegate to the 1958 NATO Conference in London, and to the UNESCO General Conference in Paris, 1964 and 1966. She has an impressive string of honors, including several dozen honorary doctor of laws degrees, including one from Yale University. She was asked by John F. Kennedy to second his nomination for Democratic Presidential candidate at the 1960 convention and in 1968 was co-chairman of Robert F. Kennedy's Oregon primary campaign. In 1972 she opposed George McGovern's candidacy; her preference was for Henry Jackson—a strange choice for a dove. Although she advocated equal rights for women and authored an equal pay bill, she did not favor Martha Griffiths' Equal Rights Amendment. She was instrumental in having women included in the Job Corps.

To summarize her votes on some key legislation of the 92nd Congress: for no-knock, state OEO veto, park logging; against SST, 18-year-old vote, Cooper-Church Vietnam War bill, family assistance, migratory workers' compensation. Called "Mrs. Education" for her lifelong interest in furthering education, she "has had tremendous power to shape the nation's educational programs" (*Congressional Quarterly Almanac*, p. 674). Nader's report finds that, formerly a flaming liberal, she now has become reactionary; she is "unpredictable"—a "political enigma" (Louise Wides, *Edith Green*, p. 29). Her votes on key legislation and her stands on other crucial problems seem to support such judgments.

Mrs. Green was encouraged to run for the U.S. Senate from Oregon. She declined, reportedly because she was appalled by the cost of such a try, and because then she could no longer say "Go to hell" to a lobbyist (Wides, p. 7). Anyway, her constituents like what she has done as well as what she is saying and doing now, and they reelect her every time with very comfortable majorities. In her eighteenth year in Congress, in 1973, she is 63 years old.

Bibliography

Works about Edith Starrett Green

"Aid to Higher Education: The One That Got Away," *Reporter* 27:28-30 (Oct. 25, 1962).

"Much More Remains To Be Done," *National Education Association Journal* 53:16-17+ (Feb. 1964).

"Congress: New Study Shows Federal Educational Budget of $2.2 Billion, $613 Million Of It For Research," J. Walsh. *Science* 141:29-31 (July 5, 1963).

"Friends and Enemies," *Newsweek* 69:30 (June 5, 1967).

"Campus Issues in 1980," excerpt from address March 1968. *PTA Magazine* 62:18-20 (Apr. 1968).

"School Busing: Are We Hurting the People We Want To Help?" excerpt from address July 3, 1969. *U.S. News* 67:72-73 (Aug. 18, 1969).

"Education Complex," *Newsweek* 76:72-73 (Sept. 7, 1970).

"Busing Has Gone Too Far," interview. *U.S. News* 72:19-21 (Apr. 3, 1972).

"Representative Edith Green: A Bare Knuckle Fighter," Norm C. Miller. *Wall Street Journal* 174:18 (Dec. 3, 1969).

Almanac, pp. 674-76.

Gruberg, p. 165.

Congressional Quarterly Almanac, 1955-70.

Congressional Quarterly Weekly Report, 1971-72.

Congressional Record, 1972.

Wides, Louise. *Edith Green, Democratic Representative from Oregon*. [Washington, D.C., Grossman Publishers, c1972] [36p.] (Ralph Nadar Congress Project. Citizens Look At Congress.)

The Green Letter [Congresswoman Edith Green's constituent report]. Several issues, 1971, 1972.

HR14592, a bill to provide Congressional due process in questions of war powers [introduced in Congress April 25, 1972].

Works by Edith Starrett Green

"Education and the Public Good: The Federal Role in Education," by the Honorable Edith Green. In *The Challenge to Education in a Changing World*, by Walter P. Reuther. Cambridge, distributed for the Graduate School of Education of Harvard University by Harvard University Press, 1964. 67p. (The Burton lecture [and] the Inglis lecture, 1963.)

MARTHA WRIGHT GRIFFITHS   (Mrs. Hicks G. Griffiths)
Democrat, Michigan
1955-

Martha Griffiths was born January 12, 1912. She attended the University
of Michigan, where she earned an LLB degree. Her husband, a probate judge,
encouraged her to pursue a political career; although he seems to have had no
such ambitions for himself. Both were for several years members of G. Mennen
Williams' law firm; Mrs. Griffiths later founded her own law business. She
served four years in the state legislature, then in 1953 became judge of the
Recorder's Court of Detroit. After losing her bid for Congress in 1952, she tried
again in 1954 and was elected to the 84th Congress, convening in 1955. Her district is the Seventeenth Michigan in northwest Detroit. It is mostly residential,
and her constituents have been white, Protestant, middle-class, and largely white-
collar; in recent years blacks have been moving in and some of the original residents have left for the suburbs. There is also quite a large group of foreign-born.
The residents work in the automobile factories and in factories that produce
machinery and equipment.

Congresswoman Griffiths is a member of the Ways and Means Committee,
one of the most important committees on which a legislator can serve. Wilbur
Mills, a hard-working, very knowledgeable, and arch-conservative Democrat from
Arkansas, has been chairman of Ways and Means for many years. Mrs. Griffiths
gets along well with the chairman. This is the only committee on which she
serves. It is also the only committee that has no subcommittees—all problems are
discussed by its full membership of 15 Democrats and 10 Republicans. The areas
of its responsibilities are revenue measures generally, taxation, tariffs, reciprocal
trade agreements and Social Security. In taxation she defers to the views of the
chairman, but she has her own ideas of several facets of the subject. She is horri-
fied by the hundreds of loopholes in its fabric and would like to close some of
the bigger ones. She thinks, for instance, that municipal bonds, now tax-free,
should be taxed like other income; but she is aware that such a view has no hope
of prevailing against its entrenched opponents. To other aspects of tax inequities she does not seem to apply the same clear-cut approach. She says she has
been for free trade from her childhood, but she can bend with the wind in that
field, too. Social Security is one of the responsibilities of Ways and Means, and
Mrs. Griffiths has worked valiantly to equalize benefits between men and women.

She has no special interest in welfare recipients, as can be clearly seen in
her acts and words as reported in the *Congressional Record*. The Congresswoman
says that welfare is a mess, but her attack does not go much beyond decrying
whatever cases of fraud are discovered. She supported HR1, which Nixon called
the most important legislation in 35 years and in which Chairman Mills took
pride. In the fall of 1972 the bill failed passage in the Senate and Nixon voiced
no regrets at the demise of this whooped-up wonder. The bill, calling for extensive revamping of the nation's welfare system had a special section, Title IV,
dealing with the Family Assistance Plan (FAP). Under its conditions a guaranteed
income of $2,400 per year would be established for a family of four without any
income. Mrs. Griffiths is in favor of this plan, while more radical people, like

Mrs. Abzug, are against it—as are also the leaders of the National Welfare Rights Organization, who want guaranteed annual income without any punitive measures. Mrs. Griffiths claimed that the welfare group's plan placed too much emphasis on assistance and not enough on job training.

Representative Griffiths seems to be only lukewarm about Revenue Sharing, one of the few good bills on which Congress and the Executive agreed and which actually became law toward the end of the 92nd Congress. Her record on the Vietnam War and on appropriations for the Defense Department is not one that would qualify her as a dove, but she spares no words when it comes to the Pentagon's wasteful methods, saying: "No one knows better than I how stupid these military people can be. The whole area of defense procurement is a monstrous disgrace. The contractors are stealing and cheating and no one in the Pentagon cares about it" (Lawson, *Few Are Chosen*, p. 97). She voted for rat control and has consistently been in favor of the Model Cities' program. She voted for the vote for 18-year-olds, and for Cooper-Church, but against SST, bombers for Chiang Kai-shek, and park logging. She was against forced busing.

Her proudest efforts have been those for equality in pay under the law for women. On occasion of the deliberations on the equal employment bill she said, "If there is any group that should not be willing to trust their rights to the federal courts it is the women. They have never won." She endorsed HR1746, a narrower version than the committee bill, which, in addition to providing cease and desist powers, also enlarged EEOC. Mrs. Griffiths was the original sponsor of the Equal Rights Amendment, HJRes208, which was approved in the House 354 to 23. She said while leading the fight: "The battle is not between women and this House but between women and the Supreme Court which has held for 98 years that women are not entitled to the equal protection of the laws." She claimed that women had been discriminated against in employment, divorce and alimony, property rights, pensions, inheritance, and some criminal laws. She also claimed women had lagged behind Negroes because the Supreme Court had refused to apply the equal rights protection clause of the 14th amendment to women. She pointed out that the Air Force still required women enlistees to be high school graduates and unmarried, conditions that were not required of men. Other forms of discrimination: the FBI refused to hire women as special agents; many schools expel unwed mothers, but not fathers. Celler, chairman of the Judiciary Committee, had refused for 20 years to let the measure come out of committee onto the floor of the House for a vote, but Congresswoman Griffiths finally dislodged it. It had rough going and was subject to many debilitating amendments; in the Senate it was even more violently opposed. One of the final amendments, offered by Congressman Wiggins, wanted to exempt women from the draft and to continue state laws for the health and safety of women, which Mrs. Griffiths opposed; the Wiggins amendment was rejected. In the summer of 1972 the Senate also passed the resolution. The amendment has by now won ratification by more than 20 state legislatures; when 38 states have approved it will become the 27th amendment to the Constitution. That will be a great victory for Mrs. Griffiths.

Another victory that it is hoped she will achieve before long is her bill for a comprehensive national health insurance program, which has gained wide support among voters. In 1970 the American public had to spend $67.2 billion for health and medical care. A year later, in 1971, the House Ways and Means Committee ended five weeks of hearings on several different health proposals. The Congress had before it, in fact, eight different plans. The Nixon administration's plan would permit federal payment for the health needs of the poor, the handicapped, and unemployed. Businessmen are against it saying its costs will ruin them and they will have to fire marginal employees. Nixon's plan, called the National Health Insurance Partnership Act, would cost the federal government $5.5 billion per year, and there would be larger, still unestimated, costs for employers and employees. Private insurance firms and Blue Cross and Blue Shield would run the program under government regulation. It would cover all those employed and under age 65, and their dependents; those over 65 would still be under Medicare; the poor and their families would also be covered. A family of four with an income of less than $3,000 per year would have no costs to assume for any medical care; others would have to pay according to a graduated schedule. Most illnesses and deficiencies would be treated medically, and hospitalization would be included.

The American Medical Association has its own plan, introduced by sponsors in both Houses. It would pay its costs by granting "medicredit": tax credits for health expenditures would be given through one's tax return. Everyone would be included; Medicare for those over 65 would continue; participation would be voluntary. Expenses are greater and benefits fewer than under the Nixon sponsored plan.

Other plans include the Health Insurance Association Plan, with still fewer benefits. The poor would have their health needs paid for by federal and state funds; Medicare would continue. The cost to the federal government would be an estimated $3.4 billion per year, while the burden to the states is not known. The Hospital Association has a voluntary "Ameriplan"; cost estimates have not been made. The Scott-Percy plan would abolish both Medicare and Medicaid; enrollment would be optional, benefits few, and costs for the sick person high; these two Senators are known as liberals. A plan advanced by Senator Pell, Democrat, Rhode Island, would provide better coverage, but no precise cost estimates have been given. Senator Javits' plan would include more benefits and would be more reasonably priced for the insured; the cost would be $10.5 billion for the first year and would rise to $68.1 billion annually in the fifth year. All the above plans are based totally or partially on private insurance carriers and would benefit them much more than the sick person.

Organized labor's plan, sponsored by AFL-CIO, the Council of Senior Citizens, and the Committee on National Health Insurance, was introduced in the Senate by Senator Edward Kennedy (S3) and in the House by Representative Griffiths (HR22). It covers everyone from the cradle to the grave; the chief co-sponsor is Congressman James Corman of California. Its cost is estimated at from $44 to $77 billion per year, but $30 billion would be rechanneled from private health insurance plans. The taxpayer pays the bill; the costs of financing the plan would be defrayed half from general revenue, and half from the Social Security payroll tax that would be applied to wages and salaries up to $15,000 per year. The worker would pay 1 percent, the employer 3.5 percent. All doctor and hospital costs would be covered, as well as up to 120 days in a skilled nursing home; prescribed drugs would be included for everyone, and dental care for children; even some types of psychiatric care would be included. The federal government would operate the plan in its entirety through a Health Security Board and would set standard charges and pay bills. Performance of doctors and hospitals would be checked by professional panels. The bills were introduced in the 92nd Congress; George Meany has said, "We will come back again and again until the Health Security Program is enacted." The Congresswoman has a battle royal on her hands, since her opponents include the AMA, hospitals, insurance companies, and President Nixon. May she stay with the struggle until it is won.

Mrs. Griffiths, besides being fourth on Ways and Means, is also fifth on the Joint Economic Committee. She credits her presence on this important committee—the only one in Congress made up of both Senate and House members—to pressure from her women colleagues. Mrs. Griffiths is the only woman member. Created pursuant to Sec. 5(a) of PL304, passed in the 79th Congress, this Committee has 20 members (10 Senators and 10 Representatives); Senator Proxmire is chairman and Representative Wright Patman is vice chairman. It has six subcommittees: Fiscal Policy, of which Mrs. Griffiths is chairman; Economic Progress; Economic Statistics; Inter-American Economic Relationships; Priorities and Economy; and Urban Affairs.

Congresswoman Griffiths has been mentioned as a candidate for a Supreme Court vacancy; she has no objection, but Nixon will have. In the meantime she keeps in close touch with her constituency and she is very popular with voters in her district. In a district questionnaire she found that 66.6 percent of her constituents supported Nixon's Vietnam policies; on unconditional amnesty for war resisters their answer was 81.7 percent no. Her constituents voiced their conviction that Nixon's present wage-price-rent control program had not been effective in combatting inflation, and they put thumbs down on his national sales tax proposal, the VAT (Value-Added Tax). They approved of national health insurance for everyone financed by employer-employee contributions matched by the federal government under Social Security; they also felt that greater federal efforts were necessary to reduce unemployment. Crime ranked highest on their concerns, and they thought that increasing federal aid to states and localities for crime control programs would be effective in reducing crime and violence. Welfare was rather low on Mrs. Griffiths' constituents' list, but 91.4 percent voted against busing as a means to achieve racial balance (*Congressional Record*, September 19, 1972. E8005). Mrs. Griffiths keeps her fingers on her constituents' pulse: like the voters she represents, she seems to have moved somewhat to the right. She travels once a week from Washington to Detroit, which in 1967 cost her $5,200 in airplane fares. She is direct, to the point, and independent in thought and action.

Bibliography

"Women in the 84th Congress," *Independent Woman* 34:22 (Jan. 1955).
"Rising Tide of Violence," address, August 27, 1960. *Vital Speeches* 26:745-47 (Oct. 1, 1960).

"Life Without a Newspaper," from an address to Congress. *U.S. News* 52:106 (June 11, 1962).
"Lady of the House Looks Into Taxes," *Business Week*, pp. 28-29 (May 23, 1964).
"From the Women: What About Our Job Rights?", *U.S. News* 61:61-62 (July 14, 1966).
Excerpt from testimony before Committee on Finance of the U.S. Senate, September 22, 1967. *Congressional Digest* 47:180+ (June 1968).
"Equal Rights For Women? Things May Never Be the Same," *U.S. News* 69:29-30 (Aug. 24, 1970).
"Ladies' Day," *Newsweek* 76:15-16 (Aug. 24, 1970).
"Martha Griffiths: Graceful Feminist," *Time* 96:10-11 (Aug. 24, 1970).
Excerpt from testimony before Subcommittee on Constitutional Amendments, May 5, 1970. *Congressional Digest* 50:16+ (Jan. 1971).
"Set Stage for New Equal Rights Battle," S. B. Conroy. *McCalls* 98:37 (May 1971).
Almanac, pp. 391-93.
Abramson, Marcia. *Martha W. Griffiths, Democratic Representative from Michigan* [Washington, D.C., Grossman Publishers, c1972]. [22p.] (Ralph Nader's Congress Project. Citizens Look At Congress.)
Congressional Quarterly Almanac, 1955-70.
Congressional Quarterly Weekly Report, 1971-72.
Congressional Record, 1972.
Gruberg, p. 165.
Lamson, pp. 87-98 and passim.

COYA G. KNUTSON
Democrat, Minnesota
1955-59

Mrs. Knutson represented the Ninth Congressional District of Minnesota from 1955 to 1959, during the sessions of the 84th and 85th Congresses. She had studied at Concordia College, Minnesota, and at the Julliard School of Music; she was a high school teacher, and she also had business experience.

From 1949 to 1956 she was a member of her county's welfare board, and she was a member of the state legislature for several years. As a farmer she had become disgusted with Eisenhower's farm program, and she easily defeated the incumbent in the 1954 general election. She was put on the House Agriculture Committee, which was her choice, and she retained this assignment throughout her incumbency. In her 1956 campaign she received out-of-state contributions to the value of $2,000 and in addition was given $1,500 from labor organizations; she had a 52.7 percent majority of votes. During the first session of the 85th Congress she introduced 31 bills and resolutions. She was among 28 Democrats who had presented a progressive program for their party, calling for adequate defense forces, a revision of immigration and naturalization laws, federal aid for school construction, improvement of water and soil conservation programs, and other forward-looking matters; the number of sponsors of these proposals eventually rose to 80. She also voted for agricultural funds, appropriating $3,191,875,539 as embodied in HR11767 (to become Public Law 459 on June 13, 1958), which included funds for a school lunch program. The committee had assigned $100 million for this purpose, which Mrs. Knutson wanted to increase by $45 million; her amendment was defeated. She would probably have been reelected in 1958 if it had not been for a public protest by her husband against her candidacy for a third term. Her political enemies gleefully published a letter purportedly asking her to "come home," and she was defeated by a Republican—the only Democrat in the 1958 election to suffer this fate. This election brought the Minnesota representation in the next Congress to five Republicans and four Democrats. This is also the only instance where the attitude of a woman representative's husband was inimical to the wife's political ambitions.

Bibliography

"Farm Women Tell How to Fight the Surplus Threat to Family Farms," *Better Farming* 125:6+ (July 1955).
"Farm Women Tell Why We Must Fight to Protect the Family Farm Now!" *Better Farming* 125:8+ (June 1955).
"Meet the Farm Woman's Congresswoman," F. Bailey. *Better Farming* 125: 116-17 (Mar. 1955).
"After Reunion With Andy, Coya Still Has a Bone to Pick," *Life* 45:34-35 (Dec. 8, 1958).
"Conspiracy Denied," *Newsweek* 52:16+ (Dec. 29, 1958).
"Out of Andy's Inn," *Time* 71:17-18 (May 19, 1958).
"When A Woman Goes Into Politics," *U.S. News* 45:42-43 (Sept. 5, 1958).
Gruberg, pp. 164-65.

KATHRYN O'HAY GRANAHAN   (Mrs. William T. Granahan)
Democrat, Pennsylvania
1956-63

William T. Granahan died on May 25, 1956, and was succeeded by his widow, who was elected to his post representing the Second Pennsylvania District, on November 6, 1956. She received a vote of 95,567, representing 62.3 percent of total votes cast. Her campaign spending was reported as $5,010.48 received and $4,282.22 spent. She served in the 85th, 86th and 87th Congresses. Her first assignment, in the first session of the 85th Congress, was on the Agriculture Committee; in the second session she was switched to Government Operations Committee and to the Post Office and Civil Service Committee, which she continued to hold throughout her service. In the first session of the 85th Congress she introduced 15 bills dealing with legislation in agriculture, education and welfare, foreign policy, military and veterans subjects, and miscellaneous matters. The second session of the 85th Congress, meeting in 1958, had a heavy Democratic majority: the House had 283 Democrats and 153 Republicans. In the first session of the 86th Congress, 1959, she introduced

21 bills. On the 1959 housing bill, which was passed on the third try after much wrangling and which became PL86-372, Mrs. Granahan offered two amendments favorable to business, both of which were rejected. She adopted a strong stand against pornographic literature. In 1962 she was named Treasurer of the United States by President Kennedy.

Bibliography

"Comstock Rides Again," *Nation* 189-411 (Dec. 5, 1959).
Congressional Quarterly Almanac, 1956-62.
Gruberg, pp. 139, 166, 279.

FLORENCE PRICE DWYER   (Mrs. Joseph Michael Dwyer)
  Republican, New Jersey
  1957-72

Mrs. Florence Dwyer has represented the Twelfth Congressional District of New Jersey since 1957, when she entered the first session of the 85th Congress. From 1949 to 1957 Mrs. Dwyer was a member of the New Jersey State Legislature. She worked for equal pay for women while serving in the Assembly, and as chairman of the Education Committee exerted herself for state school aid and for improvement of teachers' salaries. In her first try for the Congress she defeated Harrison Williams, who later became U.S. Senator from New Jersey. After her election to Congress she attended Rutgers University Law School to further her knowledge of taxation and law and to increase her effectiveness as a lawmaker.

Her district was largely suburban, with a great number of first-generation Americans, and industries include manufacturers of chemicals, drugs, machinery and equipment, etc. The population of her district has increased considerably since 1960; Mrs. Dwyer's consistent reelection to Congress may result from the fact that she is progressive and she has worked for her constituents.

Her first committee assignments were Government Operations and Veterans Affairs, but early in her career she exchanged her seat on the latter committee for one on Banking and Currency. Congresswoman Dwyer was a hard-working member of Congress; she had consistently introduced a great number of bills in a variety of fields. She was dubious about the Area Redevelopment Bill of 1959, S722, which was passed by the Senate, and reported by the House Banking and Currency Committee on May 14, 1959. In her minority report Mrs. Dwyer thought that enactment might result in nothing more than a migration or pirating of industries from the established into depressed areas; she suggested the establishment of new employment opportunities rather than the encouragement of a simple geographical shift.

The $1.4 billion omnibus housing bill introduced in Congress in 1960 was found to be inadequate by a minority group who said that its bad features outweighed its good ones and that the bill required numerous extensive amendments to make it practical; Mrs. Dwyer was a co-signer of the minority report. She is interested in helping the underdeveloped countries achieve their potential.

On the occasion of the passage of S3074 and HR11001 (signed into Public Law 86-565 on June 30, 1960) she said that the International Development Association would increase the free world's ability to do a much more effective job of helping the less developed countries strengthen their economies, and that the bill would place an increasing amount of our economic assistance on a multiple, not a unilateral basis. A bill granting funds to minimize water pollution, HR3610, was vetoed by Eisenhower, and an attempt to override it failed when the veto was upheld by 20 Democrats and Republicans who had favored passage of the bill earlier in 1959; Mrs. Dwyer was one of them. In the first session of the 87th Congress, in 1961, she sponsored a proposal by seven Republicans to put the party on record against a coalition with Southern Democrats opposing civil rights or other constructive legislation. With respect to the NLRB reorganization plan, she said that it would deprive litigants of their rights and remove Congressional curbs on arbitrary actions; the plan was killed in the House. When the House, acting on the advice of Speaker Sam Rayburn, enlarged the Rules Committee from 12 to 15 members (with eight liberal Democrats on it), so that a simple majority was sufficient to break the grip of reactionary members of the committee on progressive legislation, the 27-member House Republican Policy Committee unanimously disapproved of the Rayburn plan, calling it a packing of the Rules Committee. Mrs. Dwyer disagreed with this point of view, asserting that the Policy Committee action certainly did not represent the views of all Republicans. The reorganization plan narrowly squeaked through, 195 Democrats and 22 Republicans voting aye, 64 Democrats and 148 Republicans voting nay.

In 1962, in the second session of the 87th Congress, the President submitted a bill to form an Urban Affairs and Housing Department; 153 Republicans voted against it, while 13 Republicans, including Mrs. Dwyer and Lindsay, voted for it. In 1963, the first session of the 88th Congress, the House rebuffed Kennedy on the Area Redevelopment Bill, HR4996, which had been passed by the Senate. In a separate minority report Mrs. Dwyer supported an amendment to strengthen the bill's anti-piracy provision.

Johnson, who became President in late 1963, was embarrassed in 1964 by revelations concerning Billie Sol Estes, also a Texan. This promoter, through manipulating grain, cotton, and fertilizer stocks in complicated activities first unearthed in 1962, had brought discredit on the government and especially on the Department of Agriculture. Mrs. Dwyer was one of the investigating Representatives who pointed out the gross inefficiency and lack of communication and coordination between and within government agencies; Agriculture was criticized for failing to act energetically to halt Estes' maneuvers.

In 1965 Mrs. Dwyer introduced 43 bills. One of them dealt with Congressional reform, and a joint Committee was set up to study Congress and its operations. Mrs. Dwyer urged that House members' terms be lengthened to four years; that a central clearinghouse be set up to schedule committee and subcommittee meetings; that Congress meet for the whole year, with specific recesses; and that federal programs with money grants be reviewed every five years. Other recommendations: increased minority staffing on committees and subcommittees, additional use of temporary and ad hoc committees, and the adoption of a code of ethics for both members and staff.

In 1965 Congress voted controls on barbiturates and amphetamines, passing HR2 (enacted into PL89-74, signed on July 15); HR3416, sponsored by Congresswoman Dwyer, was identical with HR2. Its purpose was to plug up the big holes in regulating activities by which illegal traffic had flourished. She deplored the ease with which wholesale quantities of these drugs could be directly purchased, and she expressed the hope the Committee would include in the measure debated all drugs acting as stimulants or depressants.

In 1966 Mrs. Dwyer introduced 53 bills, and more often than not she supported Johnson. S3379, introduced in 1968, redesignated 3,750 acres in Great Swamp National Wildlife Region in New Jersey as a wilderness area. Mrs. Dwyer warmly supported this action, expressing her happiness at saving this last remaining island of unspoiled nature in the midst of sweeping urbanism.

In 1969 Mrs. Dwyer, as ranking Republican on the House Government Operations Committee, introduced HR13947 to establish a permanent Office of Consumer Affairs in the White House; it was co-sponsored by Leonor Sullivan, a strong defender of consumer interests. Nader had said that there was a definite need for a government agency to protect consumer interests by investigating and handling complaints, and by research, testing, and the dissemination of information. The House passed a bill establishing an independent agency with a three-member Council of Consumer Advisors to represent the consumer in federal proceedings. Liberals had sought to strengthen the agency, conservatives tried to weaken it; the result was a bill closer to Nixon's wishes than either group had wanted. The bill creating the Consumer Protection Agency and Office of Consumer Affairs in the White House was really three bills.

The preceding recital of activities demonstrates not only the multiplicity and versatility of Representative Dwyer's interests, but the difficulty of getting work done in Congress, where those who understand the needs of the twentieth century are so often stymied by a powerful conservative coalition. It must be made clear that Mrs. Dwyer sided primarily with the forces of progress. That statement is underscored by the fact that—with other women representatives like Chisholm, Griffiths, and Heckler, and with the encouragement of men like Goodell and McCarthy—she led the fight for the equal rights for women amendment, HJRes264; but the amendment did not make it through the Senate in 1970 and had to wait until 1972 for adoption. Still more evidence of her good intentions is provided in the case of the television program, "Selling of the Pentagon." On July 7, 1971, by a vote of 226 to 181, the House recommended that Dr. Stanton, president of CBS, be cited for contempt because he refused to comply with a subpoena issued by the Internal Security Committee's Investigating Subcommittee to turn over to it the film and sound recording edited from the network's controversial and award-winning documentary. Mrs Dwyer voted for recommittal of the resolution—that is, she voted to return it to the Committee, equivalent to killing it.

Congresswoman Dwyer obviously did not always vote with the Republicans or in accord with Nixon's wishes. However, she greeted Nixon's proposals to reorganize the executive branch as one of the most significant initiatives his administration had taken in domestic areas of federal government. She felt that the reorganization would revive greater respect for the institutions of our government, thus engendering more active support for its efforts to deal with public

needs. In a newsletter to her constituents she remarked that many of the bills
aimed at getting more of the good things of life for the people had been disap-
pointed because we had failed to devote adequate attention to the *how* of the government–its structure and procedures, its management and administration. Both
ends and means are essential; they must go together if anything much is to happen.

The Congresswoman's inclination, thus, is to support Nixon in his government reorganization plans and his revenue sharing. She explains that we must dis-
tinguish clearly between general and special revenue sharing; the former is the no-
strings-attached distribution of $5 billion in additional federal revenues to state
and local governments, the latter is the pooling of funds from many existing special purpose programs into a few grant repositories: education, manpower, and community development, out of which qualifying state and local governments may
draw money to spend pretty much as they see fit. In her newsletter of March 4,
1971, she expressed her disappointment at Nixon's proposal for a consumer protection law: she felt that it de-emphasized the desirability of elevating the Office
of Consumer Affairs in terms of authority, influence, status and visibility, and that
it failed to provide for a consumer advisory council.

Mrs. Dwyer has actively opposed the Vietnam War since 1966, and vigorously
urged upon Johnson and Nixon her ceasefire plan for ending the war. She has pub-
licly opposed escalating the war into Cambodia and Laos and has deplored inflict-
ing human, economic, and social desolation on the people of these countries.

Mrs. Dwyer's legislative record was progressive even before she became a Congresswoman. She was the author of New Jersey's equal pay for women law; she
introduced legislation to control air pollution, to control the sale of flammable
fabrics; and she introduced the first mandatory minimum salary schedule for public school teachers. In Congress she sponsored commuter mass transportation legislation, cost of living increases for Social Security beneficiaries and an increase in
the earnings limitation of the Social Security law.

A summary of her votes on key measures before the 92nd Congress reveals
that she voted against SST and park logging, but for farm subsidy limitation to
$20,000, the cooper-Church Vietnam War resolution, family assistance, clean water
appropriation, compensation for migratory workers and for the 18-year-old vote.
Her stance as a progressive, independent and articulate member of Congress is confirmed. COPE gave her a rating of 71, quite high for a Republican; only a Republican of her type could have held her seat so long and successfully against Democratic contenders.

Mrs. Dwyer served on the Banking and Currency Committee and on its two
subcommittees (for Consumer Affairs and Housing); she was also a ranking minority member of the Committee on Government Operations and its Subcommittee
for Intergovernmental Relations. At the end of the 92nd Congress, which terminated on January 3, 1973, she resigned her seat, which she had held for 16 years.

Bibliography

"Ladies' Day On the Hustings," M. Weston. *New York Times Magazine*, p. 32+
     (Oct. 19, 1958).
"Lady Blocks the Pork Barrel," *Life* 61:6 (Sept. 23, 1966).

Excerpt from debate, January 30, 1968. *Congressional Digest* 47:83+ (Mar. 1968).
Excerpt from remarks, August 11, 1969. *Congressional Digest* 48:298+ (Dec. 1968).
"14 Recent Issues," from *Mrs. F. P. Dwyer's Report to the People* [of her district].
Glass. *Pageant*, pp. 113-17 (July 1969).
Almanac, pp. 493-94.
Congressional Quarterly Almanac, 1957-70.
Congressional Quarterly Weekly Report, 1970-71.
Congressional Record, 92nd Congress, First Session, Thursday, June 17, 1971.
Gruberg, pp. 122, 166.

CATHERINE DEAN MAY (Mrs. James O. May)
Republican, Washington
1959-70

Mrs. Catherine May, born May 18, 1914, was elected in 1958 to represent the Fourth Washington Congressional District. She had studied at several colleges and universities, including the University of Washington and the University of Southern California, then taught English in high school and later became woman's editor, writer of special events, and news broadcaster for several North Pacific Coast radio stations. With the encouragement of her husband, a realtor and insurance man, she ran for the state legislature, where she remained for six years; she was then elected to the Congress.

Her assignment to the Agriculture Committee was a very suitable one, since her district is purely rural. One of her first actions was to join in overriding a presidential veto on a public works appropriation bill calling for outlays of $1,176,579,834. In 1960 she traveled to London as a delegate to the Atlantic Congress. On another Eisenhower veto, on water pollution grants, she voted for sustaining the veto, although in 1959 she had favored passage of the bill, along with 200 other Representatives, Democrats and Republicans. In the matter of the Colorado River Basin transmission lines, she was among 23 Republicans who split from the party to vote for federal construction, thus providing a margin for victory for this legislation, which became PL87-330. When surplus grain stocks held by the government increased to enormous amounts, a farm bill passed in 1961 (which became PL87-128) was expected to remedy this dilemma; Mrs. May did not concur in the majority opinion but stated that there was no assurance that the program would reduce surplus stocks. Again she went her own way in the Hanford atomic power project case, when the House blocked appropriations for an AEC power generator for that project; she said that the plant would prove our intention to develop peaceful use of atomic energy and that the experience gained in operating it would be very useful for private industry as it would take over the operation of large nuclear power stations.

She stood up for the sugar industry in 1961, when country-by-country sugar quotas were discussed. She said that, until additional markets were available on a permanent basis, producers would not be able to obtain loans for the construction of mills and other facilities necessary for the processing of beet sugar; however, the Congress took no further action on this subject in 1961. But in 1962 Congress once more revised the sugar quotas and this time a bill was enacted into Public Law 87-539.

In 1964 Congresswoman May became an appointed member of the bipartisan National Commission on Food Marketing, consisting of five Senators, five Representatives, and five public members appointed by President Johnson. The Committee, which operated on an authorization for an expenditure of $1,500,000, was directed to study and appraise the marketing structure of the food industry and to make interim reports; hearings were to be conducted by a minimum of at least three members. One year later the life of the National Commission was extended for one year with a funding of $2-1/2 million; it now had a second woman member, Leonor Sullivan.

The Sugar Act was given a term to run until December 31, 1971, but was criticized by Mrs. May and Robert Dole of Kansas, whose minority views expressed the opinion that the Committee on Agriculture should have adopted an amendment which tied reallocation of unfilled import quotas to the receiving countries' commitment to purchase U.S. agricultural goods for dollars.

In 1965 Mrs. May was honored by being placed on the GOP Policy and Research Committee (Charles Goodell, chairman) and on the GOP Committee on Committees (Gerald Ford, chairman) a 37-member group that makes Republican House committee assignments. In 1966 an amendment by Mrs. May to the Child Nutrition Act was accepted; its purpose was to authorize the necessary funds to extend the school milk program to children attending overseas dependent schools administered by the Defense Department. Her bias against organized labor came to the fore in the 1966 Urban Mass Transportation bill, when she offered an amendment stipulating that the provision for approval of funds that required transit workers' membership in labor organizations did not apply to federal, state, or local government; this amendment was rejected.

In a truth-in-packaging bill that permitted voluntary action on package sizes, Mrs. May opposed a stronger packaging section, saying that advocates of federal packaging size standards were more interested in a theory than in dealing with the realities of the country's food and grocery economy, and that consumers should be thankful that realists outnumbered the theorists. On meat inspection, in the 90th Congress, in 1967, Congresswoman May was against a substitute section of the bill that wanted to strengthen inspection of plants preparing meat for intrastate commerce, saying that potentially every meat producer could already be required to meet federally approved standards. Concerning federal poultry production standards she voted for a weaker provision (five Republicans against eight Democrats on the Agriculture Subcommittee on Livestock and Grains).

Between July 25 and October 31, 1969, the House Agricultural Committee held hearings on several bills dealing with food stamp programs. Included was a bill by Mrs. May, HR12222, which incorporated administration proposals for national minimum eligibility standards for food stamps and that reduced prices for stamps to insure that recipients spent no more than 30 percent of their income for stamps. Her view of the matter was liberal compared with that of

Committee Chairman Poage (Democrat, Texas), who said that deadbeats should be prevented from receiving food stamps. That year a bill that received Nixon's signature included a provision raising the fiscal 1970 authorization for the food stamp program from $340 million to $610 million. Once more on an agricultural topic, Mrs. May voted yea on a bill to exempt potatoes from the coverage of any federal marketing orders if intended for certain types of processing such as dehydration and chipping.

Mrs. May's voting record and her diligence in authoring bills were excellent; in 1969 she had a record of 100 percent attendance at 177 roll calls. She was clearly a member of the conservative coalition; her concern was for the agricultural producer and only minimally for the consumer. And though she was not always on Nixon's side, she supported him much more often than she opposed him. Mrs. May even voted for SST when many other Republicans turned it down. During the 1968 presidential election, when a massive staff ran the Nixon-Agnew campaign, Mrs. May was on a Republican key-issues committee, headed by Senator Tower, which consisted of 25 members meeting almost weekly. Her assignment to the House Agricultural Committee was her only assignment for the major part of her incumbency, but during her last two sessions she became also a member of the Joint Atomic Energy Committee.

Mrs. May lost her reelection bid in 1970, conceding to Mike McCormack, a Democrat, whom she trailed 42.4 percent to 57.6 percent.

Bibliography

"Lady You Are In Politics," *Successful Farming* 62:73+ (Nov. 1964).

"Every Man Should Have His Say," address, June 17, 1965. *Vital Speeches* 31: 622-24 (Aug. 1, 1965).

"Congresswoman Charges: Washington Consumer Aid is Deceptive Packaging," interview. *Nation's Business* 54:54-64 (May 1966).

Excerpt from address, February 20, 1966. *Congressional Digest* 45:173+ (June 1966).

"Catherine May Backs AFA," *American Forests* 75:8 (Aug. 1969).

"American Farmer," address, June 22, 1970. *Vital Speeches* 36:625-28 (Aug. 1, 1970).

Congressional Quarterly Almanac, 1959-70.

Gruberg, p. 166 and passim.

EDNA OAKES SIMPSON   (Mrs. Sid Simpson)
Republican, Illinois
1959-61

Mrs. Simpson was a member of the 86th Congress, which met from 1959 to 1961. Her committee assignments were on the House Administration and the Internal and Insular Affairs Committees.

A public works project bill appropriating $1,176,579,834 had been vetoed by Eisenhower, overridden, amended, once more vetoed, and the veto for the second time overridden; Mrs. Simpson was one of a small group of 11

Republicans who voted with the majority to override Eisenhower's vetoes. During the 86th Congress there arose a nepotism controversy and old charges of padding Congressional payrolls were aired again. It was disclosed that one Congressman had his 19-year-old son on his payroll at $11,873 per annum, a lot of money in those days. Mrs. Simpson had a Janet Simpson on her payroll at $7,438 per year, a disclosure that may have contributed to her reelection defeat in November 1960.

Bibliography

"Salute To Three Freshmen," *National Business Woman* 38:12 (Feb. 1959).
Congressional Quarterly Almanac, 1959-60.
Gruberg, p. 167.

JESSICA McCULLOUGH WEIS   (Mrs. Charles William Weis, Jr.)
Republican, New York
1959-63

Jessica Weis was a Republican Representative for New York State's Thirty-eighth District serving in the 86th and 87th Congresses. Her assignments in the 86th Congress were with the Committee for the District of Columbia, and the Government Operations Committee; in the 87th Congress she was again on the D.C. Committee, but exchanged her second assignment for membership on the Committee for Science and Astronomy. She had attended Bryn Mawr and had occupied a number of different positions in the New York Republican Party. Mrs. Weis seems to have introduced fewer bills in Congress than most active members. She died in office in 1963.

Bibliography

"Salute To Three Freshmen," *National Business Woman* 38:12 (Feb. 1959).
Congressional Quarterly Almanac, 1959-63.
Gruberg, pp. 166-67.

JULIA BUTLER HANSEN   (Mrs. Henry A. Hansen)
Democrat, Washington
1960-

Mrs. Hansen has represented the Third Washington Congressional District since 1960, when she was elected to replace the former Representative, who had died in office. This was in the second session of the 86th Congress. Mrs. Hansen was reelected to the 87th Congress and to every Congress since then, and continued to represent the District in the 93rd Congress that convened in January 1973.

Congresswoman Hansen's first assignments were to the Committee on Education and Labor and to the one for Internal and Insular Affairs. A few years later she became a member of one of the most important Congressional Committees: Appropriations. She is Chairman of its Interior Committee and is also on the Subcommittee for Military Construction. Mrs. Hansen graduated from the University of Washington and later engaged in the insurance business. She served for eight years on the Cathlamet City Council, and from 1939 to 1960, for 22 years, was a member of the state legislature, where she served for some years as Democratic minority leader and later as Speaker pro-tem.

Representative Hansen's district is largely rural, in the southwest corner of the state, near the mouth of the Columbia River, with a predominantly blue collar population; there are few urban centers. Economically the district is based on logging, saw mills, manufacture of wood products, papermaking, dairying and commercial fishing. There are few blacks but a substantial number of foreign-born in her district.

Her Interior Subcommittee of the Appropriations Committee is in charge of the Interior Department's budget and is also responsible for matters concerning the ecology. The budget for Interior and related agencies for fiscal 1973 amounted to $2,529,558,200. Mrs. Hansen is modest and has said of her responsibilities that the significance of the Subcommittee's work lies in the immensity of the land it serves and the people on it. She feels that comparatively little money has been spent on America, and that a "Marshall Plan" for the United States would not be amiss. She also acknowledges the need for better programs for the American Indians.

Mrs. Hansen has been aligned with the liberal wing of the Democratic Party. She was one of a group of Congressmen, most of whom were Democrats, who took a stand against a movement for a Prayer Amendment, believing that the House should not undertake to tamper with the First Amendment.

She was Chairman of the House Democratic group that voted to adopt modest changes in the seniority system of selecting committee chairmen; it was also agreed that no chairman of a full committee should be chairman of more than one subcommittee. These changes would have opened 40 subcommittee chairmanships for junior Representatives. It was also agreed and recommended that there should be a 30-day limit for holding legislation in the Rules Committee. Another recommendation of her committee was to permit as few as ten House Democrats to challenge the automatic naming of a committee chairman. But alas! There's many a slip twixt recommendation and realization in our system, with its many checks and balances.

On the Vietnam War, Mrs. Hansen has not taken a strong stand. In 1966 she voted, with other Democrats, for the supplementary budget, because the safety of our troops required it; the yes vote, however, was emphatically not a mandate for unrestrained and indiscriminate enlargement of the conflict.

Representative Hansen voted against ABM in the 92nd Congress, but for SST, a vote which could almost automatically be expected of a lawmaker from the Boeing state. Other votes were for the 18-year-old vote, for Nixon's Family Assistance Plan, and for migratory workers' compensation. That she also voted for park logging may reflect once more her concern for the economic interests of the state of Washington. She voted against no-knock, but also against clean water appropriations. To her credit is her stand on presidential election by direct popular vote, abolishing the Electoral College.

Mrs. Hansen is not a rough-and-tumble fighter and does not enjoy provoking the chairman of the powerful Appropriations Committee, Congressman Mahon. She is not opposed to the seniority system in Congress but she does not believe that Congressmen should expect continuous reelection throughout their lives. On the House floor she is not often heard, and the quantity of her legislation is not great. She is a gentle woman and does not want to give up all her privacy to the political job and her constituents. She favors large outlays for education and may be characterized as friendly to labor. Mrs Hansen voted for the Civil Rights Act of 1964 and the Voting Rights Act of 1965, and in 1972 she cast her yes vote for the Women's Equal Rights Amendment.

Mrs. Hansen, in addition to her substantial duties on Appropriations and on the Committee on Organizational Study and Review, serves as a member of the Executive Committee of the American Revolution Bicentennial Commission and has membership in numerous civil organizations. Her work on the Interior Subcommittee of the Appropriations Committee has been notable for her dedication to environmental protection, resource and energy management, expanding and improving Indian health and education programs, and advancing the arts and humanities.

Mrs. Hansen was born in Portland, Oregon, in 1907, and was 65 when re-elected to the 93rd Congress. She has written for newspapers and also published a prize-winning juvenile historical novel about the Northwest.

Bibliography

Works about Julia Butler Hansen

Almanac, pp. 863-64
Congressional Quarterly Almanac, 1961-70.
Congressional Quarterly Weekly Review, 1971-72.
Congressional Record, 1972.
Darmstadter, Ruth. *Julia Butler Hansen, Democratic Representative From Washington* [Washington, D.C., Grossman Publishers, c1972]. [22p.]
    (Ralph Nader Congress Project. Citizens Look At Congress.)
Gruberg, p. 167.

Works by Julia Butler Hansen

Singing Paddles, Portland, Binfords and Mort [1932].
Singing Paddles, Los Angeles, San Francisco, Sutton House Ltd. [1935]. 255p.
    "One of the prize winners in the Julia Ellsworth Ford contest."
Singing Paddles, New York, Holt and Company [1931]. 274p.

LOUISE G. REECE   (Mrs. Carroll Reece)
Republican, Tennessee
1961-63

Louise Goff Reece (Mrs. Carroll Reece) was the widow of Carroll Reece, a Representative and former Republican National Chairman, who died on March 19, 1961. She succeeded to his seat in Congress on May 24, 1961, to serve out the remainder of his term (until January 3, 1963). She was a daughter and granddaughter of two United States Senators from West Virginia, by the name of Goff. In a special election she defeated a Democrat and an Independent by a wide margin.

Congresswoman Reece's assignment was to the Public Works Committee. In the first session of the 87th Congress there raged an acrimonious controversy about the Colorado River Basin transmission line: should the federal government or should private construction money build the principal "backbone" high power transmission lines connecting the hydroelectric generating plants of the Upper Colorado River Basin? An appropriation of $13,673,000 was made to begin construction of ten backbone lines, after both Houses had agreed to a conference report which was then cleared for the President's signature. To resolve the issue the language of the bill permitted the Interior Department to use the appropriation for the declared purpose of determining whether construction was "found to be in the national interest." In the controversy 23 Republicans had split from their party vote to support federal construction; Mrs. Reece was among these rebels.

Mrs. Reece did not seek reelection to the 88th Congress.

Bibliography

New York Times Index, 1962, p. 779: "Not To Seek Reelection," (Jan. 18, 1962), 13:8.
Congressional Quarterly Almanac, 1961-62.
Gruberg, p. 167.

CATHERINE D. NORRELL   (Mrs. William F. Norrell)
Democrat, Arkansas
1961-63

Mrs. Norrell, a school teacher who had studied at the University of Arkansas, succeeded her husband after his death. She served from April 25, 1961, to January 3, 1963, as a Representative for the state's Sixth Congressional District. Her age was 60 at the time of election. Mrs. Norrell was assigned to the Post Office and Civil Service Committee, which at that time had 14 Democrats and 11 Republicans.

Bibliography

"Roads to International Understanding," address, January 15, 1963. *U.S. Department of State Bulletin* 48:214-17 (Feb. 11, 1963).
Congressional Quarterly Almanac, 1961-62.
Gruberg, p. 167.

CORINNE BOYD RILEY (Mrs. John Jacob Riley)
Democrat, South Carolina
1962-63

Mrs. Riley was elected on April 10, 1962, without opposition to represent the Second South Carolina Congressional District, a seat formerly held by her husband; she had defeated one opponent in the Democratic Primary on February 13th of that year, and she was sworn in as a member of the House on April 12. Congresswoman Riley served on the House Science and Astronautics Committee; she did not seek reelection and terminated on January 3, 1963.

Bibliography

New York Times Index, 1962.
Congressional Quarterly Almanac, 1962.

CHARLOTTE T. REID (Mrs. Frank R. Reid, Jr.)
Republican, Illinois
1963-71

Before she became a Congresswoman, Mrs. Reid was an actress. When she was urged to run for Congress, she won, becoming Representative for the Fifteenth Illinois Congressional District.

In the 88th Congress, during the controversy about school prayer, Mrs. Reid's opinion was that exclusion of religious exercises in schools "encourages agnosticism and atheism." The Supreme Court had barred official prayers and Bible reading in schools; major church groups either were divided on the issue or took no stand, and some religious leaders testified against bills introduced by proponents of school prayer. Congress thought it best to fail to act on constitutional amendments proposing religious exercise in schools.

The 89th Congress, in 1965, voted new aid programs for depressed areas; a bill to that effect was signed into law by President Johnson on August 26, 1965. The House rejected a Reid amendment that sought to reduce the annual authorization under Title I of PL89-136 from $500 million to $250 million, which she introduced, because she said Johnson had requested the smaller amount and "surely we should not press upon the President more money than he and his advisers think is needed." In 1966 Reid voted against the Colorado River Basin project; Congress failed to pass any legislation on that subject.

Increasing costs of the Vietnam War and accompanying signs of inflation induced Johnson to ask for a quick increase of $6 billion in taxes; his measure attained the status of law on March 15, 1966. In the House, 200 Democrats and 46 Republicans voted for it, while 76 Democrats and 88 Republicans opposed it. Mrs. Reid said the bill asked the taxpayer to tighten his belt while allowing the federal government to let out its own belt. She was undoubtedly right on this point, although it may be debatable whether she was on safe ground when she voted against rivers and harbors projects. She adopted the same opposing view toward a water project feasibility bill, which appropriated funds for the study of 113 water projects in 17 Western states and in Alaska. However, both bills passed and became laws.

Representative Reid had been a member of the Committee for Internal and Insular Affairs, and of the Public Works Committee; she also became one of 27 members of the GOP Policy Committee that advises on Party activities and policies. In the 90th Congress she became a member of the very important and powerful Appropriations Committee. The 90th Congress was bedeviled by multiple problems: riots, a rise in the income and excise taxes, a rise in crime, pollution, prayer controversy, Vietnam casualties. The conservative coalition sniped at Johnson and the liberal Democrats. Mrs. Reid strongly supported the House conservative coalition of Republicans and Southern Democrats, a coalition that shaped the major bills in the 90th Congress, especially in the second session of 1968.

In the Nixon presidential campaign Congresswoman Reid was heavily involved in the Republican so-called key issues drive. When Nixon came to the White House, Congress' conservative coalition increased support for the President's program in 1970; the overall support for him rose to 74 percent. Mrs. Reid's voting participation in these years was very high; she attained scores of 97, 98, and 100 percent. The rating she received from special interest groups was predictable; ADA gave her 20 percent, COPE 0 percent, but conservative groups gave her high scores.

While a member of the Internal and Insular Affairs Committee, in 1966, Mrs. Reid traveled to American Samoa, at government expense, from November 13 to December 10. In 1971 she was appointed to the 12-member House Committee on Standards of Official Conduct—six Democrats and six Republicans whose duty it was to study and investigate the conduct of House members and their employees; the Committee had the right to recommend remedial action. In 1971 the state of Illinois had redistricted Congressional areas, and only seven of 24 Representatives escaped with minor adjustments of their district lines. The bill in the legislature had met with great hostility from Republican leaders. Mrs. Reid's Fifteenth District became more rural.

Mrs. Reid had always gathered good majorities in her reelection campaigns; but she was amenable when Nixon appointed her to the Federal Communications Commission in 1971. The Congresswoman resigned her House seat on October 7, 1971, having already had her nomination confirmed by the Senate on July 29; she was 57 years old at that time.

Bibliography

Congressional Quarterly Almanac, 1963-71.
Gruberg, p. 167.
New York Times Index, 1964-68, 1970-71.

IRENE B. BAKER (Mrs. Howard H. Baker)
Republican, Tennessee
1964-65

Mrs. Baker served for less than a year, from March 1, 1964, to January 3, 1965, to fill the vacancy caused by her husband's death; she did not ask to be renominated. Congresswoman Baker represented the Second Tennessee Congressional District in the 88th Congress, having been elected by a 55.6 percent vote. She served as a member of the Committee on Government Operations.

Bibliography

Congressional Quarterly Almanac, 1964.
Gruberg, p. 168.
New York Times Index, 1964.

PATSY TAKEMOTO MINK   (Mrs. John Francis Mink)
   Democrat, Hawaii
   1965-

Mrs. Mink, born in 1927 on the island of Oahu, was one of the youngest women ever sent to Congress. She studied at the University of Hawaii and earned a J.D. degree from the University of Chicago Law School. Her husband, John Francis Mink, a geologist, is a vice-president of Earth Sciences, Inc., Washington. They have a daughter attending the University of Chicago.

Mrs. Mink practiced law in Hawaii after earning her degree and was professor of business law at the University of Hawaii from 1953 to 1962. Charter president of Oahu Young Democrats and later of the Young Democrats of the Territory of Hawaii, she became deeply interested in local and national politics and was elected to the Territory of Hawaii House of Representatives (1956-58); in 1958 she became a member of the Territorial Senate, and she was a State Senator from 1962 to 1964. In November 1964 she was elected to the 84th Congress (convening in 1965) and she won reelection to the 90th, 91st, 92nd, and 93rd Congresses in 1967, 1969, 1971, and 1973, with large electoral majorities. Her husband actively supported her candidacy as her campaign manager.

Mrs. Mink is now a member of the House Education and Labor Committee and of its subcommittees (general) on Education, (general) on Labor, and (select) on Education; she is also a member of the oversight subcommittee on poverty and of the oversight subcommittee on elementary-secondary education. Furthermore, she has membership on the House Committee on Interior and Insular Affairs and its subcommittees on Indian Affairs, National Parks and Recreation, and Territorial and Insular Affairs. She has participated in the Democratic Study Group.

When she first went to Congress she, like her colleague Spark Matsunaga, was Representative-at-large for the Territory; now she represents the Second Hawaiian Congressional District. The total population of Hawaii is about 800,000; her district has a population of 407,000 of whom about 40 percent are caucasian; 59 percent oriental, and only 1 percent black. In 1970 the voter registration was 145,000—48 percent Democrat, 12 percent Republican, 40 percent other. The caucasians of the population are well-to-do; the Japanese portion is middle class; those of Hawaiian ancestry (the majority) are very poor, and many live in slums. Her district contains part of Oahu, many smaller islands, and portions of Honolulu. The economic base is largely agricultural

(sugar cane, pineapple, and livestock); other income comes from food processing, a large number of federal offices, and tourism. The ILWU is a powerful factor; Congresswoman Mink has a good relationship not only with the longshore-
men, but also with the people in the district generally–she speaks for the sugar
and pineapple interests and the unions. Although she is thousands of miles from
home throughout most of the year, Mrs. Mink spends many weekends in her
district with her constituents; almost all her trips are financed out of her own
pocket.

Congresswoman Mink is clearly a liberal. She has sponsored and co-
sponsored a great number of bills in the fields of housing, transportation, education, and equal rights for women. She voted against ABM and SST in the 92nd
Congress, and was willing to reduce defense expenditures. She also opposed the
draft and, in April 1972, sponsored a resolution calling for an immediate end to
the Vietnam War; three months earlier she had introduced a censure motion
against Nixon because of his persistence in prolonging our involvement in Vietnam. Another head-on collision with the White House was the Amchitka affair,
when the AEC announced it would detonate a nuclear underground blast on that
Aleutian island. She attempted to force Nixon to release and publicize reports
critical of the test blast and to delete funds set aside for that purpose. Nixon dis-
regarded all opposition and "Cannikin" took place, the explosion of a five-
megaton nuclear device in a test hole 300 feet under the island.

The Congresswoman's proposals in the social and educational spheres have
not fared much better. She wants racial integration and has no objection to
busing; neither is favored by Nixon and both are totally opposed by the conservative coalition. Mrs. Mink reached Congress just in time to cast a yea vote for
the Voting Rights Act of 1965. She feels that her biggest success was the passage
of the Child Development Act of 1971, with its provisions for health care,
nutrition, education, and day care facilities for families with incomes below the
poverty line; Nixon once more used his veto in December 1971 to dash her hopes,
but she is continuing to fight for the same principles. Although Representative
Mink voted against the Higher Education Act of 1971 because it fell far short
of what she had envisioned, she put much energy into authoring and co-sponsoring an Equal Rights for Women Act (1971) and the Women's Education Act
(1972), through which she hopes to remedy the unequal education girls
receive because of the concept that woman's place is in the home. She wants
theory, methods, curricula, and textbooks changed to give women true educational equality.

Mrs. Mink has voted for the Philadelphia Plan, the commuter tax, the vote
for 18-year-olds, the Cooper-Church amendment to end the Vietnam War, the
Nixon Family Assistance Plan, and unemployment compensation for migratory
workers; she has voted against ABM, SST, no-knock, state OEO veto, park
logging, jets to Chiang, and limitation of farm subsidies to $20,000 (the latter
undoubtedly because of her protective attitude toward agricultural growers).

On July 1, 1971, the House passed HR8630, which amended the Public
Health Services Act of 1944 by extending for four years a program to train
nurses. The purpose of Mrs Mink's amendment was to increase the number of
nurses in the United States from 700,000 in 1971 to 1,100,000 in 1980, to

increase construction for nursing schools, and to provide loans and scholarships to part-time nursing students as well as to full-time ones. The amendment will help relieve the lack of qualified registered nurses, because it would permit young women unable to attend school on a full-time basis to continue studying while holding part-time jobs or tending their families.

Mrs. Mink was a member of Congress for Peace through Law. On June 24, 1971, she testified in favor of the seating of the People's Republic of China in the U.N.; she also recommended United States diplomatic relations with Peking as soon as possible, arguing that "we must recognize what is inevitable." This dovish attitude was also inherent in an amendment she offered on June 17, 1971, on Vietnam, demanding that no funds should be authorized in the 1971 defense bill for military operations in South and North Vietnam and in Cambodia and Laos after December 31, 1971; of course, it was defeated.

An amendment of hers to make the trust territories of the Pacific islands eligible for funds for adult basic education and to specify that the federal share of such funds should be 100 percent was accepted, but it was omitted later, when the bill was in conference.

Mrs. Mink opposed the transfer of legal services for the poor from OEO to the National Legal Services Corporation; she thought this was just another ruse to further dismantle the poverty program. Ichord of Missouri had added an amendment requiring that funds should not be used to provide aid to convicted criminals who brought suit against judicial or law enforcement officials, when suits arose out of acts connected with criminal conviction; this amendment was accepted although it was admitted that no such suits had ever been brought. Representative Mink opposed the Carswell nomination as an "affront to women," because Carswell had denied a woman plaintiff a hearing in a discrimination suit.

Mrs. Mink favors Congressional reforms, including an automatic age limit of 70 for House Committee Chairmen, and an eight-year limit on tenure as chairman.

She threw her hat in the ring in the Presidential election campaign in 1972, entering the Oregon Primary held on May 23, 1972; she sought 50 delegates to win the right to be nominated. Announcing her candidacy, she emphasized that she was very serious about it; her success in gaining delegate votes was nil, less even than that of Shirley Chisholm.

Congresswoman Mink is, or has been, a member of innumerable civic, political, and women's rights groups; she has received honorary degrees and honors from colleges, societies, and associations. She lists as her major interests a national day-care program, equal employment opportunities for women, comprehensive federal aid to education, a universal health care program, war against hunger and poverty, ending the war in Indochina, tax reform, student financial aid programs, equal rights for women, civil rights legislation, public housing programs and aid to the elderly—an ambitious but necessary program. Finally, she stood up for conservation in Del Norte and Humboldt Counties in California, and for area redevelopment for depressed areas.

Bibliography

"First Congresswoman From Overseas," *Life* 58:49-50+ (June 22, 1965).

Excerpts from remarks February 10, 1971. *Congressional Digest* 50:119+ (Apr. 1971).

"Hormones in the White House," *Time* 96:13 (Aug. 10, 1970).

Congressional Record, 1965-72, especially May 8, 1967, HR5171 on educational programs and day care centers; April 17, 1967, HR4257 on College Housing bill; March 23, 1971, HR6551, a bill to amend the Federal Food, Drug and Cosmetics Act concerning cosmetics that contain mercury; April 18, 1972, HR3259, introduction of the Women's Education Act of 1972.

Speech before Democratic pre-primary convention at Klamath Falls, Oregon, April 8, 1972 ("Less Than 1/3 of 1 Percent of School Children Are Bused to Achieve Racial Balance").

Speech before the annual Civil and Human Rights Conference of the United Steel Workers of America, District 31, at Conrad Hilton Hotel, Chicago, Illinois, May 2, 1972.

"Federal Legislation to End Discrimination Against Women," symposium, *Valparaiso University Law Review*, 1971. pp. 397-414.

"Micronesia: Our Bungled Trust," *Texas International Law Forum*, Winter (Jan. 1971). v.6, no. 2, pp. 181-207.

"Women's Mistake," Population Crisis Committee. *New York Times*, April 30, 1972, Sect. 12, p. 11.

Paper on U.S. China policy, May 3, 1971 (prepared for Members of Congress for Peace through Law). 14p.

"How I Found Peace of Mind," *Look* (July 27, 1971).

Life (Jan. 22, 1965).

Current Biography (Sept. 1968).

Article on child care, *Redbook* (Nov. 1969).

"The Status of Women," *Educational Horizons*, Winter 1970-71.

Men and Women of Hawaii, 1971.

"Education For All," *PHP* (Mar. 1971).

Mink listed as one of 125 brilliant achievers in America in *Town and Country* (Sept. 1971).

Almanac, pp. 184-85.

Congressional Quarterly Almanac, 1965-70.

Congressional Quarterly Weekly Report, 1971-72.

Gates, Nancy S. *Patsy T. Mink, Democratic Representative from Hawaii.* [Washington, D.C., Grossman Publishers, c1972] [29p.] (Ralph Nader Congress Project. Citizens Look At Congress.)

Gruberg, p. 168

Lamson, pp. 99-107.

LERA MILLARD THOMAS   (Mrs. Albert Thomas)
   Democrat, Texas
   1966-67

Lera Thomas, wife of long-time Congressman Albert Thomas, was elected in a special election held on March 26, 1960, to fill the unexpired term of her husband, who had died on February 15; she was sworn in on March 30, 1966. The election, in which she received 76 percent of the votes cast, brought the number of Congresswomen to 13. She represented the Eighth Texas Congressional District in the 89th Congress. Her assignment was to the Committee on Merchant Marine and Fisheries. Mrs. Thomas did not seek reelection but asked voters to vote for her husband whose name was already on the ballot for the primary; she received only 26 percent of the total vote; the election for the 90th Congress went therefore to Robert Eckhard, who took 52 percent of the vote.

Bibliography

Congressional Quarterly Almanac, 1966.
Gruberg, p. 168.
New York Times Index, 1966.

MARGARET M. HECKLER   (Mrs. John Heckler)
   Republican, Massachusetts
   1967-

Mrs. Heckler has represented the Tenth Massachusetts Congressional District since 1967, and has successfully defended her seat several times against Democratic opponents; she will again be a member of the 93rd Congress, convening in 1973. Born in 1931, she studied at New Haven's Albertus Magnus College and at Boston College Law School, and became a lawyer. Married to an investment broker, she has three children.

Her political proclivities began to appear while she was still in college. In 1963 she became a member of the Governor's Executive Council, which at that time had virtual veto power over the governor's actions; but the Council was shorn of its prerogatives by the state legislature when it was found that half of its members engaged in crooked activities. Mrs. Heckler, who belonged to the better half, continued as a member until 1966, when she ran for Congress. Her primary opponent was 84-year-old Joseph Martin, who had been the incumbent since the middle twenties and had been twice Republican Speaker of the House. Although cautioned not to run against him, she carried on a good, low-key campaign, frankly using against him arguments similar to those Martin had used in his youth against a much older contender. She won in the primary and repeated her victory in the 1966 general election against a Democratic opponent.

She is on the Banking and Currency Committee and three of its subcommittees (Consumer Affairs, Housing, and Small Business), as well as on the Veterans Affairs Committee and three of its subcommittees. Her district includes the well-to-do Boston suburbs of Wellesley, where she has her home, and Dover; it also includes the South Fall River and other small, ailing mill towns that have a great deal of unemployment and a large foreign-born citizenry. The northern part is quite safely Republican and Anglo-Saxon. In Congress Mrs. Heckler has not tried to be obtrusive, but has retained an independent stance, voting against Congressional Republican leadership and against Nixon more often than not. She urged passage of HJRes264 guaranteering equal rights to women. Her amendment to an appropriations bill for protection of American fishermen against harrassment by Russian fishing vessels along the New England coast drew no criticism.

The Congresswoman was an early opponent of the Vietnam War, and she voted against two of Nixon's pet projects: ABM and SST. She voted against jets for Chiang, thus proving herself to be a dove. Her yes votes include the 18-year-old vote, the Cooper-Church amendment, and the clean water bill. She was very angry at Nixon for vetoing her child development bill. Her stand for consumerism is not as strong as that of some other Congresswomen; she voted for compensation for losses sustained by business arising from the ban on cyclamates. Like other Representatives, she works for the interests of her constituents; she submitted, for instance, a tax credit proposal to help Catholic parochial schools. She also supported appropriations for a national commission on the cure of multiple sclerosis when one of her constituents stricken with this illness urged her to do so. She has campaigned for elimination of foreign oil import quotas in order to bring more and cheaper fuel to the cold New England states, as well as for protection of the New England textile industry. It is also pleasant to note that she approved of the publication of the Pentagon Papers on Vietnam, underlining the right of the people to know what the government does. She generally votes to support welfare programs (but not for Lockheed). She voted in favor of Adam Clayton Powell's exclusion, and is concerned with ethics in government.

Her newsletters and press releases, her legislative and committee activities, give evidence to her hard work and her liberal attitude, more liberal than that of most Republicans.

Bibliography

Almanac, pp. 356-57.
Congressional Quarterly Almanac, 1967-70.
Congressional Quarterly Weekly Report, 1971-72.
Gruberg, p. 168.
Lamson, p. 121.
Lyness, Jack. *Margaret M. Heckler, Republican Representative from Massachusetts.* [Washington, D.C., Grossman Publishers, c1972] [22p.] (Ralph Nader Congress Project. Citizens Look At Congress.)
Press release by Margaret Heckler dated June 27, 1972, and *Report from Washington* [undated, Summer 1972?].

SHIRLEY ANITA CHISHOLM   (Mrs. Conrad Chisholm)
Democrat, New York
1969-

Mrs. Chisholm was elected to the 91st Congress, meeting in 1969 and 1970; she was reelected from her Twelfth District to represent it in the 92nd Congress, and again for the 93rd Congress. Her district, which includes the Bedford-Stuyvesant section of Brooklyn, is predominantly black. She was opposed in her 1968 campaign by James Farmer, former director of CORE, but Mrs. Chisholm received 66 percent of the vote. She is the first black woman ever elected to Congress. In the 1970 election she received 82 percent of the vote. Her district is 100 percent metropolitan; employment is predominantly blue collar—men and women employed in the manufacture of apparel, food, beverages, electrical machinery, and equipment.

Congresswoman Chisholm has a Master's degree from Columbia University and is married; her husband is not interested in politics but he has supported his wife fully in her political career. Before going to Congress she was a teacher and the director of a child care center; she was a member of the New York State Legislature from 1964 to 1968. Besides being a Congresswoman, she is very busy on the lecture circuit.

In Congress she has adopted an outspoken attitude on a variety of questions. While Congress as a whole increased its support for Nixon, Representative Chisholm increased her opposition to his policies, voting against him on 65 Nixon-issue roll calls. Together with John Conyers of Michigan, she opposed the Carswell nomination in testimony before the Senate Judiciary Committee. When the House Internal Security Committee reported legislation to amend the Emergency Detention Act of 1950 she said the mere presence of that act was offensive, especially to Americans of color and to Black Panthers, who were its main targets.

In testimony before the House Education and Labor Select Subcommittee on Labor she opposed the Nixon administration's manpower training program, saying there should be a variety of programs and a public employment project. She said that worthwhile jobs exist, and that what must be done is to connect people with those jobs. What the Congresswoman means by useful, meaningful jobs is employment in health care, education, police protection, and recreation. She wants adequate housing for all, and education without discrimination is one of her goals. She places the number of jobless much higher than the Republican administration—at 5,400,000, which is 6 percent of the total labor force—and many sections of the country and the minority groups of the population are plagued by a much more serious incidence of unemployment. Her testimony before the Senate Labor and Public Welfare subcommittee attacked the Nixon proposal to give state employment agencies more responsibility for job training: "They failed to do their job; it is ludicrous to reward them for their failure." A public employment program was needed, she insisted, and matters should not be turned over to state employment agencies; manpower decentralization in the South meant that Southern whites would pay little attention to the needs of the blacks. Then she linked the need for public federal employment projects with the need for day-care centers, desperately required by women who otherwise could not take advantage of training programs. In testimony before the Select Subcommittee on Education of the House Education and Labor Committee (on May 17 and 21, 1971), she said that HR6748, providing a comprehensive child development program in the Department of Health, Education and Welfare, was a good bill, but that some sections should be reworded and amended. She announced that she and Bella Abzug would present their own day-care bill. There are 32 million working women in the United States, who have over five million children under the age of 5. Only 2 percent of these can use day care facilities; the rest face a nightmare hodgepodge of arrangements with elderly relatives, rapid turnover of sitters, and bleak custodial parking lots euphemistically called family care centers. The child care legislation for day-care centers for working mothers, co-authored by Abzug and Chisholm, appropriated five, eight, and ten billion dollars for the first, second, and third years, respectively, of the operation of the program. Legislation in this area, though not the Abzug-Chisholm version, was passed by Congress, but vetoed by Nixon.

Mrs. Chisholm favored boosting the minimum wage to $2.00 per hour, which Meany said was "long overdue." Mrs. Chisholm was one of 22 Democrats and four Republicans of the House Education and Labor Committee to endorse it, while seven other Republicans opposed it. Passage of the legislation would have added six million workers, giving them a more adequate income.

Congresswoman Chisholm's first assignment was to the House Agriculture Committee; sarcastically she characterized the stupidity of this move by saying: "All the gentlemen know about Brooklyn is that a tree grew there" (Kuriansky and Smith, *Shirley Chisholm*, p. 5). She had wanted to be assigned to the Education and Labor Committee; because of her disgust with the initial assignment, the powers that be made a second try placing her on the Veterans Committee. Since her election to the 92nd Congress the Congresswoman has served on the Education and Labor Committee.

Congress is like a factory, turning out tens of thousands of bills each year; some Senators and Representatives present scores of them, but Chisholm is comparatively frugal. In her second Congress she offered only a few, but they were of great importance. The most necessary, on child care centers, passed Congress, but Nixon axed it by his veto. A quick rundown on her votes on some of the most important measures before the 92nd Congress shows the following: she voted for the Philadelphia plan, Cooper-Church anti-war amendment, clean water appropriations, and migratory workers' compensation; she voted against ABM, SST, no-knock, and jets for Chiang Kai-shek. Her points of view and her votes may be summarized as follows: she is usually opposed to expenditures for defense or for the Vietnam War, and she is against the draft, but she testified in favor of an all-volunteer army. The Congresswoman said that she would vote against every appropriation bill for DOD. She is opposed to military aid for Spain, Greece, and Brazil, but she is quite willing to protect Israel's existence as a state. In addition to absolute opposition to ABM and SST, she is also very critical of the space shuttle. In matters of primary concern to women Mrs. Chisholm stands four-square in favor of complete legal and economic equality for women. When the Equal Rights Amendment was before the Senate Judiciary Subcommittee on Constitutional Amendments, she joined with Goodell, McCarthy, Martha Griffiths, Florence Dwyer, and Margaret Heckler in urging its passage. She looks with a jaundiced eye at protective legislation for women, agreeing with Bella Abzug that women need no protection that men have not got. Her objective was to give the EEOC direct cease-and-desist powers, while the Nixon administration, in order to emasculate the agency, preferred to have cases settled by court action. She also unequivocally favors the right of women to abortion. Her vote against HR1, the welfare bill requested by Nixon, may seem surprising, but it is explained by her contention that it is totally inadequate and demeaning to the poverty-stricken applicant. She supports federal revenue sharing and federalization of welfare, and has said that most welfare reform proposals tend to be "cosmetic."

Black Representatives announced they were forming a "shadow cabinet" to monitor federal enforcement of civil rights laws. She is a member of the Black Caucus and, as chairman of its Military Affairs Committee, she announced that Thaddeus Garrett would travel to U.S. military installations abroad to investigate racial discrimination—viz., to Germany, Italy, Greece, and Turkey to sift complaints of unequal treatment against Black American servicemen there.

Mrs. Chisholm pointed out the importance of such anti-poverty legislation as HR10351, which was passed on September 30, 1971, with a 251 to 115 vote, with amendments extending OEO for two years through fiscal 1973 and authorizing $5 billion for its program. The bill was passed after three days of debate, with most opposing Republicans and conservative Southern Democrats wanting to tighten the family eligibility provisions.

Mrs. Chisholm is for racial equality and equal opportunity and for women's rights. She has shown that she is for strict separation of church and state in religious matters. When a Mrs. Ruhlein of Cayahoga Falls, Ohio, was disturbed about remarks of her teenage son concerning the impact that absence of prayer in schools might have on the religious beliefs of the young, she approached her Representative and researched the issue with him. She then visited Senator Eastland and Representative Celler (chairmen of the Senate and House Judiciary Committees) and asked them to report out a prayer amendment. Celler did not want to hold hearings; the delay gave a group of 67 Congressmen time to evolve under the name of Congressional Committee for the Preservation of Religious Freedom. Composed of 59 Democrats and eight Republicans, this group sent a "Dear Colleague" letter to all other Representatives urging them to oppose a prayer amendment, which squashed for the time being the movement for religious interference. Mrs. Chisholm was a signer of the groups's hands-off statement.

She takes the same responsible attitude of cooperation in the women's movement. At the July 11-12, 1971, Washington meeting of the National Women's Political Caucus, it was announced that a 21-member steering committee had been formed to organize efforts on behalf of women's issues, such as passage of an equal rights amendment to the Constitution and reform of the allegedly anti-female inequality of the tax law. Mesdames Abzug and Chisholm were elected committee members. Shirley Chisholm has emphasized that she has found the discrimination against her as a woman more oppressive and onerous than that against her as a member of the black race. Women candidates for elective office now receive support in their races; 50 women announced they would run for Congress and many more wanted state and local posts, but most of them had difficult races ahead of them.

The Representative from Brooklyn is also, of course, in favor of Congressional reform. She was a member of the Committee on Organizational Study and Review appointed by the House Democratic Caucus, which was headed by Julia

Butler Hansen, and which recommended among other reform proposals that a recorded teller vote be permitted if one-fifth of a quorum requests it; it also recommended an increase in the time for a vote, schedule key votes in advance, penalize habitual absenteeism, and make changes in the seniority system.

Mrs. Chisholm's legislative record was given almost complete approval by ADA, which gave her 97 percent, Kennedy 100 percent, Wilbur Mills 22 percent, and Republican Ashbrook 8 percent.

On October 25, 1971, Mrs. Chisholm said in an interview with United Press International that she planned to enter the presidential primaries in a number of crucial states—viz., Florida, North Carolina, Wisconsin, California, and New York. She expected to announce her intention formally on January 1, 1972, and stressed that this was a "very, very serious effort." She was 47 when she said she would run for the Presidency in 1972 to challenge white supremacy, male chauvinism, and the power structure of the Democratic Party. A blunt spokesman for her race, she had little money to help her. Her financial statement in 1971 indicated that she owned no business, and had no income from any profession except that from her status as Congresswoman, reinforced by a large income from honoraria: she is much in demand as a speaker.

The Black Caucus was split on Shirley's bid; some called her "that disruptive woman." Eugene McCarthy urged voters to vote for her on March 27; the Black Panthers expressed their intention to back her on April 27; the group's national chairman, Bobby Seale, made an announcement that the membership would participate in the day-to-day campaign. Mrs. Chisholm advocated an end to the Vietnam War before POW negotiations; McGovern agreed with her. She visited the wounded George Wallace (as did Muskie, Kennedy, and McGovern), and after that assassination attempt Nixon extended Secret Service protection to her as to Kennedy and Mills. On July 1, 1972, McGovern had 1,169 delegates pledged to him, while Shirley had 35. At the end of the Democratic Convention she joined hands with McGovern and Eagleton in a symbolic gesture of unity. As a presidential candidate she had not especially stressed matters pertaining to blacks, or to women; her concerns were with the underdog generally.

Congresswoman Shirley Chisholm is a tiny woman, but she has enormous courage. She is fearless, out-spoken, direct, articulate, and shrewd.

Bibliography

Works about Shirley Anita Chisholm

"First Black Woman on Capitol Hill," *Ebony* 24:58-59 (Feb. 1969).
"As the First Black Congresswoman Puts It Herself: This Is Fighting Shirley Chisholm," *New York Times Magazine*, pp. 32-33+ (Apr. 13, 1969).
"Congresswoman Shirley Chisholm," *Vogue* 153:170-71 (May 1969).
"Number 1 Method," *Nation* 210:69-70 (Jan. 26, 1970).
"First Black Woman in the U.S. House of Representatives," *Negro History Bulletin* 33:128 (May 1970).
"Visiting Feminine Eye," *McCalls* 97:6 (Aug. 1970).
Excerpt from testimony before Constitutional Amendments Subcommittee, May 6, 1970, *Congressional Digest* 50:20+ (Jan. 1971).

Excerpt from statement to House Armed Services Committee, March 11, 1971,
    Congressional Digest 50:154+ (May 1971).
"Clear It with Shirley," *Newsweek* 78:35-36 (Oct. 18, 1971).
"Shaker-upper Wants to be Madame President Chisholm," J. Howard. *Life* 71:81
    (Nov. 5, 1971).
"Love Is Not Enough," *Parents Magazine* 46:52+ (Dec. 1971).
"On the Chisholm Campaign Trail," P. R. Wieck. *New Republic* 165:16-18
    (Dec. 4, 1971).
"In Search of a Black Strategy," *Time* 98:9-10 (Dec. 20, 1970).
"Black and Proud," *Newsweek* 79:26 (Feb. 7, 1972).
"New Kind of Candidate: She's Black," *Newsweek* 79:24-26 (Feb. 24, 1972).
"Needed: Equal Educational Opportunities For All," *School and Society* 100:
    223-24 (Apr. 1972).
"Short Unhappy Life of Black Presidential Politics 1972," S. Lesher. *New York
    Times Magazine*, pp. 12-13+ (June 25, 1972).
"Mrs. Chisholm . . . Are You Really Running for President?", V. Cadden. *Red-
    book* 139:47+ (July 1972).
Almanac, pp. 531-32.
Black Americans in Government. Text and exercises by Sheila Hobson and Hawley
    D. Goldenberg. General editor: Saunders Ready. Produced by Buckingham
    Leary Corp. [Jamaica, N.Y., Buckingham Leary Corp., 1969] . 5v. illus.
    ports.
Brownmiller, Susan. *Shirley Chisholm, A Biography.* [1st ed.] Garden City, N.Y.,
    Doubleday [1970] . 130p. illus. (Doubleday Signal Books).
Congressional Quarterly Almanac, 1969-70.
Congressional Quarterly Weekly Report, 1971-72.
Congressional Record, 1972.
Kuriansky, Joan, and Catherine Smith. *Shirley Chisholm, Democratic Represen-
    tative from New York.* [Washington, D.C., Grossman Publishers, c1972].
    [31p.] (Ralph Nader Congress Project. Citizens Look At Congress.)

Works by Shirley Anita Chisholm

Unbought and Unbossed. Boston, Houghton Mifflin, 1970. xii. 177p.

BELLA SAVITZKY ABZUG   (Mrs. Martin Abzug)
Democrat, New York
1971-

Mrs. Abzug was elected to the 92nd Congress as Representative of New
York City's Nineteenth Congressional District. She was born in 1920, a native of
New York; her father owned a butcher shop in the Jewish district. She attended
Hunter College and Columbia University. After receiving her LL.B. she became a
practicing lawyer, devoting much of her time to the defense of the underdog. It
was an easy step for her to become deeply engaged in many facets of social
reform. In 1961 she helped found the Women Strike for Peace group, whose
efforts were focused on a comprehensive nuclear test ban. In 1967 she became

identified with the Dump Johnson movement. Her husband is a stock broker and novelist who energetically supports her political career; they have two daughters.

The Nineteenth District includes the Lower East Side, Greenwich Village and the Upper West Side, harboring a very polyglot conglomeration of Chinese, Jews, Hungarians, Ukrainians, Puerto Ricans, and blacks. Although most of the population is poor, it includes many well-to-do professional and theatrical men and women, and intellectuals of liberal tendencies.

Mrs. Abzug ran against incumbent Leonard Farbstein in the primary; in the general election of 1970 she ran against Barry Farber, a radio commentator. She defeated both after campaigning hard in the streets; Mrs. Abzug was 50 when she was elected.

Her committee assignments in the 92nd Congress were on Government Operations and Public Works; she had contended vigorously for a place on the House Armed Services Committee, but the Democratic leadership did not grant her demand. In her first two years in the Congress, Representative Abzug has easily made herself one of the best known personalities in national politics through her outspokenness, honesty, and immensely hard work.

Congresswoman Abzug says that Congress needs a complete revamping. She made a beginning in this by rediscovering and using an old procedural device for obtaining information from the Executive Branch: the resolution of inquiry. She used it to bring the Pentagon Papers issue before the House in June 1971, and in October of the same year to bring the "South Vietnam non-election" before the Congress. She has used it since in other matters. Mrs. Abzug is a vigorous warrier in the fight against sex discrimination and loses no opportunity to offer amendments to various bills attacking sex discrimination (such as the Public Works Acceleration Act of 1971, and the Appalachian Regional Development Act of 1972). Other Congresswomen have since imitated her successful use of these tactics. With Representative Chisholm, Mrs. Abzug authored the Comprehensive Child Development Act, passed by the House in 1971 after extensive remodelling of its provisions. In spite of this weakening, Nixon vetoed the bill. She also had the satisfaction of proposing and having accepted a New York City rent amendment to the Economic Stabilization Act of 1971; this amendment placed these rents back under federal control. Her amendment overcame strong opposition from the Nixon Price Commission and from Senators Buckley and Javits.

Mrs. Abzug introduced the strongest water pollution bill in the House, some of whose provisions were incorporated in the legislation passed in 1972. She drafted and introduced legislation calling for a total nuclear test ban, including underground tests as well as those made in the air. That she has a heart for the elderly she proved by introducing legislation to establish a Department of Elder Affairs, with many specific benefits in Social Security and Medicare. She also testified before the Banking and Currency Committee for grants for transportation for the elderly and handicapped. For those young men who endangered their future in the United States as war resisters, she introduced an unconditional amnesty bill. For women she sought maternity leave and benefits, the right to abortion, and abolition of sex discrimination in the granting of credit. She introduced what is erroneously dubbed the "Ms. bill"—a bill that prohibits designation of the marital status of women on government documents and forms where the same information is not required of men. At the 1972 Democratic Convention she called on women delegates to elicit pledges from candidates of an equal share of jobs in government, and an equal number of cabinet posts and high administrative offices for women.

On January 18, 1972, Mrs. Abzug asked the House to censure Nixon for his Vietnam policies and procedures, because he had flouted the intent and language of a law he signed, flatly stating that he had no intention of abiding by its provisions. In June 1972 she introduced a resolution to impeach Nixon for his bombing and mining of North Vietnamese harbors. A year before, when Nixon addressed the Congress on his "new economic policy" in the summer of 1971 she had said: "Mr. Nixon is resorting to demagoguery of the worst sort to try to distract attention from his total failure in the fields of economics," using cheap rhetoric, in the "sly manner which has been his trademark for 25 years . . . to avoid the hard realities for which he is in large measure responsible." Several months before, in May 1971, she had struck out against the mass arrests and preventive detention used by the Nixon administration. In testimony before the House Armed Services Committee she stated: "I am unalterably opposed to military conscription and believe it should be dismantled. . . . Conscription . . . is involuntary servitude." And she continued: "Though not an advocate of a volunteer army, I feel that such an army is obviously a lesser evil than conscription . . . it should be a transitional part of our society" (press release dated March 1, 1971).

Her voting record proves her a vigorous defender of the underdog, and a resourceful fighter for the rights of minorities. She voted for cuts in military appropriations, for diverting funds to mass transit, and for public housing in the Forest Hills district of New York City (when all other Congressmen representing the City assumed ambivalent or opposing positions). She voted against SST and against appropriations for a space shuttle. She also opposed HR1, the Welfare Reform bill. It called for extensive revamping of the welfare system, which she opposed, because "under the guise of being a reform measure it will leave many recipients of public welfare perhaps 90 percent worse off than they are under the present system." She thought it struck out against poor people, women and children.

Representative Abzug is above all an activist, intensely energetic, and of proven integrity. A reading of the *Congressional Record* leaves one impressed by her trenchant remarks and by the enormous amount of legislation—meaningful and desperately needed—that she has introduced. Almost every issue of the *Record* attests to her ability to contribute worthwhile comments on subjects of national and international importance; she never just fills its pages with pious, harmless eulogies, as do many of her colleagues.

Of her own performance the Congresswoman feels that it is not very productive. She works 18 hours a day, seven days a week. It is often exhausting, yet she enjoys it so much that she waged a terrific battle for reelection. Her Nineteenth District was abolished and she found herself without a constituency. So she challenged William E. Ryan of the Twentieth District, although Mrs. Abzug admitted that he was a very fine, liberal Congressman. She lost, but soon thereafter Mr. Ryan died, and the Congresswoman found herself once more in a political battle, against Ryan's widow. This time she won, and she is back in the 93rd Congress.

Bibliography

Works about Bella Savitzky Abzug

"Bella," *Newsweek* 76:28-29 (Oct. 5, 1970).

"Emasculated; N.Y. City's Lower Manhattan District Subject to Garymander," *New Republic* 166:11 (Mar. 18, 1972).

"Bella and Bill," *Newsweek* 79:37 (May 8, 1972).

"Bombing Statistics," *Nation* 214:614 (May 15, 1972).

"Dilemma in the New 20th Congressional District. Bella Should Be There, So Should Ryan," A. Hill. *New York Times Magazine*, pp. 12-13+ (June 18, 1972).

"Fighting Hard," *Vogue* 157:94-95 (June 1971).

"Unfinished Business of America," *Look* 35:61 (July 13, 1971).

"Bellacose Abzug," *Time* 98:14+ (Aug. 16, 1971).

"Diary of a Fighting Congresswoman," excerpt from *Bella! Ms. Abzug Goes To Washington*. Ed. by M. Ziegler. *McCalls* 99:54+ (July 1972).

"New Women Talk Back," *Life* 72:46-50 (June 9, 1972).

"Exit Bella," *Newsweek* 80:17 (July 3, 1972).

Almanac, pp. 544-46.

Congressional Quarterly Weekly Report, 1971-72.

Congressional Record, 1972.

Facts on File, 1972.

Weinberg, Nancy, and Pauline Jennings. *Bella S. Abzug, Democratic Representative from New York*. [Washington, D.C., Grossman Publishers, c1972]. [30p.] (Ralph Nader Congress Project. Citizens Look At Congress.)

Works by Bella Savitzky Abzug

Bella! Ms. Abzug Goes to Washington. Ed. by M. Ziegler. New York, *Saturday Review Press* [c1972]. 314p. The chronicle of the Congresswoman's first year in Congress, 1971.

ELLA TAMBUSI GRASSO (Mrs. Thomas H. Grasso)
Democrat, Connecticut
1971-

Mrs. Grasso was elected to the 92nd Congress from Connecticut's Sixth District, and was reelected in 1972 to represent her district in the 93rd Congress. Of Italian extraction, she attended Mount Holyoke College, where she majored in economics and sociology, and from which she received her A.B. and M.A. degrees, graduating with the highest honors; she is a member of Phi Beta Kappa.

Mrs. Grasso is an old hand at politics. When Eisenhower swept the state of Connecticut in 1952, she, a Democrat, sailed easily into the State House of Representatives and was reelected in 1954 with a comfortable margin. In 1955 she became floor leader and in 1958 Secretary of State; she was reelected to that post twice, in 1962 and 1966. She did not want to run for Congress because she likes the close ties that bind her family, but she yielded to urgings and in 1970 beat her Republican challenger. She had spent $59,000 for her campaign, her opponent $100,000; a substantial part of her funds came from AFL-CIO. During her terms in the service of the state she had been interested in advancing education, and in aiding the handicapped; she helped to create the University of Connecticut Health Center and was instrumental in reforming election laws. She won her campaign because she personally contacted as many voters as possible, appearing at the factory gates to talk to workers. Her district, a recently formed one, is variegated; it combines urban centers, where machinery, equipment, and textiles are manufactured, with farms and rural communities laid out on rolling hills. The unemployment in her district is much higher than the national average. A good deal of it is caused by the depression that has plagued the ball bearing industry because of strong competition from Japanese imports.

Mrs. Grasso is a member of two committees: Education and Labor, where she has membership on three subcommittees (viz., Agricultural Labor, the Select Subcommittee on Labor, and the Select Subcommittee on Education) and the Veterans Committee, where she is on the subcommittees for Hospitals and for Insurance. Her seniority is low, 78th, since she is, so to speak, a freshman.

The Education Committee is concerned with education, labor, and welfare matters; its membership consists of 22 Democrats and 16 Republicans. It is a volatile committee, with much infighting and quarreling that reduce its effectiveness on the floor of the House. The Veterans Committee is more congenial; it is made up of 16 Democrats and 10 Republicans, and it is concerned with veterans' matters generally, and specifically with pensions, armed forces life insurance, rehabilitation, medical care and treatment of veterans, and veterans' hospitals.

Mrs. Grasso has been very busy introducing, sponsoring and co-sponsoring legislation in the 92nd Congress. One of her more important bills was the Emergency School Aid Act of 1971. In March 1970 Nixon had asked for $1.5 billion in appropriations for emergency federal aid to desegregate school districts, but he asked for no funds for busing. Two bills, HR2266 and HRept.92-572, were not well received; many Southern Democrats claimed that they were backdoor devices to get busing into law, and the Rules Committee refused to move the legislation to the floor of the House. Congresswoman Grasso had voted for it.

Congresswoman Grasso also voted for the Fair Labor Standards Amendments of 1971, which were to increase the minimum wage to $2.00 per hour and extend benefits to six million additional workers, but the legislation still left many millions of workers uncovered. The minimum wage for agricultural workers was to rise from $1.30 to $1.50 per hour. The increase to $2.00 would bring the annual wage close to $4,000, which at that time was very near the poverty line; Nixon wanted a smaller increase. Mrs. Grasso voted against SST, although going ahead with it would have benefitted her district (Windsor Locks would have received $5,197,481). The AFL faulted her for this stand, but otherwise found her record on matters of interest to labor quite good. She was on the House Conference Committee to iron out details of the final version of a $2.5 billion for public service jobs to ease unemployment; enactment of this bill gave her district considerable help in combatting its unemployment. An additional public works program for economic disaster areas and a comprehensive child development bill were vetoed by Nixon. Mrs. Grasso also intended to raise educational benefits for veterans to $277 per month, for three school years (nine months each), but the amount granted was reduced to $200 per month. Other legislation sponsored and supported by Mrs. Grasso dealt with liberalizing life insurance, treatment and rehabilitation of veterans and with some minor matters such as bills to return Memorial and Veterans Day to their traditional dates.

To ease the plight of the elderly she worked with others to raise Social Security payments and to liberalize medical care. She wanted to amend the Older Americans Act to provide greater benefits in nutrition, transportation, housing, etc. She was a supporter of the Cancer Act, now law, and an active leader in the fight against Sickle Cell Anemia, an illness that strikes especially at blacks, and in against Cooley's anemia; the amount involved was comparatively quite small— $8.1 million.

She helped in arranging a meeting between industrialist Vivien Kellems and Ways and Means Chairman Wilbur Mills in the matter of inequities of taxation for individuals. She is against water pollution; strip mining; dumping of waste in rivers, oceans and the air; and timber loss. For her own state she joined forces with Connecticut Senator Abraham Ribicoff to establish the Housatonic River Valley Trust to save the landscape skirting this beautiful waterway. She favors open sessions at all committee meetings, an end to the seniority system, and rotation of committee assignments, and she deplores the fact that Congress has abdicated so much of its authority to the Executive, especially in foreign affairs.

Mrs. Grasso had an 84 percent record on 320 roll calls, but missed several highly important votes on matters concerned with the Vietnam War. On this and on ABM and the B-1 manned bomber her record is somewhat spotty; she has not come out strongly for cutbacks in defense spending. On the other hand, she energetically supported projects giving impetus to the economy, such as an appropriation for $507 million for merchant ship construction in U.S. shipyards and higher appropriations for Amtrak. Representative Grasso strongly supported the Higher Education Act of 1972, now law, which, among other improvements in educational matters, evolved a new formula for aid to colleges and universities. Legislation that granted the vote to 18-year-olds (HJtRes223) was also unequivocally supported by Mrs. Grasso. She has always fought discrimination; even when still a member of the Connecticut legislature, she was instrumental in persuading her fellow law-givers to make Connecticut one of the first states in the Union to pass a housing law forbidding discrimination on the basis of race, religion, or national origin.

Mrs. Grasso's Congressional District had a population of 508,422 in 1970; the federal government spends an average of $666,865,000 there. It has a large foreign element, especially those of Italian, Polish, and Canadian origin, but there are few blacks or Puerto Ricans. Politically, 38 percent of the voters were registered as Democrats, 34 percent as Republicans, and 28 percent as other; in 1968 the district gave more votes to Humphrey than to Nixon.

Congresswoman Grasso is no shirker, she is busy on Capitol Hill and no less busy keeping in touch with the voters in her district. She spends almost one-third of the year in her district, from Friday to Sunday each week, to meet with her constituents. To make contact easier she has installed the "Ellaphone," which permits any voter in her district to call her at no cost; she receives an average of 200 calls a week while she visits her district. She has introduced a bill in Congress that would provide for free mailing of letters from citizens to Congressmen, federal officials, and the President.

Mrs. Grasso has been called an intellectual, but she is also a dynamic doer; a liberal, highly intelligent, productive Representative, she is a model legislator.

Bibliography

Almanac, pp. 133-34.
Congressional Quarterly Weekly Report, 1971-72.
Congressional Record, 1972.
Gruberg, pp. 184, 194.
Jarin, Ken, and James Burkhardt. *Ella T. Grasso, Democratic Representative from Connecticut*. [Washington, D.C., Grossman Publishers, c1972].
    [21p.] (Ralph Nader Congress Project. Citizens Look At Congress.)
Lamson, pp. 215-26.

LOUISE DAY HICKS
Democrat, Massachusetts
1971-73

Louise Hicks was elected in November 1970 to the 92nd Congress, sitting from January 3, 1971, until January 3, 1973, to represent the Ninth Congressional District of Massachusetts. Congresswoman Hicks, a widow, was born in 1919; she has two sons. Her district is the most Irish in the United States; like her predecessor, former Speaker of the House John McCormack, she is a Catholic by religion and a lawyer by profession. Printing and publishing, apparel manufacture, and insurance are the chief sources of income for her district's population of about 370,000. The relative components are 57 percent blue collar and 43 percent white collar; the black segment is considerable—27 percent of the total population. Mrs. Hicks and the NAACP do not see eye to eye, and Mrs. Hicks has quarreled with that organization.

Before 1967 Mrs. Hicks had been a member of the Boston School Board, with a clear platform against school busing. In that year she contended against Kevin White for the mayoralty of Boston with the slogan, "You know where I stand." She almost got the mayor's seat, but the more liberal White won. In 1969 she ran for the City Council and won, but in 1970 she announced her intention to go to Congress; she defeated John Moakley, a Massachusetts State Senator. Her platform was withdrawal from the U.N., but in internal politics she had a clear liberal standpoint: truth in advertising, a decrease in property taxes for the elderly, an increase in Social Security payments, improvement of Medicare, and a national health program for all. In 1971, when she was already a member of Congress, she ran another, more limited campaign for the office of mayor of Boston, but she was again turned down.

Her record in the House is liberal and urban-minded on domestic issues, but conservative on military policy and racial issues. She is a member of two

House Committees: Education and Labor, and Veterans Affairs. She is also on the General Subcommittee on Education, the Special Subcommittee on Labor, and the Select Subcommittee on Labor. Mrs. Hicks liked being a member of the Education Committee because she had experience in that field. Also among her concerns are the Veterans Affairs Committee's subcommittees on Hospitals and on Insurance. The Congresswoman is not rich by any means; she disclosed that she had had more than $5,000 income from her law practice in 1970.

Her voice was not often heard in Congress, although she has given testimony before Congressional committees, has spoken on the House floor, and has inserted items in the *Congressional Record*. On the minimum wage question she voted with other Democrats for an increase to $2.00 per hour, co-sponsoring HR6868 (22 Democrats on the Education Committee voted in favor, seven Republicans against). She supported health programs and introduced HR8423 to establish a National Sickle Cell Anemia Institute. She favored increased compensation for disabled veterans, and she introduced bills to help the elderly by giving them half-fare on transportation and by increasing Social Security checks by 50 percent; she also favored giving orphans of coal miners benefits for the black lung disease, and she co-sponsored HR7345 for a comprehensive child development program and advocated reduced taxes for single individuals.

On the other hand, she voted for continuation of secret blacklists kept by the Subversive Activities Control Board; she supported all defense expenditures and was for the Navy's F-14. Her Vietnam record is rather unclear. That she took a stand against British troops in Northern Ireland is not surprising, but it is disappointing to learn that she was for the Amchitka blast.

Mrs. Hicks' district had a population of 429,692 in 1960. In 1970, however, it had shrunk to 368,888, a decrease of 22 percent; Suffolk County lost 56,000. The fact that it was to be redistricted endangered her chances for renomination. In October 1971 the ADA released a list of 40 conservative Congressmen that it said could be defeated if newly enfranchised college students living in their districts were to vote against them. Most of these members of Congress were Republicans, but Democrat Hicks also represented such a district. Her 1970 plurality had been 32,874, and the students in her district numbered 41,312, assuring a margin of defeat if the students voted as a bloc. Something like this seems to have happened, for Mrs. Hicks was actually defeated in the 1972 general election by Independent Moakley, the man whom she had downed two years before. Mrs. Hicks was the only Democratic woman Representative not to be returned to the 93rd Congress.

Bibliography

"Breeze That Whispered Louise," *National Review* 22:1038 (Oct. 6, 1970).
"Running Back Into the Past," with reports by J. Pekkanen and R. Brigham. *Life* 71:32-34+ (Oct. 29, 1971).
Facts on File, 1972. "Defeat Due to Unfavorable Redistricting."
Almanac, pp. 355-56.
Congressional Quarterly Weekly Report, 1971-72.
Congressional Record, 1972.

Kuriansky, Joan. *Louise Day Hicks, Democratic Representative from Massachusetts.* [Washington, D.C., Grossman Publishers, c1972]. [29p.] (Ralph Nader Congress Project. Citizens Look At Congress.)

ELIZABETH B. ANDREWS (Mrs. George W. Andrews)
Democrat, Alabama
1972-73

Elizabeth Andrews was elected in a special election held April 4, 1972, in which she was unopposed. The election was to fill the seat held since 1944 by her husband, George W. Andrews, who died on December 25, 1971. Congresswoman Andrews did not seek a full term in November 1972.

A letter dated August 1, 1972, reflected her views on the military in this country. She was in favor of withdrawing from Vietnam, in view of the fact that "a military victory has been abandoned as a goal" of the war. She favored continuing the draft in some form, since she did not believe in the efficacy of an all-volunteer army. And she considered national defense as a "top priority item."

Mrs. Andrews felt that people genuinely in need must receive help, such as the old and disabled, but that our able-bodied citizens must be offered job opportunities, not welfare. She was opposed to the guaranteed annual income concept. She judged President Nixon's performance as average, but in general she supported his actions in foreign affairs, particularly the winding down of the Vietnam War.

Mrs. Andrews approved of Nixon's attempts to slow inflation through his wage and price restrictions, but she disapproved of the extravagant revenue sharing bill and the tremendously expensive welfare reform bill. She chastised his inconsistency in the school busing issue, feeling that he had done little and that contradictory remarks by him and by his cabinet members obscured any real position and served to confuse the public.

Among the bills Representative Elizabeth Andrews has introduced is one aimed at protecting welfare recipients against cuts due to Social Security increases: "a bill to amend the Social Security Act to prevent recipients of aid under the various Federal-State public assistance and Medicaid programs from having the amount of such aid or assistance reduced because of increases in monthly Social Security benefits" (HR14619, dated April 26, 1972). Another bill introduced by Mrs. Andrews would permit more outside earnings for Social Security recipients without deductions from benefits.

Her HR14778 (Medicredit national health insurance proposal) would amend the Social Security Act to provide for medical and hospital care through a system of voluntary health insurance, to be financed for low-income groups through the issuance of certificates and for other persons through tax credits.

HFRes1190, an anti-busing amendment, proposed a constitutional amendment stating that no public school student shall, because of his race, creed, or color, be assigned to attend a particular school. HR15060 would protect compensation for veterans, and for widows and dependent parents of deceased veterans.

Mrs. Andrews' Third District includes 12 Alabama counties. Mrs. Andrews had an assignment to the Post Office and Civil Service Committee and served on three of its subcommittees: Census and Statistics; Manpower, and Civil Service and Postal Facilities and Mail.

Bibliography

Congressional Quarterly Weekly Report, 1972.

SENATE

Of 71 Congresswomen, scarcely one-third made an imprint on legislation through length of service and dynamic activity. More than a third served less than two terms, many only one or only part of one term. It required nearly a quarter of a century before women were elected for longer terms, and before they became regular features in the life of the House of Representatives; now they seem to have been well established, are taken seriously and have performed commendably and substantially. This has been especially true since about the middle of the 1950s. Their number is still unjustifiably small—even in the 93rd Congress there are only 14, though they are all capable, intelligent, and progressive legislators.

What is true of Congresswomen is even more true of the women who have been Senators, of whom there have been 11 from 1922 to 1972. Nine of them served only a year or less, being used as stopgaps in sudden political crisis periods. One had two full terms of her own after acceding to her husband's seat, one had one full term of her own and then resigned, while one achieved four full six-year terms on her own initiative. For the first time in 24 years there will not be a woman Senator, unless one is appointed to fill a vacancy (of which there are none at the time of writing). What follows is a gallery of the 11 women who have graced the United States Senate since 1922.

REBECCA L. FELTON (Mrs. William H. Felton)
Independent Democrat, Georgia
1922

Mrs. Felton was sworn in on November 21, 1922, to fill a vacancy caused by the death of Senator Thomas E. Watson, Democrat of Georgia, who had been in the Senate in 1921 and 1922. On the next day the new woman Senator gave her seat up to Senator Walter George, a Democrat, who was the elected candidate for the vacancy; he served until 1937. Mrs. Felton was the first woman Senator and was undoubtedly the oldest person ever to become a freshman Senator, for her age was 88 at the time of her installation. She died in 1930, at the age of 94.

Bibliography

Works about Rebecca L. Felton

"First Woman Senator," *Literary Digest* 75:14-15 (Oct. 21, 1922).
"First Woman Senator," *Outlook* 132:272-74 (Oct. 18, 1922).
"Lady From Georgia," W. S. Ethridge. *Good Housekeeping* 76:27 (Jan. 1923).
Gruberg, p. 123.
Paxton, pp. 11-12.

Works by Rebecca L. Felton

Country Life in Georgia in the Days of My Youth; Also addresses before Georgia
Legislature, women's clubs, women's organizations and other noted
occasions. Atlanta, Ga., Index Printing Company, c1919. 299p. port.

HATTIE WYATT CARAWAY   (Mrs. Thaddeus Caraway)
Democrat, Arkansas
1931-45

Mrs. Caraway, the second women Senator, acceded to her post in 1931 and
served until 1945, for 14 years, from the 72nd through the 78th Congresses. Her
husband, Thaddeus, had been her predecessor; he had served eight years in the
House and 11 in the Senate. His wife was appointed to fill out his term, which
ran until 1933, and in 1933 and 1939 she won two full six-year terms on her
own, defeating John McClellan in the 1938 national election.

She was of humble origin and had helped in her father's country store; she
had three sons. Soft-spoken, a hard worker who got things done, she was the
kind of woman Senator that men Senators prefer. One week she received
5,000 letters, all of which she answered promptly. Hattie Caraway always voted
as "Thad would have voted"; she was retiring, and she seldom spoke on the Senate floor. But she could boast of many firsts: she was the first woman chairman
of a Senate committee, the first woman Senator to conduct Senate hearings, first
to preside over Senate sessions, the first to be a Senior United States Senator.
Serving on the Committee for Agriculture and Forestry, she became an advocate
of farm and labor groups. For her state she obtained an aluminum plant, con-
structed and owned by the federal government, operated by the Aluminum
Company of America, and helped get other government operations for the
economic benefit of her constituents. She always voted for a large army, navy
and air force, and she supported lend lease. However, she claimed to be a constant advocate of peace. Her economic principles were conservative: she wanted
wartime federal controls and restrictions abolished without delay. She did not
get the Party's nomination to serve in the 79th Congress and was defeated by
William Fulbright, who became Senator for Arkansas in 1945.

Bibliography

"Five Democratic Women," M. Davis. *Ladies Home Journal* 50:114+ (May
   1933).
"Hattie and Huey," H. B. Deutsch. *Saturday Evening Post* 205:6-7+ (Oct. 15,
   1932).
"Woman Who Holds Her Tongue," G. Creel. *Colliers* 100:22+ (Sept. 18, 1937).
"Biography" in *Current Biography* (Mar. 1945).
"Ladies of Congress," A. Porter. *Colliers* 112:22 (Aug. 28, 1943).
"Last of the First," *Time* 44:19 (Aug. 7, 1944).
"Women in Congress," *State Government* 10:203-204 (Oct. 1937).
Gruberg, pp. 124, 136, 291.
Paxton, pp. 15-28 and passim.

ROSE McCONNELL LONG   (Mrs. Huey Pierce Long)
Democrat, Louisiana
1936-37

Mrs. Rose Long was temporarily appointed to the Senate after the assassination of her husband, Huey Long. She served for less than a year and did not seek reelection; she vacated her seat to Allen Ellender, who served as Senator from Louisiana from 1937 until his death in 1972.

Bibliography

"Huey Long's Widow in the Senate," *Christian Century* 53:252 (Feb. 12, 1936).
"Lady From Louisiana," *Time* 27:12 (Feb. 10, 1936).
"Senator's Widow Gets Job that Death Twice Vacated," *Newsweek* 7:12 (Feb. 8, 1936).
"Third Woman Senator," *Literary Digest* 121:34 (Feb. 15, 1936).
Gruberg, p. 124.
Paxton, p. 129.

DIXIE BIBB GRAVES   (Mrs. Bibb Graves)
Democrat, Alabama
1937-38

Mrs. Graves served four months as United States Senator in 1937, and then resigned. She was appointed by her husband, Bibb Graves, governor of Alabama, to the Senate seat vacated when Hugo Black was appointed to the Supreme Court of the United States by Franklin Delano Roosevelt.

Bibliography

"Family Seat," *Time* 30:15 (Aug. 30, 1937).
New York Times Index, 1938.
Gruberg, p. 125.
Paxton, p. 129.

GLADYS PYLE
Republican, South Dakota
1938-39

Gladys Pyle was never sworn in, because the Congress was not in session between her election and the expiration of her term.

Bibliography

"In-between Senators," *Time* 32:10 (Dec. 19, 1938).
Gruberg, p. 125 and passim.
Paxton, p. 130.

VERA C. BUSHFIELD (Mrs. Harlan J. Bushfield)
Republican, South Dakota
1948-49

Ten years after Gladys Pyle, South Dakota had another Republican woman Senator for a brief time. Vera Bushfield, who held the Senate seat for two months and then resigned, had been appointed to fill the vacancy left by the death of her husband, Harlan Bushfield.

Bibliography

New York Times Index, 1948.
Gruberg, p. 125.

MARGARET CHASE SMITH (Mrs. Clyde H. Smith)
Republican, Maine
1949-73

Margaret Chase Smith, U.S. Senator from Maine, was born in Skowhegan, Maine, in 1899, one of six children. Her father was a barber, and her mother worked occasionally as a waitress and as a clerk in a dimestore. Margaret went to work for the same store at the age of 12, and she later became a switchboard operator. While still in her teens she was a schoolteacher for a while, and she later became associated with the Skowhegan *Independent Reporter*, whose founder and publisher was Clyde H. Smith. They were married in 1930. Clyde Smith, a liberal Republican, was a life-long politician; he was elected to Congress in 1936, with his wife working as his secretary and his campaign manager. He died in 1940, and his wife was elected to take his seat. She was reelected three times, until she forsook the House in 1948 to run for the Senate. During her career she ran three more times, to serve four full six-year terms.

She was always a proponent of a strongly armed United States. While in the House she expressed unity of foreign policy as her post-war aim, and she said that nothing was too good for those who had risked their lives in combat—that they must be assured of good jobs and wages. Her first committee assignment in the House was on the District of Columbia Committee, one not especially cherished. She wanted and was given membership on the committee that was then the Naval Affairs Committee, later absorbed into the Senate Armed Services Committee.

While in the Senate Margaret Smith was known for her nearly unsurpassed attendance at roll calls; she attained a maximum of 2,000 in a 10-year period from 1955 to 1965, and a certificate of recognition was tendered her by fellow Republican Senators Aiken and Dirksen. Later, because of illness, she had to abdicate her number-one roll call status to Senator Proxmire, who could boast a 100 percent attendance record to her 93 percent. To curb absenteeism, Senator Smith offered SJRes192 as a constitutional amendment; its aim was to expel any Congressman or Senator who had an attendance record of less than 60 percent or fewer than 200 roll call votes in a session. Attendance on the floor is frequently deplorable: 15 Representatives and eight Senators missed at least 40 percent of roll calls in the first session of the 92nd Congress, 1971.

Mrs. Smith was never a woman of many words; she had learned that freshmen Senators were to be seen, not heard. Being independent of mind, however, and therefore unpredictable, one day early in her senatorial career she rose to speak on the floor of the Senate. She had been in the Senate scarcely a year and a half. On June 1, 1950, she spoke in a clear, firm, but not loud voice for about 15 minutes—her target was Senator Joseph McCarthy of Wisconsin, who had put fear into the hearts of some of his fellow Senators, while others were too complacent to respond to his irresponsible charges of rampant communism in the government (and especially in the State Department). With the encouragement of six other Republican Senators, Mrs. Smith made her declaration of conscience, never referring by name to McCarthy, but demanding an end to his cynical, self-serving accusations. The Senator from Wisconsin had his revenge on Senator Smith; he ridiculed her as Snow White and her co-sponsors as the six dwarfs, and he kicked her off the Senate Permanent Investigating Committee on which he had earlier asked her to take membership. The vacancy was filled by Richard Nixon. McCarthy continued his harrassment, and because of his influence Senator Smith's relations to President Eisenhower were strained during much of his administration. McCarthy also seems to have had a hand in trying to defeat Mrs. Smith in her 1954 reelection campaign, but his encouragement of her Republican primary opponent backfired: she polled five times as many votes as her challenger.

Senator Smith has always been a supporter of military strength for the United States; as early as 1943 she came to the then House Naval Affairs Committee, which later merged with the Military Affairs Committee to become the Armed Services Committee; she was on this committee throughout her Senate career. She fought for permanent regular status for women in the armed forces; one of the first battles in which she was involved concerned the appointment of Waves to non-combatant duties overseas (Women Appointed for Volunteer Emergency Service); the Wacs (Women Army Corps) already served there. Later she tangled with Khrushchev, and she voted against the Nuclear Test Ban Treaty. She had a commission in the Naval Reserve as a Lieutenant Colonel. In the summer of 1972, Defense Secretary Laird demanded that Congress appropriate funds for a new Trident submarine and for building the B-1 bomber; Admiral Moorer backed him up, saying that Congress *must* provide the necessary funds if we did not want to fall back into obsolescence. Mrs. Smith agreed with them and expressed her fear of what would happen if Congress did not supply the weapons program requested.

It may be stated that Senator Smith usually sided with the Pentagon. She has supported continued spending for the Vietnam War, and she voted against the Mansfield proposal for withdrawal of all U.S. troops from Indochina after prisoner-of-war release. She also voted against banning the use of defoliant chemicals in Vietnam, against reduction of our military forces in Europe, and against a volunteer army. (On this subject, however, she expressed herself as follows in a letter to the author: "I support an all-volunteer armed force if it can be obtained in the necessary quality and quantity manpower at an acceptable cost to the American taxpayer." September 1, 1972.)

Always holding her cards close to her chest, she would never divulge in advance how she planned to vote. Thus she voted against the ABM, although she had been expected to vote favorably, and against the SST—both projects near to Nixon's heart. Nor did Mrs. Smith vote unfailingly for Eisenhower's bills: she voted against Lewis Strauss's nomination for Secretary of Commerce and against McCone's nomination for the AEC; she was hostile to the promotion of actor Jimmy Stewart to Brigadier-General and relaxed her opposition only after several years during which Stewart had improved his standing. But she voted again for the military when she cast a yes vote for the space shuttle.

On the internal, social scene, her status is mixed. She voted against busing, against cutting penalties on marijuana use, against funds for mass transit, increased funds for HEW, Headstart, and manpower training, and even against unemployment compensation for migratory farm workers. She is strongly for law and order, and voted for no-knock and preventive detention of persons accused of committing crimes in Washington, D.C. In 1972 she and Stennis introduced a proposal, S2139, to curb drug abuse among soldiers and to hold any man for 30 days beyond his tour of duty if he had a drug abuse dependence problem. She voted, like all Republicans, for Kleindienst as Attorney General; 19 Democrats opposed his nomination.

In the civil rights sphere she voted for the Civil Rights Act of 1964 and for the Voting Rights Act of 1965; in 1972 she supported the Equal Rights Amendment, but she does not consider herself a feminist, and militant women's groups give her a low mark.

Maine is larger than the other five New England states put together, but although it is well supplied with natural resources, the state is economically poor. Aroostook County is the potato empire of the world, but unemployment is above the national average. Besides potatoes and dairy products, poultry, canned and preserved fruits and vegetables, the state produces seafoods, lumber and wood products; it also has paper mills and manufactures footwear and other leather products. It is said that she has not exerted herself strongly on behalf of her Maine constituency. But she had no qualms about voting against limiting farm subsidies to $20,000 for each farmer, and she opposed legislation that would require further financial disclosures by members of Congress. In matters of Congressional organization she approves of seniority.

Her unwillingness to pour forth a flood of words has already been commented on. Her legislative output was also relatively modest. In 18 months of the 92nd Congress she introduced only five bills of her own, all of minor importance; she co-sponsored 16 bills with other Senators, mostly for the military and for the country's defense; her remarks in the Senate are usually on defense matters.

On June 1, 1970, just 20 years after her declaration of conscience, Mrs. Smith issued a second declaration of conscience against two groups whom she despises—leftists and moonlighting Senators. Her view was that the Vietnam War was only a convenient rallying point for the extremism that exploded into murder, arson and assault. Even Agnew did not escape criticism from the Senator for having overreacted to the TV networks and their commentators. Although she was ousted from a coveted committee early in her Senate career in Nixon's favor, and although her relationship to him remained cool, she has stated that she supported him on Vietnam and she rates his performance excellent.

She was a high-ranking member of several very important Senate committees: she sat on the Senate Aeronautical and Space Sciences Committee as second-ranking minority party member. This committee is concerned with aeronautical and space activities (except those primarily associated with the development of new weapons systems or military operations), also it has charge of NASA. Its membership includes six Democrats and five Republicans. She was also the third-ranking minority member of the Appropriations Committee; this committee has 13 Democratic and 11 Republican members. It is, of course, the counterpart of the House Appropriations Committee and studies all proposed expenditures of government agencies and programs. The annual presidential budget is the chief target of scrutiny. Senator Smith was ranking minority member of the Armed Services Committee and would have become chairman in the event of a Republican Congressional landslide and her reelection. Military proposals, strategic planning, and central intelligence are the focus of considerations of this committee. Mrs. Smith was also on several committees concerned solely with Republican Party matters and on five of the subcommittees of the above-named Senate committees.

In 1964 Mrs. Smith was nominated for Republican Party presidential candidate; her New England colleague Senator Aiken made the nominating speech. In 1972 she confounded those who had guessed she would retire. She announced that she would seek a full term and she trounced her Republican primary opponent; in November, however, she was defeated by Democrat Hathaway, which thus ended her 32-year Congressional career.

Margaret Chase Smith was one of the most powerful and respected members of the Senate. She was tenacious, well prepared, and a good shrewd politician. Symington said of her that her approach to problems was always cogent, while others see her as a bundle of contradictions. Her vote has not infrequently gone against her party, and it has just as often gone against progressive impulses. She feels at home with the military and stresses armed might; she understands armaments and the nature of power as few women have (Graham, *Margaret Chase Smith*, p. 172). But she also supported women's rights, although moderately, as well as some social and economic improvements. President Wilson once said of Senators that some of them grow, while others just swell. She cannot be classed with the second category, but her critics generally seem to agree that she has not grown in 24 years in the Senate. She was not a great or memorable Senator, but she was hard-working, knowledgeable, persistent, independent, and incorruptible—a Senator of whose character and accomplishments both men and women may well be proud.

Bibliography

Works about Margaret Chase Smith

Newsweek 15:36 (May 27, 1940).
"Why I Am for Thomas E. Dewey," *Womans Home Companion* 71:38 (Nov. 1944).

"Biography" in *Current Biography* (Feb. 1945).

"Ladies of Congress," A. Porter. *Colliers* 112:22 (Aug. 28, 1943).

"Challenge to Women," *Independent Woman* 28:101-102+ (Apr. 1949).

"Ballot Box Autopsy," *Newsweek* 32:19 (Sept. 27, 1948).

"Career Woman," *Newsweek* 32:26 (July 5, 1948).

"Her Nomination a Victory For Us All," *Independent Woman* 27:225 (Aug. 1948).

"Lady from Maine," *New Republic* 119:8 (July 5, 1948).

"Madame Senator," *Scholastic* 53:14 (Sept. 29, 1948).

"Our BPW in the Senate," E. Curtice. *Independent Woman* 27:292-94+ (Oct. 1948).

"Our BPW Senator Feted," *Independent Woman* 28:37+ (Feb. 1949).

"Senator from the Five-and-Ten," B. Smith. *Saturday Evening Post* 221:36-37+ (Sept. 11, 1948). Same abridged with title: "Lady from Maine," *Readers Digest* 53:13-16 (Dec. 1948).

"Yard of Pump Water," *Time* 52:21 (July 5, 1948).

"Antiquing," *Hobbies* 55:63 (Feb. 1951).

"Free Citizen Votes Intelligently," *Scholastic* 57:5 (Oct. 18, 1950).

"Growing Confusion," address in Senate, June 1, 1950. *Vital Speeches* 16:552ff (July 1, 1950).

"Tribute to Our Education," *Independent Woman* 28:335 (Nov. 1949).

"And A Woman Shall Lead Them," H. L. Ickes. *New Republic* 122:16 (Jan. 19, 1950).

"Candid Columnist," *Newsweek* 34:60-61 (Sept. 12, 1949).

"Lady from Maine," *Newsweek* 35:24-26 (June 12, 1950).

"McCarthy Gets His Lady," *Time* 57:9 (Feb. 5, 1951).

"Mrs. Smith Really Goes to Town," L. Rixey. *Colliers* 126:20-21+ (July 29, 1950).

"Surprising Mrs. Smith," J. Ripley. *Christian Science Monitor Magazine*, p. 5 (Nov. 11, 1950).

"Two Members of Congress Named to Unesco National Committee, *U.S. Department of State Bulletin* 22:651 (Apr. 24, 1950).

"Woman's Conscience," *Time* 55:19 (June 12, 1950).

"Women in Congress," *National Education Association Journal* 38:283 (Apr. 1949).

"No Place for a Woman?", *Ladies Home Journal* 69:50+ (Feb. 1952).

"Russia's Rebirth," *Colliers* 128:83 (Oct. 27, 1951).

"We Can Forfeit Freedom," *Nation* 173:13 (July 7, 1951).

"Why Vote for Eisenhower?", *Womans Home Companion* 79:38-39 (Nov. 1952).

"Committee Coup," *Newsweek* 39:20 (Jan. 28, 1952).

"Margaret Chase Smith Sues Crown, Lait and Mortimer," *Publishers Weekly* 161: 2007 (May 17, 1952).

"Maverick from Maine," D. Aikman. *Nation* 173:207-210 (Sept. 15, 1951).

"Their Hats Were In the Ring," *Independent Woman* 31:226 (Aug. 1952).

"Will Margaret Chase Smith Ever Be President?", A. Fields. *Coronet* 31:96-100 (Nov. 1951).

"Women in the 83rd Congress," M. L. Temple. *Independent Woman* 32:59 (Feb. 1953).

"Those Who Speak Loudest," *Nation* 177:493 (Dec. 12, 1953).
"Woman, the Key Individual of Our Democracy," address, June 7, 1953. *Vital Speeches* 19:657-59 (Aug. 15, 1953). Excerpts, *Independent Woman* 32: 354+ (Oct. 1953).
"Senator Abroad," *Time* 64:95 (Nov. 8, 1954).
"Senator McCarthy's Political Power," Maine Primary. *Christian Century* 71: 811 (July 7, 1954).
"Six Most Powerful Women; Selected by Editors of the *Womans Home Companion*," *Womans Home Companion* 82:18 (Jan. 1955).
"Smith Beats Jones," *Time* 64:9 (July 5, 1954).
"Strange Alliance," *New Republic* 131:5 (Aug. 16, 1954).
"Women in the 84th Congress," *Independent Woman* 34:20 (Jan. 1955).
"Bomb for Barbarians?", *Time* 62:12 (Aug. 24, 1953).
"McCarthyism: First Test," H. Lavine. *Newsweek* 43:23-24 (Apr. 5, 1954).
"Maine: Can Jones Beat Smith?", E. Donahue. *New Republic* 130:10-11 (May 17, 1954).
"Maine's for the Lady," *Newsweek* 43:21-22 (June 28, 1954).
"Mighty Smith Is She," *Colliers* 132:50-51 (Aug. 7, 1953).
"Mrs. Smith and the Jones Boy," *Look* 18:97-98 (June 15, 1954).
"Mrs. Smith Comes to Washington," E. Churchill. *American Mercury* 77:73-76 (Sept. 1953).
"One Senator's Conscience," M. Frakes. *Christian Century* 70:570-1 (May 13, 1953).
"People of the Week," *U.S. News* 37:14 (July 2, 1954).
"Billion Dollar Prescription," *Saturday Review* 39:43-45 (Apr. 21, 1956).
"Cotton Textile: Imports from Japan," letter. *U.S. Department of State Bulletin* 33:1065-67 (Dec. 26, 1955).
"Impatience and Generosity," *Vital Speeches* 21:1230-3 (May 15, 1955).
"Guessing Game," *Newsweek* 45:31 (May 23, 1955).
"Kitchen for a Lady Senator," M. Davidson. *Ladies Home Journal* 73:204-206 (Nov. 1956).
"Hot Potatoes from the Senator," *Senior Scholastic* 72:8 (Feb. 14, 1958).
"Lady Said No," *Newsweek* 51:24 (Mar. 3, 1958).
"Right Man for the Big Job," *New York Times Magazine*, p. 27+ (Apr. 3, 1960).
"As Maine Goes," *Time* 76:13-16 (Sept. 5, 1960).
"Gentlewoman from Maine," *Ladies Home Journal* 78:65+ (Jan. 1961).
"However Maine Goes, It Goes Feminine," *New York Times Magazine*, p. 20 (Oct. 23, 1960).
"Ladies in the Club," *New Republic* 143:6 (Oct. 10, 1960).
"Ladies of Maine," *Time* 75:15-16 (Mar. 7, 1960).
"Lady Balks Again," *Newsweek* 53:37 (Mar. 23, 1959).
"Lady Senator vs. the General," *U.S. News* 46:21 (June 29, 1959).
"One Star for Jimmy?", *Newsweek* 53:35 (Feb. 23, 1959).
"Political First," *National Business Woman* 39:2 (Oct. 1960).
"Core of our Trouble in Latin America," excerpt from report, March 24, 1962. *U.S. News* 52:68 (Apr. 9, 1962).
"Is Romney to be a Sacrificial Lamb for Republicans in '64?", *U.S. News* 52:13 (Feb. 26, 1962).

"Capability vs. Credibility," *Newsweek* 58:23 (Oct. 2, 1961).

"Capability vs. Credibility," *Time* 78:16 (Sept. 29, 1961).

"Credibility and Incredibility," *Commonweal* 75:60-61 (Oct. 13, 1961).

"Lady from Maine," *Nation* 192:314-15 (Apr. 15, 1961).

"Mrs. Smith Advises and Does Not Consent," S. Lansdowne. *America* 105:788 (Sept. 23, 1961).

"Nikita, the Devil and the Ball Player," *Time* 78:29 (Oct. 20, 1961).

"No Failure of Will," *America* 106:7-8 (Oct. 7, 1961).

"This Red-Or-Dead Nonsense," M. Ascoli. *Reporter* 25:26-28 (Oct. 12, 1961).

Excerpt from address, March 24, 1962. *Congressional Digest* 42:79+ (Mar. 1963).

"Candidate Smith?", *Newsweek* 62:34 (Nov. 18, 1963).

"Hey, Look Me Over," *Newsweek* 63:19-20 (Feb. 24, 1964).

"Lady from Maine: Her Record, Her Views," *U.S. News* 56:16 (Feb. 3, 1964).

"Lady in the New England Snow," M. McGrory. *America* 110:246 (Feb. 22, 1964).

"Lady of Maine," K. Crawford. *Newsweek* 63:30 (Feb. 10, 1964).

"Madame Candidate," *Time* 83:23 (Feb. 7, 1964).

"Maggie vs. May," *Newsweek* 61:23-24+ (Apr. 8, 1963).

"Maggie's List," *Time* 81:21 (Mar. 1, 1963).

"Margaret Chase Smith: Woman of Courage," by F. Graham, Jr. Review. *Saturday Review* 47:42-43 (Apr. 18, 1964). By C. B. Luce.

"Mom and Pop; Goldwater-Smith Ticket," *Reporter* 29:24 (Nov. 21, 1963).

"Twenty-four Hours in the Life of Margaret Chase Smith," H. Markel. *McCalls* 91:116-17+ (May 1964).

"What Is Maggie Smith Up To?", Mr. Cheshire. *Saturday Evening Post* 237:30-32 (Apr. 18, 1964).

"Without Portfolio," C. B. Luce. *McCalls* 91:18 (June 1964).

"Woman for President?", *U.S. News* 56:34-36 (Feb. 10, 1964).

"Womans Right," *Newsweek* 63:22-23 (Feb. 10, 1964).

"Sick Movies: A Menace to Children," *Readers Digest* 91:139-42 (Dec. 1967).

"Woman to Woman; Questions and Answers," see issues of *McCalls.*

"Surprising Lady from Maine," *Newsweek* 74:21 (Aug. 18, 1969).

"Remembrance of Christmas," *House Beautiful* 112:56-57 (Dec. 1970).

"U.S. Faces Choice Between Anarchy and Repression," address, June 1, 1970. *U.S. News* 68:45-46 (June 15, 1970).

"Voice of Reason," *Time* 95:18 (June 15, 1970).

"We Talk To. . .," interview. *Mademoiselle* 71:298 (Aug. 1970).

"Church Women United Honor Margaret Chase Smith," *Christian Century* 87:559 (May 6, 1970).

"Is America Going Isolationist?", interview. *U.S. News* 70:27-28 (June 28, 1971).

"It's Time to Speak Up for National Defense," *Readers Digest* 100:66-71 (Mar. 1972).

"Declaration of Conscience," by M. C. Smith. Review. *Saturday Review* 55:66-67 (Apr. 15, 1972).

"Roll Call," *Commonweal* 96:3-4 (Mar. 10, 1972).

"On the Alliance;The Vitalizing of Forces for Evolutionary Change and the Military," *Inter-American Economic Affairs* 16:89-95, Summer 1962.

"Try for White House by Mrs. M. C. Smith Roils GOP Primary Outlook," Henry Gemmil. *Wall Street Journal* 163:1+ (Jan. 28, 1964).

"A Woman for President? Hurdles in the Path of M. C. Smith," *U.S. News* 56: 34-36 (Feb. 10, 1964).

"Defense Spending: Changing Attitudes," *Defense Management Journal* 6:2-5 (Winter 1970).

"From M. C. Smith: U.S. Faces Choice Between Anarchy and Repression," *U.S. News* 68:45-46 (June 15, 1970). Address delivered in the Senate on June 1, 1970.

"Senator Smith Warns Nation Anew About Extremism," [gist of a speech made in the Senate, June 1, 1970]. *Congressional Quarterly Weekly Report* 28: 1476 (June 5, 1970).

"Is the Great Lady from Maine Out of Touch?", B. Price. *New York Times Magazine*, pp. 38-40+ (June 11, 1972).

Congressional Record, 1972.

Congressional Quarterly Almanac, 1945-70.

Congressional Quarterly Weekly Report, 1970-71.

Almanac of American Politics, pp. 313-16.

Cook, Gay, and Dale Pullen. *Margaret Chase Smith, Republican Senator from Maine.* [Washington, D.C., Grossman Publishers, c1972]. [26p.] (Ralph Nader Congress Project. Citizens Look At Congress.)

Fleming, Alice (Mulcahy). *The Senator from Maine: Margaret Chase Smith.* New York, Crowell, 1969. 136p. (Women of America) for juvenile readers.

Graham, Frank, Jr. *Margaret Chase Smith: Woman of Courage.* New York, John Day [c1964]. 187p. ports. "Not intended to be a formal biography of Margaret Chase Smith. It is, rather, designed to describe the professional life of a United States Senator."

Gruberg, passim.

Lamson, Peggy. *Few Are Chosen*, pp. 3-29 and passim.

Paxton, pp. 75-81.

Works by Margaret Chase Smith

Declaration of Conscience. Ed. by William C. Lewis, Jr. Garden City, N.Y., Doubleday, 1972. ix, 512p.

EVA BOWRING   (Mrs. Arthur Bowring)
Republican, Nebraska
1954

Mrs. Rebecca Felton had been the first woman Senator for Georgia, followed by Mrs. Caraway for Arkansas, Mrs. Long for Louisiana, Miss Pyle and Mrs. Bushfield both for South Dakota. Now another small state sent two more women Senators to Washington, both in 1954. Mrs. Bowring was the first of the two to be appointed, but her term lasted only seven months.

Bibliography

"Cowbells in Politics," *U.S. News* 36:16 (Apr. 30, 1954).
"Farm (and City) Policy," *Time* 64:13 (July 5, 1954).
"I Could Use a Horse," *Newsweek* 43:23 (May 10, 1954).
"Lady From Bar 99," *Time* 63:28 (Apr. 26, 1954).
"Lady From the Sandhills," R. G. Donovan. *Independent Woman* 33:204-206 (June 1954).
"Senate's Woman Rancher," *Scholastic* 64:16 (Apr. 28, 1954).
Gruberg, pp. 127, 141.

HAZEL HOLLAND ABEL   (Mrs. George P. Abel)
Republican, Nebraska
1954-55

The second woman Senator from Nebraska was Hazel Abel, whose two-month term was only to fill out the remainder of the late Senator Dwight P. Griswold's term.

Bibliography

"Lady from Nebraska," *Newsweek* 44:20 (Dec. 20, 1954).
Gruberg, p. 127.

MAURINE BROWN NEUBERGER   (Mrs. Richard Neuberger)
Democrat, Oregon
1960-66

Mrs. Neuberger, whose husband, the U.S. Senator from Oregon, died in office of a cerebral hemorrhage, was elected to one full term in Congress. A 1929 graduate of the University of Oregon, she had taught English and physical education in high school for 12 years. Being an excellent grassroots campaigner, she helped her husband achieve election to the Oregon State Senate in 1948. She had been active in the League of Women Voters, and she was herself elected to the Oregon House of Representatives; while there she occupied herself with consumer and education legislation. Since their salaries as elected officials in the Oregon legislature were small, they made their living chiefly by free-lance journalism. She had two terms in the Oregon legislature, from 1951 to 1955. While her husband was United States Senator, she worked with him, without salary, in his office.

Mrs. Neuberger advocated federal medical aid to old people, also federal aid to education and an improved federal housing program. One of her early measures in the U.S. Senate was to authorize federal financial contributions to presidential and Congressional candidates, and to put ceilings on election expenditures. She also voted for a five-year program for educational television facilities, temporary extension of unemployment compensation, and an increase in the minimum wage; but she voted against billboards on highways. Her committee assignments were Agriculture and Forestry, and Banking and Currency. She was

also a member of the special committee on aging, which was to study and investigate problems of the aging and to report its findings to the Senate; that special
committee could make recommendations, but it could not report legislation.
Health, education, and consumer problems were her areas in the Senate. She
wanted women to be active in politics; feeling that they were less corruptible
than men.

Although she was the daughter of dairy farmers, she helped kill a milk
control law that kept prices too high; she also fought for an end to the prohibition against colored margarine. In the first session of the 87th Congress, she
worked for area redevelopment and for billboard control; in the 88th Congress
her main thrusts were against air pollution and for Congressional ethics; she
advocated strong regulation of cigarette advertising. A bill to require truth in lending was recommitted, thus killed, because of strong opposition from private finance companies, bankers, department stores and other business interests. Along
with Senators Douglas, Joseph Clark, Proxmire and Muskie, she voted against
recommittal.

In the 89th Congress, in 1965, the Senate unanimously confirmed the nomination of Carl Bagge to the Federal Power Commission. Mrs. Neuberger voted
against him because she questioned his role in a dispute over a plan for a racially
integrated housing project in Deerfield, Illinois. In the second session of the 89th
Congress, in 1966, Mrs. Neuberger introduced more than 100 bills. One of them
was to save a section of the Oregon coast near Coos Bay; her original bill had
called for a sanctuary of 44,000 acres (1963) but it was later scaled down to
30,000. Nevertheless, it did not carry, and the Senate took no further action in
1966. Mrs. Neuberger voluntarily retired at the close of 1966; she was 59. In her
stead Oregonians elected Mark Hatfield.

Bibliography

"Crusaders Widow," *Newsweek* 55:42-43 (Mar. 21, 1960).
"Madam Senator from Oregon," R. Cahn. *Saturday Evening Post* 234:24-25
        (Jan. 7, 1961).
"People of the Week," *U.S. News* 48:25 (Mar. 21, 1960).
"Let's Stop the Ladies from Joining the Ladies," *McCalls* 88:110-11+ (Sept.
        1961).
"Head Winds, Filibuster by Liberals," *Time* 80:11 (Aug. 10, 1962).
"Lady from Oregon," W. S. White. *Harpers* 223:98+ (Oct. 1961).
"Hazards of Teenage Smoking," excerpt from "Smoke Screen: Tobacco and
        the Public Welfare," *Parents Magazine* 39:51+ (Jan. 1964).
"Tobacco and the Public Welfare," *PTA Magazine* 58:10-11 (May 1964).
"Jar of Hope," *Newsweek* 65:64 (May 31, 1965).
Gruberg, pp. 127-28 and passim.
Current Biography, 1961.
Congressional Quarterly Almanac, 1961-66.
"The View From the Highway: America's Newest Roads [Interstate Highway
        System Inaugurated by Congress in 1956] Are in Danger of Becoming
        Corridors Lined with Billboards if the States Do Not Soon Take Advantage
        of the Federal Law," *Country Beautiful* 2:22-27 (Mar. 1963).

"Footnotes on Politics by a Lady Legislator," *New York Times Magazine*, p. 18, (May 27, 1951).

ELAINE EDWARDS (Mrs. Edwin Edwards)
Democrat, Louisiana
1972

For about six months in 1972 there were two United States women Senators—one of them was Mrs. Margaret Chase Smith, who was serving her fourth full six-year term; the other was Mrs. Elaine Edwards. She had been placed in the Senate as a "strictly interim appointment" to succeed Senator Allen Ellender of Louisiana after his death in July 1972. The appointment was made by Edwin Edwards, governor of Louisiana, Mrs. Edwards' husband. Before being elected governor, he had represented a Louisiana district in the House. As soon as Ellender's full-term successor was elected in November, Mrs. Edwards resigned her post. She presided several times over the sessions of the Senate, once preventing threatened fisticuffs between Norris Cotton of New Hampshire and Jacob Javits of New York.

With Mrs. Edward's departure and Mrs. Smith's defeat, there is an all-male Senate for the first time in nearly 20 years.

Bibliography

Newsweek, p. 40, with portrait (Aug. 14, 1972).
Congressional Quarterly Weekly Report, 1972.

A CHRONOLOGICAL LIST
HOUSE OF REPRESENTATIVES

Name	Party	State	Years Served
Miss Jeannette Rankin	R	Montana	1917-19; 1942-43
Mrs. Alice M. Robertson	R	Oklahoma	1921-23
Mrs. Winifred Sprague Mason Huck	R	Illinois	1922-23
Mrs. Mae Ella Nolan	R	California	1923-25
Mrs. Florence P. Kahn	R	California	1925-37
Mrs. Mary T. Norton	D	New Jersey	1925-51
Mrs. Edith Nourse Rogers	R	Massachusetts	1925-60
Mrs. Katherine Langley	R	Kentucky	1927-31
Mrs. Pearl P. Oldfield	D	Arkansas	1929-31
Mrs. Ruth Hanna McCormick	R	Illinois	1929-31
Mrs. Ruth Bryan Owen	D	Florida	1929-33
Mrs. Ruth Baker Pratt	R	New York	1929-33
Mrs. Effiegene Wingo	D	Arkansas	1930-33
Mrs. Willa B. Eslick	D	Tennessee	1932-33
Mrs. Virginia Ellis Jenckes	D	Indiana	1933-39
Mrs. Kathryn O'Loughlin McCarthy	D	Kansas	1933-35
Mrs. Marian Williams Clarke	R	New York	1934-35
Mrs. Isabella Greenway	D	Arizona	1934-37
Mrs. Caroline O'Day	D	New York	1935-43
Mrs. Nan Wood Honeyman	D	Oregon	1937-39
Miss Jessie Sumner	R	Illinois	1937-47
Mrs. Bessie Hawley Gasque	D	South Carolina	1939
Mrs. Clara G. McMillan	D	South Carolina	1940-41
Mrs. Florence R. Gibbs	D	Georgia	1940-41
Mrs. Frances P. Bolton	R	Ohio	1940-69
Mrs. Katharine Edgar Byron	D	Maryland	1941-43
Mrs. Veronica Boland	D	Pennsylvania	1942-43
Mrs. Clare Boothe Luce	R	Connecticut	1943-47
Miss Winifred C. Stanley	R	New York	1943-45
Mrs. Willa E. Fulmer	D	South Carolina	1944-45
Mrs. Emily Taft Douglas	D	Illinois	1945-47
Mrs. Helen Gahagan Douglas	D	California	1945-51
Mrs. Chase Going Woodhouse	D	Connecticut	1945-47; 1949-51
Mrs. Helen Douglas Mankin	D	Georgia	1946-47
Miss Eliza Jane Pratt	D	North Carolina	1946-47
Mrs. Georgia L. Lusk	D	New Mexico	1947-49
Mrs. Katherine St. George	R	New York	1947-65
Mrs. Reva Beck Bosone	D	Utah	1949-53
Mrs. Cecil M. Harden	R	Indiana	1949-59

Name	Party	State	Years Served
Mrs. Edna E. Kelly	D	New York	1949-69
Mrs. Vera Buchanan	D	Pennsylvania	1951-55
Mrs. Elizabeth Kee	D	West Virginia	1951-65
Mrs. Marguerite Stitt Church	R	Illinois	1951-63
Miss Ruth Thompson	R	Michigan	1951-57
Mrs. Leonor K. Sullivan	D	Missouri	1953-
Mrs. Gracie Pfost	D	Idaho	1953-63
Mrs. Elizabeth Farrington	R	Hawaii	1954-57
Mrs. Iris Blitch	D	Georgia	1955-63
Mrs. Edith Green	D	Oregon	1955-
Mrs. Martha Griffiths	D	Michigan	1955-
Mrs. Coya Knutson	D	Minnesota	1955-59
Mrs. Kathryn O. Granahan	D	Pennsylvania	1956-63
Mrs. Florence P. Dwyer	R	New Jersey	1957-72
Mrs. Catherine May	R	Washington	1959-70
Mrs. Edna Simpson	R	Illinois	1959-61
Mrs. Jessie McCullough Weis	R	New York	1959-63
Mrs. Julia Butler Hansen	D	Washington	1960-
Mrs. Louise G. Reece	R	Tennessee	1961-63
Mrs. Catherine D. Norrell	D	Arkansas	1961-63
Mrs. Corinne Boyd Riley	D	South Carolina	1962-63
Mrs. Charlotte T. Reid	R	Illinois	1963-71
Mrs. Howard H. Baker	R	Tennessee	1964-65
Mrs. Patsy T. Mink	D	Hawaii	1965-
Mrs. Lera M. Thomas	D	Texas	1966-67
Mrs. Margaret M. Heckler	R	Massachusetts	1967-
Mrs. Shirley A. Chisholm	D	New York	1969-
Mrs. Bella Abzug	D	New York	1971-
Mrs. Ella T. Grasso	D	Connecticut	1971-
Mrs. Louise D. Hicks	D	Massachusetts	1971-73
Mrs. Elizabeth Andrews	D	Alabama	1972

A CHRONOLOGICAL LIST
SENATE

Name	Party	State	Years Served
Mrs. Rebecca L. Felton	Ind. D	Georgia	1922
Mrs. Hattie W. Caraway	D	Arkansas	1931-45
Mrs. Rose McConnell Long	D	Louisiana	1936
Mrs. Dixie Bibb Graves	D	Alabama	1938-39
Miss Gladys Pyle	R	South Dakota	1938-39
Mrs. Vera Bushfield	R	South Dakota	1948-49
Mrs. Margaret Chase Smith*	R	Maine	1949-73
Mrs. Eva Bowring	R	Nebraska	1954
Mrs. Hazel Abel	R	Nebraska	1954-55
Mrs. Maurine B. Neuberger	D	Oregon	1961-67
Mrs. Edwin Edwards	D	Louisiana	1972

---

*Served in House of Representatives before becoming Senator, as Republican from Maine (1940-48).

AN ALPHABETICAL LIST
HOUSE OF REPRESENTATIVES

Name	Party	State	Years Served
Abzug, Mrs. Bella S.	D	New York	1971-
Andrews, Mrs. Elizabeth	D	Alabama	1972-
Baker, Mrs. Irene B.	R	Tennessee	1964-65
Blitch, Mrs. Iris	D	Georgia	1955-63
Boland, Mrs. Veronica B.	D	Pennsylvania	1942-43
Bolton, Mrs. Frances P.	R	Ohio	1940-69
Bosone, Mrs. Reva Beck	D	Utah	1949-53
Buchanan, Mrs. Vera	D	Pennsylvania	1951-55
Byron, Mrs. Katharine Edgar	D	Maryland	1941-43
Chisholm, Mrs. Shirley A.	D	New York	1969-
Church, Mrs. Marguerite Stitt	R	Illinois	1951-63
Clarke, Mrs. Marian Williams	R	New York	1933-35
Douglas, Mrs. Emily Taft	D	Illinois	1945-47
Douglas, Mrs. Helen Gahagan	D	California	1945-51
Dwyer, Mrs. Florence P.	R	New Jersey	1957-72
Eslick, Mrs. Willa B.	D	Tennessee	1932-33
Farrington, Mrs. Elizabeth	R	Hawaii	1954-57
Fulmer, Mrs. Willa L.	D	South Carolina	1944-45
Gasque, Mrs. Bessie Hawley	D	South Carolina	1938-39
Gibbs, Mrs. Florence R.	D	Georgia	1940-41
Granahan, Mrs. Kathryn O.	D	Pennsylvania	1956-63
Grasso, Mrs. Ella Tambusi	D	Connecticut	1971-
Green, Mrs. Edith	D	Oregon	1955-
Greenway, Mrs. Isabella	D	Arizona	1933-37
Griffiths, Mrs. Martha W.	D	Michigan	1955-
Hansen, Mrs. Julia B.	D	Washington	1960-
Harden, Mrs. Cecil M.	R	Indiana	1949-59
Heckler, Mrs. Margaret M.	R	Massachusetts	1967-
Hicks, Mrs. Louise D.	D	Massachusetts	1971-73
Honeyman, Mrs. Nan Wood	D	Oregon	1937-39
Huck, Mrs. Winifred Sprague Mason	R	Illinois	1922-23
Jenckes, Mrs. Virginia Ellis	D	Indiana	1933-39
Kahn, Mrs. Florence P.	R	California	1925-37
Kee, Mrs. Elizabeth	D	West Virginia	1951-65
Kelly, Mrs. Edna F.	D	New York	1949-69
Knutson, Mrs. Coya	D	Minnesota	1955-59
Langley, Mrs. Katherine	R	Kentucky	1927-31
Luce, Mrs. Clare Boothe	R	Connecticut	1943-47
Lusk, Mrs. Georgia L.	D	New Mexico	1947-49

Name	Party	State	Years Served
McCarthy, Mrs. Kathryn O'Loughlin	D	Kansas	1933-35
McCormick, Mrs. Ruth Hanna	R	Illinois	1929-31
McMillan, Mrs. Clara G.	D	South Carolina	1939-41
Mankin, Mrs. Helen Douglas	D	Georgia	1946-47
May, Mrs. Catherine	R	Washington	1959-70
Mink, Mrs. Patsy T.	D	Hawaii	1965-
Nolan, Mrs. Mae Ella	R	California	1921-25
Norrell, Mrs. Catherine D.	D	Arkansas	1961-63
Norton, Mrs. Mary T.	D	New Jersey	1925-51
O'Day, Mrs. Caroline	D	New York	1935-43
Oldfield, Mrs. Pearl P.	D	Arkansas	1929-31
Owen, Mrs. Ruth Bryan	D	Florida	1929-33
Pfost, Mrs. Gracie	D	Idaho	1953-63
Pratt, Mrs. Eliza Jane	D	North Carolina	1946-47
Pratt, Mrs. Ruth Baker	R	New York	1929-33
Rankin, Miss Jeannette	R	Montana	1917-19; 1942-43
Reece, Mrs. Louise G.	R	Tennessee	1961-63
Reid, Mrs. Charlotte T.	R	Illinois	1963-71
Riley, Mrs. Corinne Boyd	D	South Carolina	1962-63
Robertson, Miss Alice M.	R	Oklahoma	1921-23
Rogers, Mrs. Edith Nourse	R	Massachusetts	1925-60
St. George, Mrs. Katherine	R	New York	1947-65
Simpson, Mrs. Edna	R	Illinois	1959-61
Stanley, Miss Winifred C.	R	New York	1943-45
Sullivan, Mrs. Leonor K.	D	Missouri	1953-
Sumner, Miss Jessie	R	Illinois	1939-47
Thomas, Mrs. Lera M.	D	Texas	1966-67
Thompson, Miss Ruth	R	Michigan	1951-57
Weis, Mrs. Jessie McC.	R	New York	1959-63
Wingo, Mrs. Effiegene	D	Arkansas	1930-33
Woodhouse, Mrs. Chase Going	D	Connecticut	1945-47; 1949-51

AN ALPHABETICAL LIST
SENATE

Name	Party	State	Years Served
Abel, Mrs. Hazel	R	Nebraska	1954-55
Bowring, Mrs. Eva	R	Nebraska	1954
Bushfield, Mrs. Vera	R	South Dakota	1948-49
Caraway, Mrs. Hattie W.	D	Arkansas	1931-45
Edwards, Mrs. Edwin	D	Louisiana	1972
Felton, Mrs. Rebecca Latimer	Ind. D	Georgia	1922
Graves, Mrs. Dixie Bibb	D	Alabama	1937-38
Long, Mrs. Rose McConnell	D	Louisiana	1936-37
Neuberger, Mrs. Maurine	D	Oregon	1961-67
Pyle, Miss Gladys	R	South Dakota	1938-39
Smith, Mrs. Margaret Chase*	R	Maine	1949-73

*Mrs. Smith also served in the House, 1940-48, before being elected to the Senate.

ABBREVIATIONS AND DEFINITIONS
OF TERMS

ABM: Antiballistic missile system, called "Safeguard." An amendment to delete funds for its further development was defeated in the Senate 50:50, but Agnew's tiebreaking vote tipped the scales in favor of ABM.

Act: A bill, passed by both Houses, signed by the President, or passed over his veto, thus becoming a federal law.

Amendment: Proposal to alter language or stipulation of a bill or an act.

Appropriations Bill: Funds for federal outlays first have to be authorized by Congress; then an appropriation bill is introduced, usually in the House, which actually approves and appropriates the funds named in the authorization bill.

Bill: Legislation that originates in House or Senate. Written by a member, a bill is placed in the hopper, a box on the Clerk's desk where bills are collected. Bills may be either private or public. Private bills are for the benefit of specified individuals, public bills are for general legislation. The period of time from the introduction of a bill to its becoming public law is long and the way is devious; most bills introduced never become law.

Committee: Discusses bills introduced and prepares them for a vote in the House, or disregards them. The House has 21 standing (permanent) committees, the Senate has 17; almost every full committee has one or more subcommittees (the total is more than 200). There are also several important joint committees with members from both Senate and House, and there are special and ad hoc committees.

Committee of the Whole: It takes a hundred or more representatives on the floor of the House to form the Committee of the Whole. It is generally concerned with important legislation, and it is a way of speeding up action. When the Committee of the Whole sits, the Speaker's place is taken by a chairman.

Conference: Designated House and Senate members meet to iron out differences in bills passed by either House on the same subject. The members of the Conference meeting are appointed by the leadership of the House and Senate. Their report is sent to both Houses for approval or rejection; it cannot be amended by the whole body, and if not accepted must be returned to the Conference committee for further action.

Congressional Record: The daily proceedings in both Houses, reported verbatim. A Digest at the end of each issue reports the highlights of remarks made on the floor and committee action.

Consent Calendar: Any bill on the Union Calendar or House Calendar, normally called for action on the first or third Monday each month.

Cooper-Church: After Nixon invaded Cambodia in April 1969, Senators Church and Cooper attached an amendment to a military appropriation bill prohibiting use of funds for military operations in Cambodia without specific Congressional authorization after June 30, 1970.

Clean Water Funds: HR14159, introduced in 1969, for $1 billion in appropriations to fight water pollution.

Commuter Tax: HR2076, defeated August 3, 1970, which would have allowed federal agencies to withhold municipal taxes from the paychecks of their employees.

Eighteen-year-old Vote: The bill to give the right to vote to citizens 18 years old or older, pursuant to HR4249, the Voting Rights Act.

Family Assistance Plan: HR16311, a welfare reform bill, passed April 16, 1970. Its purpose was to provide a national minimum of $1,600 per year to a family; it was first supported by Nixon, later sabotaged by him; died in Senate.

Farm Subsidies Limit: A bill to limit to $20,000 per year the federal payments to an individual farm for growing nothing. Senator Eastland had received subsidies of nearly $150,000 for one year.

House Calendar: It lists public bills for action, but not bills whose purpose is to raise revenue.

Jets to Chiang: A bill to provide more than $50 million for funds for military jets to Taiwan.

Joint Resolution: Like a bill, it requires approval by both Houses of the Congress and the President to become law.

Law: A bill approved and passed by both Houses and signed by the President; a bill also becomes law if a presidential veto is overridden.

Lobby: A group of persons seeking to influence legislation before the Congress, either to pass or defeat it. The right to lobby is inherent in the first amendment ["petition the government for a redress of grievances"]. Used as verb and noun.

Majority Leader: The chief strategist and floor spokesman of the majority party in House and Senate, chosen by the membership to channel legislation and procedure.

Majority Whip: Assistant to the majority leader in both House and Senate; the minority party has its own minority leader and minority whip.

Migratory Workers Compensation: Unemployment compensation for migratory agricultural workers, if six or more such workers are employed for six months a year by an employer, the compensation to be paid by the federal-state compensation system. If it had passed, it would have made eligible for unemployment payment hundreds of thousands of poorly paid workers.

No-Knock: Legislation for a separate law system for the District of Columbia, containing a provision allowing entry of a dwelling without notice, with a search warrant by police officers. Passed.

Override Veto: If the President vetoes legislation, both Houses may override the veto by a two-thirds vote of House and Senate; the bill then becomes law over the President's veto.

Park Logging: A bill strongly backed by the timber industry—and just as strongly condemned by conservationists—to allow more tree cutting in national forests; it was defeated February 26, 1970.

Philadelphia Plan: Gives federal government the right to force use of minority labor on federal construction projects; objected to by white construction workers; Nixon dropped the plan.

Quorum: A majority in either House; requires the presence of 51 Senators and of 218 Representatives. However, if the House sits as a Committee of the Whole, a quorum consists of only 100.

Recommit: A motion made on the floor to return a piece of legislation to the committee that originated it. This is usually tantamount to killing it.

Record Vote: The most meaningful vote taken by the Congress. It requires an alphabetic roll call of the membership; each member answers "yea," "nay," or "present" (if he declines a vote). A record vote is required to override a veto, and also if a record vote is demanded by 15 members present. This vote provides a clear record of the stand taken by a member.

SST: Supersonic Transport Plane. Funds for continuation of the building program were denied by rather narrow majorities in both Houses in March and May, 1971.

Select or Special Committee: A committee set up for a specific purpose for a limited time.

Standing Vote: Members approving a bill stand up and are counted; then those who opposed stand up to be counted. This type of vote does not provide a record of how each member voted.

Teller Vote: A vote used in the House only, in which members file past a teller to be counted either for or against a measure.

Union Calendar: A bill appropriating money or raising revenue is placed on the Calendar, in chronological sequence, by the committee reporting it.

Veto: President disapproves of a bill or joint resolution and refuses to sign it into law. He must do this within 10 days after receipt if the Congress is in session, otherwise it becomes law anyway. If Congress submits a bill to him within 10 days of its adjournment, he may "pocket veto" it by taking no action. This does not apply to a constitutional amendment, which needs no presidential signature.

Voice Vote: Used in both Houses; members simply say "aye" or "no" in chorus. The presiding officer then decides the result, which makes it a questionable device. However, it is used not infrequently when something is decided "without objection."

SUBJECT BIBLIOGRAPHY

This selective bibliography is arranged by subject. Books listed in this bibliography are indexed by author beginning on page 174. It should be noted that books and articles by and about individual women members of Congress are listed at the end of each members biographical sketch.

ABORTION

Schulder, Diane, and Florynce Kennedy.

Abortion Rap. New York, McGraw-Hill, 1971. xvi, 238p.

Describes legal cases presented to New York Court on behalf of more than 100 plaintiffs, some of whom tell harrowing stories of illegally performed abortions. Includes evidence from medical personnel and others. The evidence did not reach trial because the state of New York moderated its abortion laws. Interesting and at times gripping, but poorly organized. Includes cases of unwed mothers; abortion clinics; and abortion in London (illegal) and Japan (legal). Contains remarks of legal personnel, of women called, and of such non-legal experts as theological scholars, health workers, and researchers.

BIOGRAPHICAL DICTIONARIES

Current Biography. New York, H. W. Wilson, 1940– .

Current Biography, which is now in its fourth decade, aims to provide the reference librarian, the student and researcher with brief, objective, accurate, and well-documented biographic articles about living leaders in all fields of human accomplishment the world over. New and updated biographic sketches supersede earlier, outdated ones; newspapers, magazines, authoritative reference books and news releases of governmental and private agencies provide the facts. The articles run from two to three pages in length, with key to pronunciation of name, birth date, profession, address, and other information available; there are references at the end of the article and portraits are found for most biographees. Ten-year indexes for 1951-60 and 1961-70 reveal only a few Congresswomen, namely Green, Griffiths, and Mink. The 1972 edition lists not a single Congresswoman.

Foremost Women in Communications: A Biographical Reference Work on Accomplished Women in Broadcasting, Publishing, Advertising, Public Relations and Allied Professions. New York, Foremost American Publishing Company, 1970. xxii, 788p. ports.

Index to Women of the World from Ancient to Modern Times. Biographies and portraits by Norma Olin Ireland. Westwood, Mass., F. W. Faxon, 1970. 573p.

Notable American Women 1607-1950: A Biographical Dictionary. Edward
T. James, ed. Cambridge, Mass., Belknap Press of Harvard University
Press, 1971. 3v.

This work has articles on 1,359 women. (The *Dictionary of American
Biography*'s 15,000 entries include only 700 women.) All subjects had
ended their active careers by 1920, and were dead by 1950. The signed
articles, which vary from 400 to 7,000 words in length, were prepared by
738 contributors. The biographees are arranged alphabetically by name; in
volume 3 there are classified lists of biographees such as feminists, peace
advocates, and political figures. Among political personalities are Senators
Caraway and Felton, and Congresswomen Huck, Kahn, Langley, O'Day,
Robertson, and Ruth Hanna McCormick Simms, usually known as Ruth
Hanna McCormick. To be included, biographees had to possess distinction
in their own right, and the distinction had to be of more than local signifi-
cance; the only women entered on their husbands' credentials are the wives
of presidents. The associate editor has supplied an interesting introduction
narrating the development of the American woman's status. Each article
concludes with a bibliography. Since the scope of the work in general pre-
cluded inclusion of women who distinguished themselves after 1920, there
are included only a handful of the 81 Congresswomen who served between
1917 and 1972.

Who's Who in America. 1972-1973. Chicago, Marquis Who's Who, 1972.

Who's Who in America for 1972-1973 has entries for the president,
vice-president, members of the cabinet, federal judges governors of states,
state attorneys-general, heads of universities and colleges, generals and
admirals; additionally, it covers many outstanding personalities in business,
the professions, the arts and sciences, as well as the members of Congress
serving in the 92nd Congress. The articles follow the same specifications
for inclusion, but vary greatly as to length; Bella Abzug, for instance, has
11 lines, Patsy Mink 18, and so forth. This publication is now in its 37th
edition and entries for Congresswomen no longer in active service may be
found in previous editions.

*Who's Who in American Politics, 1971-72: A Biographical Directory of
United States Political Leaders.* 3rd ed. Ed. by Paul A. Theis and
Edmund L. Henshaw, Jr. New York, Bowker, 1971– . xxv, 1171p.

This biographic directory of United States political leaders compiled
by the Jaques Cattell press, lists 15,800 political leaders. *Saturday Review*
said of its first (1967-68) edition that it "filled a genuine need in reference
literature." Its editorial Advisory Committee consists of six members,
among whom is listed Governor Ronald Reagan of California. On its intro-
ductory pages are listed the president and his cabinet, the state delegations
to the 92nd Congress, and the governors and lieutenant governors of the
states, with a geographic index for political leaders from all states including U.S. possessions such as American Samoa, Guam, Puerto Rico, and

the Virgin Islands. Among women, Abzug rates 7 lines, Chisholm 25, and Sullivan 10, to give some examples.

Who's Who in Government, 1972-1973. Chicago, Marquis Who's Who, 1972. 785p.

The more than 16,000 listings in this first edition provide biographic data about men and women in all branches of the federal government, with selected entries for officials in local, state and international government. It is useful for businessmen, students, researchers and scholars. It has two indexes, one of which lists biographees by department, bureau, office, or agency, while the other lists biographees by topic, such as census statistics, foreign aid, drug abuse, etc. In the majority of cases men and women supplied their own data, which was reviewed before it was written in sketch form, then sent back for verification by the biographee, rechecked and then put in final form. The key to information includes name, position, vital statistics, parents, education, marital status, children, career, career-related activities, civil activities, political activities, military record, political affiliation, religion, writings, address, and other facts. In the index of biographees by topic, Hansen, for instance, appears listed under Appropriations—House, Heckler under Banking and Currency, Smith under Armed Services. For members of Congress, committee memberships, Washington address, and election data may be found. Such information is also available from Congressional Quarterly Weekly Service, which also provides much more pertinent factual data on voting, political activities, speeches etc. *Who's Who in Government* gives Abzug 11 lines, Chisholm 20, Green 25, Griffiths 13, Hansen 15, and Dwyer only 7.

Who's Who of American Women. 8th ed., 1974-1975. Chicago, Marquis Who's Who, 1973. xiv, 1072p.

Another source of vital statistics and biographic information is *Who's Who of American Women*, now in its 8th edition, also a Marquis publication. It claims that its accounts are based on a continuing examination of newspapers, magazines, journals, books by and about women, and the output of all other communications media and that of research associations. Most of the biographees have furnished their own data. Admission is based on two factors: the position of responsibility held and the achievements in the subject's field. All Congresswomen have been entered with accounts of varying length—e.g., Abzug has 12 lines, Chisholm 24, Dwyer 4, Green 27, and so forth.

Women Members of the 83rd Congress. Washington, U.S. Women's Bureau, 1947— .

Published at irregular intervals. Title varies. Varies in size from a few looseleaf pages to 45 pages for the 87th Congress. Mostly brief biographical remarks with hints of legislative interests in some cases. Available from 81st to 90th Congresses.

CIVIL RIGHTS

Fraenkel, Osmond R.

The Rights We Have. New York, T. Y. Crowell, 1971. x, 246p.

Discusses rights under the Constitution and the Bill of Rights: the right to self-expression, to privacy, to freedom of religion, to freedom of association and assembly, to due process of law, and many others. There are 54 headings and many subsections. The author warns the citizen not to bank too confidently on the laws given the individual citizen; the Supreme Court has many times provided contradicting interpretations of the Constitution.

CONGRESS—Books

Biographical Directory of the American Congress, 1774-1971. Washington, D.C., Government Printing Office, 1971. 1972p.

This work incorporates the salient facts of all annual issues in one large volume of nearly 2,000 pages. Presented by the Joint Committee on Printing, it contains 10,800 individual biographies, starting with a listing of executive officers from 1789 to 1971, proceeding to the Continental Congress, and thereafter to the 1st through 91st Congresses and their members. There are, on an average, seven biographies to the page; the members of the 92nd Congress serving their first term in 1971 (54 of them) are given only one line each. Biographies of the others are found on pages 487 to 1,972, arranged alphabetically by name. This is a good retrospective tool. Senator Caraway receives 16 lines, Chisholm 10, Heckler 11, Mink 18, Dwyer 9; Abzug and other novices have to be satisfied with one line each. Mrs. Andrews and Mrs. Edwards, who had only temporary appointments, are, of course, not named at all.

Congressional Quarterly Service.

Congressional Roll Call: A Chronology and Analysis of Votes in the House and Senate, 91st Congress, 1st Session. Washington, D.C., 1970. 51, 81H, 46S, 8Ap.

If a Congressman objects to a vote having been taken because he thinks a quorum was lacking, there may be an automatic roll call vote. (Quorum for the Senate is 51; for the House 218; and for the Committee of the Whole, 100.)

The Almanac of American Politics: The Senators, the Representatives, Their Records, States and Districts. By Michel Barone, Grant Ujifusa, and Douglas Matthews. Boston, Gambit, 1972. xxv, 1030p. ports.

The title is self-explanatory. There are about two pages for each member of Congress; their records are for the first session of the 92nd Congress. To be kept up to date.

Congressional Quarterly Almanac. Washington, Congressional Quarterly, 1945– . v.1– .

Has about 1,600 pages annually. Distills and reorganizes the information from the weekly issues, with important issues treated in depth. Good index.

Congressional Quarterly Weekly Report, 1943– . v.1– . Washington, Congressional Quarterly, Inc.

Analyzes major issues and pressures; gives committee assignments, votes, lobbies; discusses and analyzes legislation.

Congressional Quarterly Service.

Congress and the Nation: A Review of Government and Politics in the Postwar Years. Washington, 1965-69. 2v. illus.

Vol. 1, 1945-1964; Vol. 2, 1965-1968. Chapters are as follows: (1) politics and national issues; (2) foreign policy; (3) national security policy; (4) economic policy; (5) labor; (6) agriculture; (7) national resources and power; (8) health, education, and welfare; (9) veterans; (10) federal-state relations; (11) Congress, the executive and the courts; (12) statehood and territories; (13) election law; (14) lobbies; (15) civil rights; (16) civil liberties and internal security; (17) investigations.

Congressional Quarterly Service.

Guide to the Congress of the United States: Origins, History and Procedure. Washington, 1971. xxxi, 639, 323a, 21b p.

(1) Origins and development of Congress; (2) Congress at work; (3) powers of Congress; (4) housing and support of Congress; (5) Congress and the electorate; (6) pressures on Congress (Constitution, lobbies, executive branch, Supreme Court, internal pressures).

Congressional Quarterly Service.

Members of Congress 1945-70. Washington, 1970. 47p.

Green, Marc J., James M. Fallows, and David R. Zwick.

Who Runs Congress? Preface by Robert C. Fellmeth. Introduction by Ralph Nader. New York, Grossman Publishers, 1972. x, 307p. (Ralph Nader Congress Project). (A Bantam-Grossman Book).

Archaic rules of procedure and seniority, encroaching executive power, and influence of lobbies strip Congress of independent action. Tells what Congressmen do and how they stay elected. Critical, with copious examples of undemocratic behavior.

Manley, John F.

> *The Politics of Finance: The House Committee on Ways and Means.*
> Boston, Little, Brown and Company, 1970. 395p. (The Study of
> Congress Series).

> A study of what many observers consider the most important Con-
> gressional Committee, concerned with tax policy, Medicare, social welfare
> issues, reciprocal trade, and tariff control questions. Based on interviews
> with 30 members. Recruitment to Committee. Examines Wilbur M. Mills
> in action and examines his crucial role in the Committee. Other chapters
> deal with relations with the rest of the House membership, interaction
> with the Senate, and executive-legislative relations. In addition to inter-
> views, uses public records back to 1933 and roll call votes. Many tables
> and figures.

Mayhew, David.

> *The 92nd Congress and Its Committees.* Washington, The Center of
> Information on America, 1971. 22p. (Grass Roots Guides).

> Dr. Mayhew is a member of the Department of Political Science at
> Yale University.

National Journal: Intelligence Reports on Federal Policy Making. Washing-
> ton, D.C., Center for Political Research, 1969 .

> This publication, which began publication in 1969, is published by
> the Center for Political Research, appears weekly, has articles on important
> topics, records roll call votes and other crucial information, and is similar
> in nature to the *Congressional Almanac*, although less extensive in scope.

Saloma, John S., III.

> *Congress and the New Politics.* Boston, Little, Brown and Company,
> 1969. xix, 293p. (The Study of Congress Series).

> The body of the book evaluates six major functions of Congress:
> representation, lawmaking, oversight and control of administration, investi-
> gation, education and information, and constituent service. In the author's
> judgment contemporary Congress has demonstrated considerable vitality,
> innovative response, and adaptation. Reform of Congress is not a target of
> this work.

Tacheron, Donald G., and Morris K. Udall.

> *The Job of the Congressman: An Introduction to Service in the U.S.
> House of Representatives.* Indianapolis, Bobbs-Merrill, 1966. xv,
> 446p.

> The freshman Congressman is "a lost soul." He finds his role insignifi-
> cant, and the rules of the House are a closed book to him. This book is
> meant to be an orientation for new members. Explains functions of

Congress, powers of the House, organization and operation of the Congressman's office, committee assignments, conflict of interest, parliamentary practice and other topics. Many practical and useful appendixes. Donald Tacheron is Associate Director of the American Political Science Association; Morris Udall is a member of Congress, Second District, Arizona. Many members of Congress contributed to the contents of the book.

U.S. Congress.

> *Official Congressional Directory, 1809-19– .* v.fold, plans. Annual. Washington, U.S. Printing Office.

This annual is published by the U.S. Government Printing Office. It lists Senators and Representatives alphabetically by state, then numerically by Congressional districts. After the biographical paragraphs, there is information on the Senators' and Representatives' terms of service; the committees of Senate and House and their subcommittees, membership in committees and subcommittees; joint committees, commissions and boards; Senate and House committee assignments; the names of administrative assistants and secretaries; and statistical information. This is followed by a description of the Capitol, the capitol buildings and grounds, listings of the Executive Office and the Departments, names of foreign diplomatic representatives, the members of the press galleries and other galleries for the news media, and finally maps of Congressional districts and a long detailed index. There are, on an average, two to three biographical paragraphs for each member of Congress, preceded by an exact outline of the member's district, which may run to more than eight lines. Bella Abzug's district requires ten lines for the description, while her biography and her activities need only 13 lines; Mink has 26 lines, Sullivan 23, Grasso 16. For Senator Smith, there is simply the term "Republican" after her name, and nothing else. Usually listed are vital statistics, education, religious affiliation, membership in associations, election facts, and membership of committees. The *Official Congressional Directory* has appeared annually since 1809.

Zinn, Charles J.

> *How Our Laws Are Made.* Washington, D.C., Government Printing Office, 1969. vi, 57p. (91st Congress, 1st Session. House of Representatives. Document No. 91-127. Presented by Mr. Celler).

A clear, but simplified exposition of the way in which bills are introduced, considered, voted on, accepted, rejected, given final form and sent to the President for signature to become public law. Most of the more than 25,000 bills annually placed into the hopper originate in the House; only a few hundred survive the intense scrutiny to which they are subjected and are enacted into law. With facsimile reproduction of samples. Without index.

CONGRESS–Periodical Articles

"Moonlighting Congressmen," *New Republic*, pp. 6-7 (July 8, 1972).

"The Nader Look," *New Republic* 167:10 (July 22, 1972).

"Nader's Biggest Raid," *Time*, p. 15 (July 31, 1972).

"The New House," *New Republic* 167:7 (July 22, 1972).

"New Look in Store for Congress in '73," *U.S. News*, p. 56 (June 5, 1972).

"The Record Congress is Taking to the Voters," *U.S. News*, pp. 13-14 (Oct. 30, 1972).

"Women in Congress," *Congressional Quarterly Weekly Report*, pt. 2, p. 1745 (1970).

ENVIRONMENT

DeBell, Garrett, ed.

The Voter's Guide to Environmental Politics Before, During and After the Election. Foreword by David Brower. New York, Ballantine Books, 1970. xix, 305p. (Friends of the Earth Series).

Fifteen chapters, by various authors, on recycling, transportation, air pollution, pesticides, the wilderness, stable population and other environmental topics; chapters 11 to 15 discuss regulating the industrial complex, reforming Congress, and understanding Congressional voting records, and they tell how your Congressman voted and how to influence your Congressman. Records all Congressmen's votes on conservation. Many have dismal records; Congresswomen have, on the whole, better records than men. On ten important bills the best records were scored by Dwyer and Griffiths, and the highest favorable score was obtained by Sullivan. (Records taken in the 91st Congress.)

FAMILY

Schur, Edwin M., ed.

The Family and the Sexual Revolution: Selected Readings. Bloomington, Indiana University Press, 1968 (c.1964). xv, 427p.

Contains 28 essays by prominent social scientists and philosophers. Part I, changing sex standards; Part II, the woman problem; Part III, birth control. Contributors are both men and women; among those represented are Alfred C. Kinsey, Bertrand Russell, Piterim A. Sorokin, Margaret Mead, Mirra Komarovski, Bronislaw Malinowski. Intended as a collection of throught-provoking materials, with emphasis on values and policy and a bias toward unconventional views, meant to express diversity of opinion.

UNEMPLOYMENT

"Why America's Unemployment Stays So High," *U.S. News*, p. 53 (Dec. 20, 1971).

WELFARE

"Welfare Myths vs. Facts. HEW's Own Report," *U.S. News*, pp. 54-55 (Dec. 20, 1971).

WOMEN

Beauvoir, Simone de.

The Second Sex. Translated and edited by H. M. Parshley. New York, Knopf, 1957. xxx, 732, xiv p.

First published in France, in 1949, with the title: *Le deuxième sexe.* First published in the U.S. in 1953 (c.1952). A "serious, all inclusive . . . uninhibited work" (p.v). Central thesis: "Since patriarchal times women have in general been forced to occupy a secondary place in the world in relation to man" (p.vii). The myth of woman's secondary position, created by men, is investigated in the works of Montherlant, Lawrence, Claudel, Breton, and Stendhal. Written with deep intellectual discernment and a wealth of scholarship.

Herold, J. Christopher.

Love in Five Temperaments. London, Hamish Hamilton, 1961. xii, 291p. ports.

Five essays on French women of the era of Louis XIV and XV. These women, some of them exceedingly ambitious, others modest, some from the lower classes, some highly and coldly intellectual, others ruled by passionate hearts, were acquainted and associated with all the great literary and scientific lights of that dazzling age. Written with deep understanding, in polished prose. With an excellent bibliography.

Mead, Margaret.

Male and Female: A Study of the Sexes in a Changing World. New York, William Morrow and Company, 1949. xii, 477p.

Gives an anthropologist's view of several primitive tribes of New Guinea, with a chapter on the sexes in contemporary America. With a wealth of detail and deep understanding. Bibliographies.

Mencken, Henry Louis.

In Defense of Women. Rev. New York, Knopf, 1928 (c.1922). xvi, 210p.

First published in 1918; written in the usual exhilerating Mencken style. "My own belief . . . is that the grant of the ballot to women marks the . . . beginning of an improvement in our politics, and, in the end, in our whole theory of government" (p.137). Women are clearheaded, practical, more intelligent; women are nearly always against war; men are sentimental and given to posturing.

Millett, Kate.

Sexual Politics. Garden City, N.Y., Doubleday, 1970. xii, 393p.

An "essay composed of equal parts of literary and cultural criticism" (p.xii). Sex, according to the author, has "a frequently neglected political aspect." A systematic overview of patriarchy as a political institution. Shows male chauvinism in the literary productions of D. H. Lawrence, Henry Miller, Norman Mailer, and Jean Genet. Bibliography.

Women Studies Abstracts. Vol. 1, No. 2, Spring 1972. Ed. by Sara Stauffer Whaley. Rush, N.Y., Women Studies Abstracts, 1972. 99p.

Issued quarterly since Winter 1972, this work has three or four abstracts to the page on education, sex characteristics and employment, society and government, sexuality, family, women in history and literature, and the women's liberation movement. Over 2,000 periodicals are examined (in English and some foreign languages) and articles and books appearing since July 1971 are abstracted. The second issue of 1972 has an essay by Sara Stauffer Whaley on American women in national political life (pp. 1-9, 88-97), discussing Chisholm at some length and taking exception to Senator Smith's remark, "Sex doesn't matter in politics." The index has references to some Congresswomen, especially Bella Abzug. This is a useful publication which we hope will continue.

WOMEN IN AMERICA—Books

America's Twelve Great Women Leaders During the Past Hundred Years, as Chosen by the Women of America. A compilation from the *Ladies Home Journal* and the *Christian Science Monitor*. Chicago, Associated Authors Service, 1933. 55p. ports.

Contents: Jane Addams, founder of Hull House; Susan B. Anthony, woman suffrage leader; Clara Barton, founder of Red Cross; Carrie Chapman Catt, suffragist; Mary Baker Eddy, founder of Christian Science; Julia Ward Howe, composer of the "Battle Hymn of the Republic"; Helen Keller, deaf and blind lecturer; Mary Lyon, founder of Mt. Holyoke College; Amelia Earhart, aviator; Harriet Beecher Stowe, author of *Uncle Tom's Cabin*; Frances E. Willard, founder of the Woman's Christian Temperance Union; Mary E. Woolley, president of Mt. Holyoke.

Amundsen, Kirsten.

The Silenced Majority: Women and American Democracy. Englewood Cliffs, N.J., Prentice-Hall, 1971. viii, 184p.

Examples of discrimination against women in many spheres of public and everyday life. She remarks that her academic discipline has virtually neglected the "woman question."

Andreas, Carol.

Sex and Caste in America. Englewood Cliffs, N.J., Prentice-Hall, 1971. xiv, 146p.

Sex roles are assigned to male and female through education and customs of public life. The doctrines of St. Paul, the teachings of Freud, and the advertising emanating from Madison Avenue strengthen the male in his disregard of the rights of women, and law and morals do the same. But the present offers new possibilities for solving the age-old problem of sexism.

Bardwick, Judith M.

Psychology of Women: A Study of Bio-cultural Conflicts. New York, Harper and Row, 1971. vii, 242p.

Author disagrees totally with the Freudian view that anatomy is destiny. Differences between men and women derive from differences in reproductive systems, from inborn temperamental differences, and from sex-linked cultural values. Data are from middle-class American white women, especially college undergraduates. "In our culture . . . men and women apply masculine criteria to their performance." Well-documented, scientific, but quite within comprehensibility of the layman. Dr. Bardwick, a psychologist, teacher at the University of Michigan, is married and has three children.

Beard, Mary R.

America Through Women's Eyes. New York, Macmillan, 1933. 558p.

The place of women in the evolution of American society is firmly established. This book illustrates "the share of women in the development of American society, their activity, their thought about their labor and their thought about the history they have helped to make" (p. 9). From the early period to the 1930s, with many lengthy excerpts from women's writings; Mary Beard's narrative links the excerpts.

Bell, Raley Husted.

Woman from Bondage to Freedom. New York, The Critic and Guide Company, 1921. xv, 230p.

Woman's condition from prehistory to World War I, with chapters on woman and religion, law, the feminist movement, woman suffrage, marriage, birth control, divorce, freedom of choice in selecting a mate, and child-bearing. The publisher of the book was one that specialized in works on the woman question, sex life, morality, population, birth control, family planning, and kindred subjects.

Bennett, Margaret.

> *Alice in Womanland; or, the Feminine Mistake.* Englewood Cliffs, N.J., Prentice-Hall, 1967. 189p. illus.

By two women who have written under this pseudonym for women's and general magazines. Pokes fun at today's various formulas for relieving the great female complaint.

Benson, Mary Sumner.

> *Women in Eighteenth-Century America: A Study of Opinion and Social Usage.* New York, Columbia University Press, 1935. 343p. (Studies in History, Economics and Public Law, No. 405).

The position of eighteenth century American women in theory and fact. Four of the nine chapters are devoted to an analysis of European influences; chapters 7 and 8 deal with women in early American literature, and in law, politics, and in church life. There are also individual observations and experiences, and observations made by American travellers and by foreign observers. Bibliography. Restricted to a discussion of the higher classes.

Bernard, Jessie.

> *Academic Women.* University Park, Pa., The Pennsylvania State University Press, 1964. xxv, 331p.

Written by a sociologist and educator, from the point of view of the academician and the woman, this is an objective study of the woman academic's role. "This book should be helpful to career-minded women. . . ." (p. xxiii). The author claims to have "never experienced professional discrimination from my colleagues, because of my sex" (p. ix).

Exhaustive study; contains many extracts from autobiographical writings and letters, to elucidate statements. Bibliographical notes.

Bird, Caroline.

> *Born Female: The High Cost of Keeping Women Down.* By Caroline Bird, with Sara Welles Briller. Rev. ed. New York, David McKay Company, 1970. xiv, 302p.

The history of discrimination against women and a source book for the women's liberation movement. When Helen Gahagan Douglas made a gallant fight in 1945 and again in 1948 to get the Federal Equal Pay Act passed, unions and employers said it was unworkable and would bring a depression. "Sex is becoming a less useful way to classify workers and to organize work"; it will become a "personal characteristic only slightly more consequential than the color of one's hair, eyes–or skin"; a frankly feminist book. Author takes issue with Harvard sociologist Talcott Parson's distinction between men (instrumental-adaptive, doing things to the physical environment, and making policy for the family, firm and nation) and women (expressive-integretive, registering emotions, and integrating individuals into the group). She also points to Mme. Curie and Marion Goeppert Mayer, only women Nobel Prize winners in physics.

Blanc, Marie.

Les américaines chez elles. Nouv. éd., revue et augmentée. Paris, Hachett, 1904. 358p.

Excellent first-hand report of a French woman traveller in the United States, one of scores of foreigners who have left illuminating records of sojourns in America. Emphasis on higher and lower middle classes; their freedom is compared with that of European women. Only cursory examination of the doings of the highest society, Anglomaniacs who annually travel to Europe's capitals and watering places. Her travels took her to Chicago, Boston, Washington, New Orleans, and other Eastern and Southern places. Covers women's clubs, salons, homes for the poor, Chautauquas, women's prisons, workers' homes, woman's suffrage, education, charities, Christian Science, Helen Keller, Julia Ward Howe, etc.

Blumenthal, Walter Hart.

American Panorama: Patterns of the Past and Womanhood in its Unfolding. Worcester, Mass., Achille J. St. Onge, 1962. 47p.

"Failure of historical writings to accord recognition to the subordinated sex as a fulcrum of our national rise to power and prestige" (p. 7). From Blackstone, through the fathers of the country, to Allan Nevins, most books do not once mention the contributions of women to the development of the United States. The Iroquois gave their women the "rights of suffrage, nomination and recall even prior to the time New Englanders were hanging hapless harridans as witches" (p. 30).

Blumenthal, Walter Hart.

Brides from Bridewell: Female Felons Sent to Colonial America. Rutland, Vt., Tuttle, 1962. 139p. illus.

England sent female prisoners to Virginia and Maryland, while France sent her prisoners to New Orleans. A slightly higher class of women was that of indentured servants. Maryland had in 1755 a population of 50,695 men and 37,622 women; 1,507 of the men were convicts, and 386 of the women were convicts. Among the servants were 3,576 adult males and 1,049 minors, as well as 1,824 adult and 422 minor females. Thirty percent of the total population were Negro slaves. Adult convicts comprised about 6.3 percent of the adult white population. The first shipment of female felons occurred in 1619. In all, more than 33,000 women prisoners were shipped between 1619 and 1868 (after the American Revolution many criminals were transported to Australia).

Bradford, Gamaliel.

> *Portraits of American Women*. Boston, Houghton Mifflin, 1924 (c.1919). x, 276p. ports.

> Abigal Adams, Sarah Alden Ripley, Mary Lyon, Harriet Beecher Stowe, Margaret Fuller Ossoli, Louisa May Alcott, Frances Elizabeth Willard, Emily Dickinson. With the exception of Miss Willard, all were born in New England.

Breckinridge, Sophonisba P.

> *Women in the Twentieth Century: A Study of Their Political, Social and Economic Activities*. New York, McGraw Hill, 1933. xi, 364p. (Monographs: Recent Social Trends in the United States. A series of monographs prepared under the direction of the President's Research Committee on Social Trends).

> Investigates three aspects of women's lives in the first third of the twentieth century: their varied organizations, their search for gainful occupation, and their relation to government. Activities incidental to family life are not examined, nor is this meant to be a thorough review of the women's movement. The President's Research Committee was named by President Hoover in December 1929. Women in Congress are discussed on pages 296 to 301; candidates for office, most of whom did not get elected, are on pages 301 to 305.

Chesnut, Mary Boykin.

> *A Diary from Dixie*. Edited by Ben Ames Williams. Boston, Houghton Mifflin, 1949. xii, 572p. port.

> First published in 1905. Author died in 1886. Written during Civil War years by a Southern lady who was politically well informed, intelligent, independent, articulate, and interested in people.

Cooper, A.

> *A Voice from the South: By a Black Woman of the South*. New York, Negro Universities Press, 1969. iii, 304p. port.

> Originally published in 1892. The Negro woman has a double problem: the race problem and the woman problem. Written by a highly educated lady with a powerful and effective command of the English language.

Diamonstein, Barbaralee.

> *Open Secrets: Ninety-four Women in Touch with Our Time*. New York, Viking Press, 1972. xxxvi, 474p. ports.

Fifty-six questions submitted to American women, all highly educated and with substantial accomplishments. The questions are here answered, sometimes in great detail, by 94 respondents. Included are some women in political life, such as Bella Abzug and Shirley Chisholm. The main criterion for inclusion was whether the women were "genuinely in touch with our times." Comments range from superficial to penetrating and original. Analysis of questions and answers by editor is on pages xi to xxxvi.

Earle, Alice Morse.

Colonial Dames and Goodwives. Boston and New York, Houghton Mifflin, 1895. 315p.

Replete with quaint and amazing information on the lives of many different types of women, their home lives and duties, travel, and participation in patriotic acts. Margaret Brent, of Maryland, was the first woman in America to demand the vote and representation; she came to the province in 1638.

Epstein, Cynthia Fuchs.

Woman's Place: Options and Limits in Professional Careers. Berkeley and Los Angeles, University of California Press, 1970. x, 221p.

"Women's talents are underutilized" (p. 2). Why this is so and how it occurs is focal point of this book. There are few women at the top, even in the USSR. Rapid social changes should lead to the opening of opportunities.

Farber, Seymour M., and Roger H. L. Wilson, editors.

The Challenge to Women. New York, London, Basic Books, 1966. xii, 176p.

Stresses the dangers of overpopulation, a "problem particularly concerning women." Many of the contributors to the 13 chapters of the book are women in academic positions. The articles are from a symposium held at the University of California Medical Center. "Social problems . . . often emerge as unintended by-products of decisions made for quite admirable ends," and "social systems resist modification in a variety of ways" (p. 27). Authors argue for greater similarity of the social roles of the sexes. Blue-collar women want men to rule.

Friedan, Betty.

The Feminine Mystique. New York, Norton, Rev. ed. 1974.

A landmark book in the modern women's movement. "I came to realize that something was very wrong with the way American women are trying to live their lives today" (p. 9). Reviews the period since World War II and offers a new life plan for women, away from the conventional role to the search for identity, independence, and equality with men. Much of the proof for the author's thesis is derived from the contents of women's magazines. The feminine mystique is the image to which women try to conform in contradistinction to the reality of their lives; this produces a schizophrenic split that causes frustration, unhappiness, and a loss of self-respect.

Gilman, Charlotte Perkins.

> *Women and Economics: A Study of the Economic Relation Between Men and Women as a Factor in Social Evolution.* Edited by Carl N. Degler. New York, Harper and Row, 1966. xxxix, 356p. (Harper Torchbooks. American Perspectives). Originally published in 1898.

Written by a life-long socialist whose interest "was always intellectual and social, rather than political or partisan."

Ginzberg, Eli.

> *Life Styles of Educated Women.* By Eli Ginzberg with Ivar E. Berg, Carol A. Brown, John L. Herma, Alice M. Yohalem, and Sherry Gorelick. New York and London, Columbia University Press, 1966. ix, 224p.

This book is based on a questionnaire answered by 311 women who met three criteria: pursuit of education beyond college, demonstration of a high order of intellectual ability (one-third acquired doctorates), and membership in a generation with markedly broadened options. The women questioned were those who had attended Columbia University in the immediate post-war years (p. 15). A companion study is entitled *Educated American Women: Self-Portraits.*

Ginzberg, Eli.

> *Educated American Women: Self-Portraits.* By Eli Ginzberg and Alice M. Yohalem. New York, Columbia University Press, 1967 (c.1966). xii, 198p.

Harbeson, Gladys Evans.

> *Choice and Challenge for the American Woman.* Cambridge, Schenkman Publishing Company, 1967. xvii, 185p.

The personal desire for a larger measure of self-fulfillment is universally felt by educated American women. This book discusses new designs in education that are intended to prepare them for assuming the dual role of homemaker and paid employee. Methods are suggested to keep professional and cultural interests alive during the child-rearing period. Bibliography is on pages 137 to 145. Selected readings (excerpts from writings by women authors on British, Russian and Swedish women) covers pages 147 to 185.

Jensen, Oliver Ormerod.

The Revolt of Women: A Pictorial History of the Century of Change from Bloomers to Bikinis, from Feminism to Freud. New York, Harcourt, Brace, 1952. 224p. (A Picture Press Book).

Lerner, Gerda, ed.

Black Women in White America: A Documentary History. Pantheon Books, 1972. 630p.

Collection of documents, letters, statements, manuscripts, articles, etc., written or dictated by American women, most of them black, from the 1830s to 1970. A record of outrageous treatment they received, but also a record of courage and endurance. The editor's introduction reveals deep understanding for these women.

Lewis, Edwin C.

Developing Woman's Potential. Ames, Iowa State University Press, 1968. ix, 389p.

By a psychologist who is interested in the efficient use of human resources. Growing up; the female personality; the homemaker; employed women; career women; higher education for women.

Lifton, Robert Jay, ed.

The Woman in America. Boston, Houghton Mifflin, 1965. ix, 293p.

Twelve essays by Erik Erikson, Robert Lifton, Esther Peterson, Alice Rossi, David Riesman, Diana Trilling, and others, on the psychology of women, women in contemporary literature, working women, equality of the sexes, etc. Also contains essays on Jane Addams and Eleanor Roosevelt.

Marryat, Frederic.

A Diary in America. With remarks on its institutions. Edited, with notes and introduction by Sydney Jackman. New York, Knopf, 1962. xxvi, 487, ix p. port.

Consists of remarks on society and women. Captain Marryat visited America in 1837.

Rainwater, Lee, Richard P. Coleman, and Gerald Handel.

Workingman's Wife: Her Personality, World and Life Style. Preface by W. Lloyd Warner. New York, Oceana Publications, 1959. xiv, 238p.

The psychological world of the workingman's wife, day in, day out, her behavior as a consumer, her strategy in marketing, and her response to advertising. Based on research studies conducted over several years, in several different areas, and on interviews with 600 women in Chicago,

Louisville, Trenton, and Tacoma. Readers of McFadden publications were interviewed (*True Romance*, *True Stories*, and *True Experience*).

Reeves, Nancy.

Womankind Beyond the Stereotypes, with Parallel Readings Selected and Annotated by the Author. Chicago, New York, Aldine Atherton, 1971. xii, 434p. illus.

"This book is an effort to discern images of woman in the mirrors of our century and of the century that looms ahead." The first part is entitled "Stereotypes: The Traditional Model of Woman Through the Ages"; the second part notes and scrutinizes three assumptions (that woman, having been outside the historial sweep, should remain so; that anatomy is destiny; and that sex-linked traits are primary). The third part (pages 109 to 145) consist of readings from men and women authors to parallel the discussion in the first two parts.

Reische, Diana, ed.

Women and Society. New York, H. W. Wilson Company, 1972. 234p. (The Reference Shelf, v. 43, no. 6).

Contains 29 brief essays from magazines and daily papers, in four sections: (1) challenge to the status quo; (2) most important target of women's groups: elimination of discrimination in jobs and salaries; (3) role women have played in various societies throughout history; (4) female biology and behavior—which is crucial?

Roesch, Roberta.

Women in Action—Their Questions and Their Answers. New York, John Day Company, 1967. 249p.

Tries to answer the question: For what am I living? Looks at education, jobs, and motherhood, and appraises the problems of the young woman, the middle-aged woman, and the old woman. Seeks a middle ground between apathy and belligerence. "Both worlds—inside and outside the home—are good worlds for women" (p. 24).

Ross, Ishbell.

Charmers and Cranks: Twelve Famous American Women Who Defied the Conventions. New York, Harper and Row, 1965. xii, 306p.

The author, who has written many other books on women, provides portraits of: Hetty Green, Wall Street financier; Mrs. Frank, who left $2 million to Mrs. C. C. Catt for suffrage work; Victoria Woodhull, exponent of free love and fighter for the woman's movement; Carrie Nation, hatchet swinger to demolish saloons; Isadore Duncan, great dancer; Aimee Semple McPherson, bewitching evangelist; and other unconventional American women.

Sapieha, Virgilia, Ruth Neely, and Mary Love Collins.

Eminent Women: Recipients of the National Achievement Award.
George Banta Publishing Company, 1948. xi, 162p. ports.

Sixteen women, fourteen Americans, who received the Gold Medal of
the National Achievement Award, established 1930. Among the women
who served on the award committee were Mrs. Eleanor Roosevelt, Dr.
Beatrice M. Hinkle (science), and Dr. Marjorie Nicholson (letters). Frances
Grimes designed the medal. Sixteen recipients whose achievements are
honored are Dr. Florence Sabin, histology professor, Johns Hopkins Medical School; Frances Perkins, Secretary of Labor under F. D. Roosevelt;
Katherine Cornell, actress; Rachel Crothers, dramatist; Carrie Chapman
Catt; Margaret Mead; Dr. Florence B. Seibert, who succeeded in isolating
the active principle of tuberculin; Anne O'Hare McCormick, foreign correspondent for the New York Times; and others. The most moving essays are
those on Frances Perkins, Josephine Aspinwall Roche (coal mine owner
and official in the federal government, also under FDR), and Carrie
Chapman Catt.

Sinclair, Andrew.

The Emancipation of the American Woman. New York, Harper and
Row, 1966 (c.1965). xxix, 401p.

Covers history from the time of the Pilgrims, but with emphasis on
the years from 1830 to after World War II. The introduction gives a good
birdseye view of the movement and its phases, the women and men who
were responsible, the dynamics, etc. The movement was complex and
included abolitionism, temperance, and woman's suffrage. The movement
is still going on. What does the future hold? It is now based in urban centers, which are radical; the small towns which berthed it in the earlier era
have now become fortresses of reaction. The first edition of the book was
called *The Better Half.*

Smith, Page.

*Daughters of the Promised Land; Women in American History: Being
an Examination of the Strange History of the Female Sex from the
Beginning to the Present with Special Attention to the Women of
America, Illustrated by Curious Anecdotes and Quotations by Divers,
Authors, Ancient and Modern.* Boston, Little, Brown and Company,
1970. x, 392p.

"American women have indeed a history, moving, dramatic and
absorbing, and in fact essential to any proper understanding of the larger
history of the American people" (p. x). A well-organized, comprehensive
treatment, written well and humorously by a solid historian.

U.S. Citizens' Advisory Council on the Status of Women.

> *Women in 1971.* Washington, D.C., U.S. Govt. Print. Off., 1972. 61p.

The council was established by Executive Order 11126 by President Kennedy in 1963, on the recommendations of the President's Commission on the Status of Women (Mrs. Eleanor Roosevelt, chairman). First chairman of the council was Miss Margaret Hickey, followed by Senator Maurine Neuberger; present chairman, Mrs. Jacqueline G. Gutwillig. There is a brief note on appointments of women to high political posts in 1971, followed by a rundown of recent events with regard to the Equal Rights Amendment. There are also brief reports on Supreme Court decisions on education, equal employment opportunities, child care, etc.

U.S. Civil Service Commission. Manpower Statistics Division.

> *Study of Employment of Women in the Federal Government, 1970.* Prepared for the Federal Women's Program. Washington, D.C., U.S. Govt. Print. Off., 1971. 236p. mostly tables.

Compared with the 1969 figures, there was a net decrease of 7,067 full-time women's jobs. They represented 33.2 percent of the total white collar work force (1,981,722). The losses were in civil service grades 1 through 6; women in grades 13 and above increased by 470 (6.6 percent) to 7,539, which compares with an increase of 3.6 percent for men in these grades. Fifty-five percent of all federal white collar workers are in grades 1 to 6.

Wharton, Anne Hollingworth.

> *Colonial Days and Dames.* Philadelphia, Pa., J. B. Lippincott, 1908 (c.1894). 248p. illus.

Presents information gathered by talking with men and women who lived in the first quarter of the nineteenth century. They tell how our great cities looked before the advent of the railroad, the steamboat, and the telegraph, and they reach back through their family traditions, placing the reader in touch with scenes of the Revolution and of Colonial days. There are glimpses of social and domestic life North and South, gathered from these oral recollections and from diaries and letters.

Wolff, Janet L.

> *What Makes Women Buy: A Guide to Understanding and Influencing the New Woman of Today.* New York, McGraw-Hill, 1958. xiv, 294p. (McGraw-Hill Series in Advertising and Selling).

Discusses influences, problems, and desires of modern women. Practical handbook for merchants with women customers. At the end of each chapter specific feminine guideposts place the information into easy to use form.

WOMEN IN AMERICA—Periodical Articles

"Bias Charges in Hiring: AT&T Fights Back," *U.S. News*, pp. 66-68 (Aug. 14, 1972).

"Closing Pay Gap for Women: New Rules," *U.S. News*, p. 56 (June 5, 1972).

"Do Women Discriminate Against Each Other?", *National Public Account-ant*, v. 16, p. 16ff. (Oct. 1971).

"The Polls: Women's Role from Roosevelt to the Present," *Public Opinion Quarterly*, v. 35, pp. 275-90.

"Symposium on the Legal Rights of Women," *New York Law Forum*, v. 17, no. 2, 1971. pp. 335-598.

WOMEN IN POLITICS

Duverger, Maurice.

The Political Role of Women. Paris, Unesco, 1955. 221p.

Discusses the part played by women in elections and political leadership. Based on surveys in France, the German Federal Republic, Norway, and Yugoslavia. The surveys were undertaken by Unesco's Department of Social Sciences (1952 and 1955) at the invitation of the United Nations Commission on the Status of Women, whose nine members included three women.

Menzies, Sutherland, pseud.

Political Women. Port Washington, N.Y., Kennikal Press, 1972. 2v. First published in 1873.

Provides portraits of Anne de Bourbon, sister of the great Condé; Anne of Austria; the Princess Palatine; Duchess of Portsmouth; Princess des Ursins, etc. The choices are not as arbitrary as might seem, but are rather guided by instances in the adventurous game of politics, not restricted to private machinations but played on the grandest scale and in the most conspicuous areas, "when peace and war, crowns and dynasties have trembled in the balance, and even the fate of a nation has been at stake."

WOMEN IN POLITICS—England

Brookes, Pamela.

Women at Westminster: An Account of Women in the British Parliament 1918-1966. With a foreword by Mary Stokes. London, Peter Davies, 1967. xv, 287p. ports.

American-born Viscountess Astor was the first woman M.P. Since then there have been more than 25 in the House of Commons, and about 20 in the House of Lords. This book tells what kind of women have sat in

Parliament, what were their contributions, and how they have differed from men in their political impact.

Mann, Jean.

> *Woman in Parliament*. Long Acre, London, Oldhams Press Limited, 1962. 256p. ports.

> Relates Mrs. Mann's experiences as a Laborite woman member of Parliament from Scotland, 1942 to 1962, with glimpses of her fellow women M.P.'s. The greatest number of women incumbents was registered from 1945 to 1951; by 1951 the number had dropped from 24 to 17. Interesting remarks on men's and women's abilities and ways of behaving politically. Most women members are highly educated but do not do much reading; have common sense, like to dress well, get much attention from male M.P.'s. Many have entered Parliament by taking seats left vacant by a husband either by death or removal to the House of Lords. Written in vivid and energetic style.

WOMEN IN POLITICS—Germany

Bremme, Gabriele.

> *Die politische Rolle der Frau in Deutschland: Eine Untersuchung über den Einfluss der Frauen bei Wahlen und ihre Teilnahme in Partei and Parlament*. Göttingen, Vandenhoeck and Ruprecht, 1956. 288p. (Schriftenreihe des Unesco Institutes für Sozialwissenschaften, Köln, Bd. 4).

> Woman's political role in Germany. An investigation of women's influence in elections and their participation in party and parliament. Election participation of women in the Weimar Republic and since 1945 and an analysis of various factors that influence woman's participation. Votes of men and women cast for various parties from 1919 to 1933, and from 1946 to 1956. The second part concerns itself briefly with women in party and parliament in the Weimar Republic and more extensively with the role of women in the political life of the Bundes Republic. It concludes with a review of the difficulties and potentialities of women's political participation in Germany. Women cast fewer votes for the radical parties than men. There are statistical tables of election participation of men and women on pages 231 to 256.

WOMEN IN POLITICS—United States (Books)

Chamberlin, Hope.

> *A Minority of Members: Women in the U.S. Congress*. New York, Washington, London, Praeger Publishers, 1973. ix, 374p. ports.

> A gallery of 80 women who went to Congress as Representatives or Senators from 1917 through 1972. Most of them are arranged in groups of

from three to seven, under a catchy phrase such as "In Search of an Image"; "Winds of Change"; "From Peace to War"; "On Merit"; or "On the Wane." Some, like Jeannette Rankin, Rebecca Felton, Frances Bolton, Margaret Chase Smith, Leonor Sullivan, and six others, are treated singly. Personal interviews, diaries, letters, and personal documents provide a firm basis for documentation.

The space devoted to each women varies from one page to 19 pages, and does not necessarily denote the woman's Congressional importance. For instance, Mrs. Norton and Mrs. Rogers, Congresswomen of solid importance, get five and four pages, respectively, while Mrs. Rebecca Felton, who served in the Senate for exactly one day, is allotted 19 pages. Senator Margaret Chase Smith, who served for nearly three and a half decades with substantial accomplishments, receives 13 pages, and Leonor Sullivan, one of the most outstanding advocates of consumerism, is dealt with in seven pages. However, the book concentrates on biographic details and events, providing warm, human glimpses of these mini-minority members (80 out of more than 10,000 lawmakers in Congress from 1789 through 1971). Written in vivid, interesting style, the biographies provide a welcome view of the Congresswomen's personal lives.

There is a postscript (about five pages) devoted to the five newcomers among Congresswomen in 1973, followed by an alphabetical list of all women who ever served in Congress and an index, chiefly of names. There is no bibliography and there are no bibliographic footnotes. There are eight pages of photographs, with additional pictures on the dustjacket.

Gruberg, Martin.

Women in American Politics: An Assessment and Sourcebook. Oshkosh, Wisc., Academia Press, 1968. viii, 336p.

The only comprehensive treatment of American women in politics, at all levels and in all spheres of politics: as voters, in the party, in legislative, executive and judicial positions, appointive and elective, with a thorough survey of women's organizations of all types. Sections of special note: women in the national government since 1920, Congresswomen and Senators (pages 117 to 131), and a somewhat more extensive treatment of Congresswomen from 1917 to 1967, by year of entry into the House (pages 151 to 168). This section, which covers 65 women, is mostly biographical, with some remarks on their achievements. There are copious bibliographic notes and a long and useful bibliography.

Harriman, Mrs. F. J. (Hurst).

From Pinafores to Politics. New York, Holt, 1923. 359p. illus. ports.

Autobiography of a woman in politics. The author, a wealthy Democrat, was a supporter of Reform Mayor Mitchel of New York and of President Wilson. She advocates women's entry into politics and their work for peace. Clear, fresh, modestly written.

Lamson, Peggy.

Few Are Chosen: American Women in Political Life Today. With a foreword by Maurine B. Neuberger. Boston, Houghton Mifflin, 1968. xxxii, 240p. ports.

With special emphasis on Senator Margaret Chase Smith, Congresswomen Frances P. Bolton, Martha Griffiths, Patsy T. Mink, Margaret M. Hickler, and Ella T. Grasso, and women in high executive or ambassadorial posts.

Paxton, Annabel.

Women in Congress. Richmond, Va., Dietz Press, 1945. 134p. ports.

The pioneering work on women in Congress; each Senator and Congresswoman is briefly appreciated. Sympathetically written but somewhat uncritical.

Republican Party. National Committee 1960-1964. Women's Division.

The History of Women in the Republican National Convention and Women in the Republican National Committee. Researched and compiled by Josephine L. Good under the direction of Clare B. Williams. Washington, D.C., 1963. 58p.

Roosevelt, Eleanor.

It's Up to the Women. New York, Frederick A. Stokes Company, 1933. x, 263p. port.

Mrs. Roosevelt calls on women to do their part to overcome the Great Depression.

Roosevelt, Eleanor, and Lovena A. Hickok.

Ladies of Courage. New York, Putnam's Sons, 1954. vii, 312p.

From Elizabeth Cady Stanton and other women's rights fighters, through the New Deal, and Republican administrations: women who fought for political rights and office, some of whom were elected as mayors, judges, state legislators, governors, or Congresswomen. Includes a chapter offering a profile of Mrs. Roosevelt, and another on how to break into politics.

Ross, Ishbel.

Sons of Adam, Daughters of Eve. New York, Evanston and London, Harper and Row, 1967. viii, 340p. ports.

A large gallery of women in America; first ladies, Congresswomen, executives, reformers, and many others.

Sanders, Marion K.

The Lady and the Vote. Illus. by Charles E. Martin, Boston, Houghton Mifflin, 1956. viii, 172p. illus.

Practical hints by a woman with some experience in politics. Calls herself one of the "lesser battle-axes," or "cryptofeminists," who at one time ran for office but was "clobbered." Says most lesser battle-axes are blessed with supremely cooperative husbands. Humorously written.

Young, Louise M.

Understanding Politics: A Practical Guide for Women. New York, Pellegrini and Cudahy, 1950. 330p.

Intended to stimulate and stir women's political consciousness by presenting the realities of politics from the precinct level to the national scene. Part I: The political arena in general with regard to the patterns of participation for women citizens; Part II: Specific emphasis on the role of women in actual politics. Especially for younger women's use. Book grew out of watching politicians, and especially women politicians, at work. By now the factual material is quite out of date, though the main points may still be valid. Not exceptionally enlightening.

WOMEN IN POLITICS–United States (Periodical Articles)

"American Candid," J. Brady. *Harpers Bazaar* 105:61 (July 1972).

"Beauty, the Beast and the Militant Woman: A Case Study in Sex Roles and Social Stress in Jacksonian America," Carroll Smith Rosenberg. *American Quarterly*, v. 23, pp. 562-84 (1971).

"Crusade for Morality," address, June 10, 1970, M. Rountree. *Vital Speeches* 36:597-602 (July 15, 1970).

"1872 Was Not the Year of the Woman," E. Anthony. *Harpers Bazaar* 105:88 (July 1972).

"Election Countdown '72," E. Hardwick. *Vogue* 160:8 (Aug. 15, 1972).

"Eve's Operatives: Women Delegates of the Democratic Convention," *Time* 100:25-26 (July 24, 1972).

"Good Will Toward Women," *New Republic* 165:5-6 (Dec. 25, 1971).

"History of the Rise of the Unusual Movement for Women Power in the U.S., 1961-68," W. Hinckle and M. Hinckle. *Ramparts Magazine* 6:22-31 (Feb. 1968).

"How to Deradicalize: Republican National Convention," *Time* 100:17-18 (Sept. 4, 1972).

"How Women are Doing in Politics," *U.S. News* 69:23-27 (Sept. 7, 1970).

"In America the Great Brain Divide," M. Ellmann. *Vogue* 153:152+ (May 1968).

"Insiders Guide for the Politically Innocent," M. A. Guitar. *Mademoiselle* 75:132-33+ (June 1972).

"Men, Women and Politics," Lenore Romney. *Look* 35:11 (Apr. 6, 1971).

"New Woman, 1972: Where She Is and Where She's Going," symposium. *Time* special issue on women. *Time* 99:25-103 (Mar. 20, 1972).

"Now Women Talk Back," *Life* 72:46-50 (June 9, 1972).

"Petunia in an Onion Patch," Mrs. M. W. Evers. *Ladies Home Journal* 89: 113+ (Apr. 1972).

"Politics is Women's Work," *The Economist*, pp. 51-52 (Oct. 23, 1971).

"Up with Women in Politics," J. Egan. *McCalls*, v. 98:47 (Sept. 1971).

"What Do Women Want at the Conventions?", P. Pierce. *McCalls* 99:42 (July 1972).

"What Do Women Want in a President?", *Ladies Home Journal* 85:24 (Sept. 1968).

"What Politicians Don't Know about Women," interview, edited by J. L. Block, J. Muskie. *Good Housekeeping* 174:88-89 (Apr. 1972).

"Which Ms. has the Movement, Betty and Gloria and Shirley and Bella," N. Gittelson. *Harpers Bazaar* 105:80-81+ (July 1972).

"Women and Politics," Karen de Crow. *Mademoiselle*, v. 70, p. 34 (Feb. 1970).

"Women and Politics," Margaret Mead. *Redbook*, p. 50+ (Nov. 1970).

"Women Candidates: The Voters Verdict," *U.S. News* 69:30 (Nov. 16, 1970).

"Women and Politics in the U.S. and Canada," R. R. Boyd. *Annals American Academy* 375:52-57 (Jan. 1966).

"Women in Congress," F. L. Gellen. *Trans-action* 6:36-40 (Oct. 1969).

"Women in Government," interviews with six in top jobs. *U.S. News*, pp. 72:62-9 (Jan. 17, 1972).

"Women in Politics: How are They Doing?", *Life*, p. 46 (June 9, 1972).

"Women Need Politics," interview by B. Diamonstein. *Vogue* 159:100+ (Feb. 15, 1972).

"The Women on the Hustings," *Time* 96:11 (Aug. 17, 1970).

"Women's Political Caucus," *U.S. News* 71:67-68 (Aug. 16, 1971).

"Women's Role in the Soviet Union: Ideology and Reality," Alice Schuster. *Russian Review*, v. 30, no. 3, pp. 260-67 (July 1971).

WOMEN LEADERS

Anthony, Susan Brownell, defendant.

> *An Account of the Proceedings of the Trial of Susan B. Anthony, on the Charge of Illegal Voting at the Presidential Election in November 1872, and on the trial of Beverly W. Jones, Edwin T. Marsh and William B. Hall, the Inspectors of Election by whom the Vote was Received.* Rochester, N.Y., Daily Democrat and Chronicle Book Print, 1874. vii, 212p.

Bloomer, Dexter C.

> *Life and Writings of Amelia Bloomer.* Boston, Arena Publishing Company, 1895. 387p. ports.

Burnett, Constance Buel.

> *Five for Freedom.* New York, Abelard Press, 1953. 317p.

> Lucretia Mott, 1793-1880; Elizabeth Cady Stanton, 1815-1902; Lucy Stone, 1818-1893; Susan B. Anthony, 1820-1906; Carrie Chapman Catt, 1859-1947.

Cook, Jennie C.

> *Constitutional Equality, a Right of Woman; or, A Consideration of the Various Relations Which She Sustains as a Necessary Part of the Body of Society and Humanity, with Her Duties to Herself, Together with a Review of the Constitution of the United States, Showing that the Right to Vote Guaranteed to All Citizens. Also a Review of the Rights of Children.* New York, Woodhull, Claflin, 1871. 148p. ports.

Dorr, Rheta Louise (Childe).

> *Susan B. Anthony: The Woman who Changed the Mind of a Nation.* Illustrated from photographs. New York, F. A. Stokes Company, 1928. xiii, 367p. ports.

Flexner, Eleanor.

> *Century of a Struggle: The Woman's Rights Movement in the United States.* Cambridge, Mass., The Belknap Press of Harvard University Press, 1959. xix, 384p. ports.

> From 1800 to 1920. Woman's rights were more bitterly opposed by the vested interests than were the popular election of Senators and the federal income tax. Chapter 22 discusses the opponents of woman suffrage: the South, women in high society, brewers, liquor industry, saloons, political machines (Tammany Hall) and business (which was very circumspect in its opposition). The fear was that women were in favor of cleaning up

politics, were relatively unsusceptible to bribes and threats, and were more militant and in favor of disturbing reforms; they were for sewage control, abolition of child labor, better schools, and protective legislation for women workers. Bibliographic references and notes on pages 339 to 373.

Godwin, Mary Wollstonecraft.

A Vindication of the Rights of Woman, with Strictures on Political and Moral Subjects [by] Mary Wollstonecraft. Edited with introduction, chronology and bibliography by Charles W. Hagelman, Jr. New York, W. W. Norton, 1961. 295p. First edition 1792 by J. Johnson, London, xix, 452p.

Harper, Ida (Husted).

The Life and Work of Susan B. Anthony, Including Public Addresses, Her Own Letters and Many from Her Contemporaries During Fifty Years; A Story of the Evolution of the Status of Woman. Indianapolis and Kansas City, Bowen-Merrill Company, 1898-1908. 3v. illus. ports.

Lerner, Gerda.

The Grimké Sisters from South Carolina: Rebels Against Slavery. Boston, Houghton Mifflin, 1967. xiv, 479p. illus. ports.

Sarah and Angelina Grimké were from a South Carolina slave-holding family; Sarah was born in 1792, Angelina was 13 years her junior. They could not bear the treatment meted out to slaves and moved to Massachusetts to support the anti-slavery movement. Angelina was supremely eloquent and gave innumerable lectures; she married Theodore Weld, who became a leader of anti-slavery forces. Angelina may also be considered a forerunner of the women's franchise movement. Constantly harried by the press, politicians, and the rabble, the sisters (like most outspoken reformers of that and present times) were in constant physical danger. They spent most of their later lives in Pennsylvania. Gerda Lerner has written a beautiful, well-documented book, with an excellent bibliography (pages 437 to 457).

Lutz, Alma.

Crusade for Freedom: Women of the Antislavery Movement. Boston, Beacon Press, 1968. xi, 338p. ports.

Discusses Maria Weston Chapman, Lydia Child, Abby Kelley Foster, Lucretia Mott, Elizabeth Cady Stanton, the Grimké sisters, and others, and their relationship to Frederick Douglass, William Lloyd Garrison, Wendell Phillipps and their work in the American Anti-Slavery Society, the Boston Female Antislavery Society and the Massachusetts Antislavery Society. "Women made an outstanding contribution to the abolition of Negro slavery, and at a time when the participation of women in public reform movements was frowned upon. . . . This book tells their history." Lucy

Stone said: "Slavery is set down in the hearts of the people of this country deeper than they themselves know." These women believed wholeheartedly in the American dream of equal rights for all, and they helped turn public sentiment in favor of the 13th, 14th, and 15th amendments (p. ix). Bibliography (pages 319 to 331), manuscript collections, newspapers and magazines, and general reference works.

Lutz, Alma.

Susan B. Anthony: Rebel, Crusader, Humanitarian. Boston, Beacon Press, 1959. 340p. illus.

Riegel, Robert E.

American Feminists. Lawrence, University of Kansas Press, 1963. 223p. illus.

Discusses the industrial revolution to some extent, but more especially the women reformers who were responsible for the changed and improved position of American women. This book describes a sufficient number of pioneer feminists to furnish the basis for at least some conclusions about the factors that produced a crusader (p. vi). Chapter 10, "Why a Feminist?", presents some interesting conclusions: the nineteenth century was rich in reformers, from vegetarians to anarchists, feminists, abolitionists, and temperance advocates. They came predominantly from the Northeast, with a scattering from the Middle West, and a few from the South. Most of them were physically and mentally vigorous, and lived long lives. They derived from the prosperous middle classes, lawyers, doctors, businessmen, bankers, ministers, and were generally born in urban surroundings; few came from rural sections. They were well educated, of superior intelligence, not original, theoretic, or abstract, but with warm involvement in the lot of the underdog. They held themselves to be pure and unselfish; most of the women were married and had children. As to religion they generally adhered to the smaller sects—many were Quakers, and some were strongly attracted to occult beliefs such as theosophy, spiritualism, mesmerism. Their husbands also were usually reformers. They were moved by a desire for importance and power, had a drive to excel, were able and aggressive; they were also jealous, which resulted in many splits in the movement. The author asserts that on the whole the condition of women was far from terrible, but that, of course, is not true of poor women, who suffered frightfully.

Sachs, Emanie.

"The Terrible Siren": Victoria Woodhull (1838-1927). New York, Harper and Brothers, 1928. xiv, 423p. illus. ports.

Victoria and her sister, Tennessee, aided by Commodore Vanderbilt, set up a brokerage house in Wall Street. They lectured and wrote on spiritualism, free love, and woman's enfranchisement. Victoria stole a march on Susan Anthony and Elizabeth Stanton in petitioning the Congress for granting the vote to women. Bewitchingly beautiful, with enormous courage and stamina, she was brilliant in everything she did, though of mean ancestry and little education. She ran for President of the United States in 1872, with Frederick Douglass on the vice-presidential spot (against his wishes). She advocated a revolution in the family, but later she embraced respectability.

Stanton, Elizabeth Cady.

> *History of Woman Suffrage.* Edited by Elizabeth Cady Stanton, Susan B. Anthony and Matilda Joslyn Cage. Illustrated with steel engravings. Rochester, N.Y., C. Mann, 1887-1922. 6v. illus. maps. ports.

Vol. 1: 1848-61; Vol. 2: 1861-76; Vol. 3: 1876-85; Vol. 4: 1885-1900; Vol. 5-6: 1900-1920.

WOMEN'S LIBERATION

Robins, Joan.

> *Handbook of Women's Liberation.* Edited by Roger Lovin with an introduction by Judith Brown. North Hollywood, Calif., NOW Library Press, 1970. 279p. illus.

Joan Robins writes from her experience of the Western modern liberationist. Contents: what is women's liberation about; UCLA Women's Liberation Front; how the movement got started; an interview with Marlene Dixon; on the beginnings; how we organize (consciousness raising); programs (child care); groups (places where women's groups are located; black women; man-hating; lesbians; dirty old men; and so forth. There is a bibliography on pages 253 to 276.

Stambler, Sookie, comp.

> *Women's Liberation: Blueprint for the Future.* New York, Ace Books, a Div. of Charter Communications, 1970. 283p.

Three dozen articles, some reprinted, written by women active in the various factions of the movement. Arrangement is under the following headings: women on women; women on men (e.g., man as an obsolete life form); women on law and education; women on sex and sex roles; women on liberation; women and the arts; and women's struggle: a historical overview.

WOMEN'S MAGAZINES

White, Cynthia L.

Women's Magazines, 1693-1968. London, Michael Joseph, 1970.
348p. tables. (Michael Joseph Books on Live Issues).

Part 1, pre-war history of the women's press. Part 2, the vast expansion of the women's press in post-war Britain. Also covers the women's press in America, with appendices. Bibliography on pages 328 to 337. Based on the author's Ph.D. thesis, University of London.

AUTHOR INDEX TO BOOKS LISTED
IN THE BIBLIOGRAPHY

Full bibliographic description and annotations for these books will be found in the subject-arranged bibliography; page references are provided to the complete entry. Only books—no articles—are included in this alphabetical author and short-title listing.

Almanac of American Politics, p. 146.

America's Twelve Great Women Leaders During the Past Hundred Years, p. 152.

Amundsen, Kirsten. *The Silenced Majority*, p. 153.

Andreas, Carol. *Sex and Caste in America*, p. 153.

Anthony, Susan Brownell, defendant. *An Account of the Proceedings of the Trial of Susan B. Anthony, on the Charge of Illegal Voting at the Presidential Election in November 1872, and on the trial of Beverly W. Jones, Edwin T. Marsh and William B. Hall, the Inspectors of Election by whom the Vote was Received*, p. 169.

Bardwick, Judith M. *Psychology of Women*, p. 153.

Beard, Mary R. *America Through Women's Eyes*, p. 153.

Beauvoir, Simone de. *The Second Sex*, p. 151.

Bell, Raley Husted. *Woman from Bondage to Freedom*, p. 153.

Bennett, Margaret. *Alice in Womanland*, p. 154.

Benson, Mary Sumner. *Women in Eighteenth-Century America*, p. 154.

Bernard, Jessie. *Academic Women*, p. 154.

Biographical Directory of the American Congress, 1774-1971, p. 146.

Bird, Caroline. *Born Female*, p. 154.

Blanc, Marie. *Les américaines chez elles*, p. 155.

Bloomer, Dexter C. *Life and Writings of Amelia Bloomer*, p. 169.

Blumenthal, Walter Hart. *American Panorama*, p. 155.

Blumenthal, Walter Hart. *Brides from Bridewell*, p. 155.

Bradford, Gamaliel. *Portraits of American Women*, p. 156.

Breckinridge, Sophonisba P. *Women in the Twentieth Century*, p. 156.

Bremme, Gabriele. *Die politische Rolle der Frau in Deutschland*, p. 164.

Brookes, Pamela. *Women at Westminster*, p. 163.

Burnett, Constance Buel. *Five for Freedom*, p. 169.

Chamberlin, Hope. *A Minority of Members*, p. 164.

Chesnut, Mary Boykin. *A Diary from Dixie*, p. 156.

INDEX OF NAMES AND SUBJECTS